I0138910

ANTISLAVERY
IN THE
DISSENTING
ATLANTIC

ANTISLAVERY, ABOLITION, AND THE ATLANTIC WORLD

R. J. M. Blackett, Series Editor

James Brewer Stewart, Editor Emeritus

ANTISLAVERY

IN THE

DISSENTING ATLANTIC

Archives and
Unquiet Libraries
1776–1865

BRIDGET BENNETT

Louisiana State University Press
Baton Rouge

Published by Louisiana State University Press
lsupress.org

Copyright © 2025 by Louisiana State University Press
All rights reserved. Except in the case of brief quotations used in articles or reviews,
no part of this publication may be produced or transmitted in any format or by any
means without written permission of Louisiana State University Press.

DESIGNER: Michelle A. Neustrom
TYPEFACE: Adobe Caslon Pro

COVER ILLUSTRATION: Map from *The Physical Atlas*,
William Blackwood & Sons, 1848.

LIBRARY OF CONGRESS CATALOGING-IN-PUBLICATION DATA

Names: Bennett, Bridget, author.
Title: Antislavery in the dissenting Atlantic : archives and unquiet libraries, 1776–1865 /
    Bridget Bennett.
Description: Baton Rouge : Louisiana State University Press, 2025. | Series: Antislavery,
    abolition, and the Atlantic world | Includes bibliographical references and index.
Identifiers: LCCN 2024047651 (print) | LCCN 2024047652 (ebook) | ISBN 978-0-8071-8371-7
    (cloth) | ISBN 978-0-8071-8413-4 (pdf) | ISBN 978-0-8071-8412-7 (epub)
Subjects: LCSH: Antislavery movements—England—Yorkshire—History—19th century. |
    Antislavery movements—Pennsylvania—History—19th century. | Slavery—Religious
    aspects—Society of Friends. | Slavery—Religious aspects—Moravian Church. |
    Ackworth School—History—19th century. | Richardson, Anna, 1806–1892. | Armistead,
    Wilson, 1819?–1868. | Abolitionists—Great Britain—Biography. | Abolitionists—United
    States—Biography.
Classification: LCC HT1162 .B45 2025 (print) | LCC HT1162 (ebook) | DDC
    326/.8094281—dc23/eng/20241230
LC record available at https://lccn.loc.gov/2024047651
LC ebook record available at https://lccn.loc.gov/2024047652

CONTENTS

ACKNOWLEDGMENTS

This book would not have been possible without the generous support of the Leverhulme Trust, which awarded me a Major Research Fellowship in 2019. The fellowship started in the autumn of 2020, during a time in which COVID had changed everything: many libraries and archives had been closed, travel (especially international travel) was restricted or impossible, and in consequence it was not a good time to be working on a book. Like many others, I had to work from home and got used to Teams and Zoom to keep me in touch with colleagues and students, family and friends. The Leverhulme Trust remained understanding throughout and gave me an extension to the fellowship, enabling me to complete my research. I am profoundly grateful and would like to thank Reena Mistry and Nicola Thorp in particular for their assistance at various points.

Once some restrictions had lifted, it became possible to visit libraries and archives once more. It was very unsettling to travel from Leeds to London on virtually empty trains to work in an almost empty British Library. The strange experience of going online to book short slots at the library well in advance, before managing the rigid restrictions governing access and all elements of working, is one I had hoped never to repeat. However, in an uncanny manner, work on the book was once again interrupted in its final stages, this time by a catastrophic cyberattack on the British Library. Thus, both starting on my fellowship and finalizing the manuscript coincided with significant problems accessing the library collection on which it most depended. The experience only reinforces my sense of the value of libraries, something with which many of the figures I write about in the pages of the book would concur. The book has changed considerably because of the pandemic. Since I could not access the U.S. archives I had planned to visit until international travel to the United States was once more allowed, I had to rethink my ideas about the kind of book I wanted, and was able, to write.

As all of us who undertake this kind of work know, research and writing are profoundly collaborative. The seeds of this book are in an undergraduate research scheme that brought me together with Neko Mellor several years ago. I didn't realize then how things would turn out. Working with her was a great pleasure and I'm glad to be able to acknowledge that here. I also encountered Joe Williams at that time, and have greatly enjoyed working with him on a number of occasions over the years.

During that early period, I was lucky enough to be helped by Lee Dalley from the Workshop Theatre at the University of Leeds, who (among other things) recorded my young children reading from nineteenth-century newspapers for a website Neko and I cocreated. He once again graciously stepped in with this book, taking one of the photographs I use in its pages.

At the opening of the project exhibition at the Stanley and Audrey Burton Gallery at the University of Leeds, a power cut meant that things went awry at the very last minute. But abandoning our plans, Joe Williams, Ayesha Bennett, and Iona Bennett all bravely gave live performances and saved the day. Malcolm Chase came to that opening and told me about the extraordinary census entry that has become part of this story, and book. I wish he was still with us so that I could thank him again for his generosity and knowledge.

Once I started developing my plans further, I was fortunate to benefit from the expertise of Celia Wolfe, the archivist at Ackworth School. She put me in touch with Jane Alden Stevens, who in turn told me about her ancestor Hannah Hoyle, whose embroidered samplers are discussed in the book's opening chapter. I greatly enjoyed our email conversations as we discovered more about Hannah, especially when I found the ship's manifest giving details about her arrival in the United States, and I knew the first person I had to tell was Jane. Thank you, Jane, and I hope you enjoy the book.

I have benefited from the expert knowledge of archivists and libraries in many places, including the American Antiquarian Society; Boston Public Library; British Library at St. Pancras and at Boston Spa in West Yorkshire; Historical Society of Pennsylvania; Fulneck Moravian Church archives; Houghton Library; John Rylands Library; Leeds Central Library; Leeds Library on Commercial Street; Library Company of Philadelphia; Library of the Society of Friends; the Moravian Archives in Bethlehem, Pennsylvania; the Moravian Church Archive and Library in London; the Newberry Library; Newcastle Lit & Phil; the Special Collections of the Brotherton Library at the University of Leeds; Quaker and Special Collections at Haverford College, Pennsylvania; and the West Yorkshire Archives.

For facilitating my research in various ways, I'd like to thank Melissa Atkinson, Brianne Barrett, Layla Bloom, Claire Drone-Silvers, Carl Hutton, Connie King, Michaela Koller, Tom McCullough, Tony Mehew, Paul Peucker, Antony Ramm, Jane Riley, Lorraine Seymour, Hilary Smith, and Aidan Thackray. I thank *Atlantic Studies* for permission to reprint a revised version of an article that is incorporated into chapter 3.

I have delivered papers at conferences and seminars on both sides of the Atlantic, where audiences have made me think more clearly about what I wished to communicate. In addition, having learned the craft of Zoom and Teams, I have been able to participate in a number of conferences and seminar series while still based at home during the pandemic. I love the fact that this makes international conversations so much easier, and more environmentally sustainable, but it does not replace face-to-face interactions. The largely online group Nineteenth-Century Americanists in the North was especially important during the time of intense pandemic restrictions. Individuals I have encountered in libraries, conferences, or other institutions have been generous with suggestions and ideas, including (but certainly not limited to) Elena Furnaletto, Daisy Hay, Ilka Brasch, Lukas Etter, Gisa Mackenthun, Katie Sampeck, Ellen Gruber Garvey, and Cameron Seglias.

I also learned a lot from the walks I have taken, exploring the landscape in which my subjects lived and worked. Particularly memorable walks include a long solitary circuit in the countryside around Ackworth School on a surprisingly hot late summer day, a convivial group walk close to Fulneck Moravian Settlement and its beautiful environs in bluebell season, and walks in Leeds, Newcastle, and Philadelphia in all weathers. This supplements book knowledge and (for me at least) brings subjects to life in new and surprising ways. Intrigued by reading about the licorice plants growing in the vicinity of Ackworth School in the nineteenth century, for instance, I am now successfully growing my own.

I continue to learn from the wonderful, resourceful, and intelligent postgraduate students I have been fortunate enough to work with at Leeds. Thanks especially to Mashael Alhammad, Lloyd Belton, Anastasia Cordone, Tara Deshpande, Emily Ennis, Adrienne Mortimer, Yishi Pan, Charlie Salway, Arththi Sathananthar, and Georgia Walton for all you have taught me and continue to teach me. I have also had the good fortune to be surrounded by a remarkable group of colleagues and former colleagues. In particular, I thank Manuel Barcia, Hamilton Carroll, Tony Crowley, Kate Dossett, Sam Durrant, Claire Eldridge, David Fairer, Denis Flannery, Alaric Hall, Ed Larrissy, Katy Mullin, Jim Mussell, Brendon Nicholls, Jay Prosser, Nick Ray, Jane Rickard, and Andrew Warnes for their readings, conversation, support, and suggestions. Recently I have had the opportunity to work more closely with Clare Barker, Fiona Douglas, Brett Greatley-Hirsch, Hazel Hutchison, Christiana Gregoriou, John McLeod, Pam Rhodes, Julia Snell, Matthew Treherne, Rob Walker, and Matt Woodcock, and all have, in various ways, offered encouragement and support.

But many other colleagues have contributed to this work and to my life in the School of English at Leeds, and I thank you all and apologize for not naming you in person. Coffees, lunches, chats in the photocopying room, and day-to-day interactions have all played their part in sustaining me, especially in tough times.

I am hugely indebted for the insights, comments, and arguments of colleagues and friends both new and older, from my own sustaining international networks: BAAS, BrANCA, BrANCH, C19: The Society of Nineteenth-Century Americanists, C19: Americanists Abroad, and C19th Americanists in the North. I thank Bruce Baker, Michelle Coghlan, Thomas Constantinesco, Duncan Faherty, Erin Forbes, Katie McGettigan, Genevieve Johnson-Smith, Erin Pearson, Matthew Pethers, Michaël Roy, Andy Taylor, Kristin Treen, and Tom Wright. Ben Offiler, Jesús Sanjurjo, Ed Sugden, and Rachel Williams have all given helpful advice about parts of the book, and Cécile Roudeau and Graham Thompson have both been hugely supportive. Discussions with John Barnard, Elleke Boehmer, Hermione Lee, Gail Marshall, and

Steve Matthews have always been welcome and enjoyable. Emily Cuming has followed the project from its inception, encouraging me as she pursued her own book project and helping me to keep going.

An extra big thank-you to Clare Elliott and Fionnghuala Sweeney, who have followed my progress for a long time and who have offered invaluable and varied kinds of support and inspiration, repeatedly and often at short notice. It would not be the same book without you two, while conferences would also be much less enjoyable. Richard Blackett has encouraged this project from the start. His modeling of academic rigor and personal sense of fun are much appreciated. Rand Dotson has been reflective and quick to respond to email—who can ask for more? Matt Mason offered invaluable feedback while Todd Manza has been a rigorous and sympathetic copy editor with fine instincts and great tact. The LSU team have been great to work with, and my gratitude is extended to them all, especially to Neal Novak.

My friendship with Charlotte Jones and Julia Thackray has gone back more years than we have all noticed, as they remind me periodically. I thank them both for advice, support, and conversations, and for our walking holidays. Though I'm glad that we continue our ambition of aging disgracefully, we seem to manage it with alarming ease. Reflecting on my days of early adulthood when I met them both, I also want to thank Sophie Verhagen and to remember Clare Tarplee, whose premature death remains an ongoing source of sadness. I'm happy to have a group of sustaining friends in this period of later adulthood, either locally or further afield, who include Emma Brown, Gaby Chiappe, Jocelyn Ferguson, Dom Gray, Susie Godsil, Lucy Morris, Alison Morse, Kate Newman, Will Rea, Mark Sofilas, Cat Wilkinson, and Stuart Wilkinson. Sandra (Sandy) Staley and Adriana Panait have helped me remain flexible and happy, despite long hours spent at my desk. Daniela Bernadelle and Andreas Wegmann were around at a key period in the completion of the book, bringing food and laughter and ensuring, in the words of Herr Zwiebel, that none of us were on our own. Kiran Dhillon likes to ask about the book. Here's her answer (finally). Fin Armstrong and Niko Nikov have been a welcome addition to my world in too many ways to be counted.

My final thanks are of course to my extended family, who know more than most about the difficulties of writing and of living with writers. This encompasses all Bennetts, Martinez-Bennetts, Divanis, Mukherjees and Velanis, an expanding group which now encompasses nine decades, three generations, five continents and many memories. Sadly, my father, Duncan Bennett, is no longer a living member of this diverse and multilingual group, but he is remembered here with love and with admiration for how he coped with adversity. My mother, Josephine Bennett, is always a great cheerleader, and it was her who made me realize that I should think more about Ackworth School. Thanks for everything, and onwards and upwards, Josie! Ayesha Bennett and Iona Bennett continue to be stalwarts. Their enthusiasm for life, smart and analytical questions, and belief that the book would get done have been invaluable throughout. Sanju Velani has been there from the start, as always, and will be delighted that the book is finished. Sanju, though my acknowledgments are not as original or even as whimsical as the ones you add to your Big Sums, they are just as heartfelt. My thanks, and love, go to them all.

ANTISLAVERY
IN THE
DISSENTING
ATLANTIC

Prologue

On 1 January 1859, the *Leeds Intelligencer* reported on a meeting, or "soiree," of the Leeds Young Men's Anti-Slavery Society held in Leeds Town Hall at the end of the previous year.[1] The newly opened municipal building was designed to house the law courts and to be a location for elements of the city's business. It was also intended to display the standing of an industrial city particularly known for its manufacture of textiles, notably flax and wool. It was the latest in a series of elaborate residential and nonresidential edifices erected in Leeds, bespeaking the growing confidence and wealth of the luckier parts of its population, many of them merchants. The antislavery meeting took place in the building's centerpiece, the vast and grand space of Victoria Hall, the home of what was at that point the largest pipe organ in Europe. Navigating through the smoke-filled streets of a city in West Yorkshire on a midwinter evening in bad weather was likely to put off the fainthearted. But the oldest of the attendees were long-standing antislavery activists and they were keen to recruit a new generation of young men to their ranks. Besides, they were accustomed to overcoming more significant adversities than the challenge of Yorkshire weather.

The local nature of the meeting belies larger ambitions. It sets the scene for the extensive transatlantic crosscurrents of people and ideas, material objects, print and letters discussed in the pages of this book. *Antislavery in the Dissenting Atlantic* engages with a historically situated set of transatlantic relationships, chiefly but not exclusively centered on communities of dissenters in Yorkshire, Newcastle, and Pennsylvania in the decades roughly between the American Revolution and the passing of the Thirteenth Amendment in 1865. The considerable reach of the many figures I investigate was profoundly rooted in homegrown forms of local connectedness. Yet that does not mean they should be thought of as merely parochial or provincial. Their public antislavery labor and transnational purview were the product of deeply held private convictions nurtured in the communities, schools, and families from which they came. These communities were locally situated, but they maintained an international connectedness and were outward looking. For instance, patterns of migration meant that families often were physically split across an Atlantic divide while keeping up through extensive correspondence. They shared local news and information by sending clippings and books across the Atlantic, either using the burgeoning postal system or handing packages to individuals who were making the journeys themselves. This kept geographically scattered families and their communities in regular contact, allowing them to be up to date with their activities, including those related to antislavery. A number of the figures I discuss were connected with Ackworth School near Pontefract in West Yorkshire, a pioneering establishment offering formal education for boys and girls whose families were members of the Society of Friends. These included Quaker children from other parts of the world, taking the ideas and lessons inculcated in West Yorkshire to places as far away as Australia and Russia. There also were regular visitors from the United States who shared ideas, books, and even the patterns that were used for embroidered samplers—including those I discuss in this book.

As we know, the extent to which transatlantic antislavery and abolition shaped the eighteenth and nineteenth centuries cannot be overstated.[2] This book addresses the many ways in which antislavery was encouraged and sustained, sometimes in the face of considerable opposition and attack. *Antislavery* is an inclusive word, covering a range of different positions, encompassing both egalitarianism and paternalism while at the same time obfuscating such distinctions. It is not my intention here to probe all the ways in which the individuals I study understood antislavery, nor how their beliefs changed over time. Throughout the pages of this book, we will encounter figures whose beliefs coalesced to a large degree but were sometimes profoundly at variance with one another when it came to ideas about political and racial equality. Nonetheless, they were willing to work together for a larger common cause. Their contributions to that cause took many forms, including letter writing, petitioning, public speaking, writing and editing books and tracts, and pedagogy.

Antislavery frequently had abolition as its desired political outcome, as it did for those who attended the meeting that evening. Theirs was a moral position, profoundly connected to their religious beliefs. Some of the speakers had amassed considerable wealth and believed it was now their duty visibly to engage in philanthropic activities, including antislavery. Since several were well known and influential, the organizers had the means to hold the meeting in a grand location. This meant that it commanded newspaper coverage, and in consequence was recorded for posterity in print. So we know that the meeting comprised a small but committed collection of individuals. A number of them were religious dissenters whose theological beliefs and doctrinal practices, emerging from the Protestant Reformation, positioned them not just outside of the fold of the established church in Britain but also outside of many social and educational institutions. Even those who were not (in this specific sense) dissenters were engaged in acts of what can best be defined as dissent. They were participants in what I term the dissenting Atlantic.

In order to explain this, I turn to formal definitions. The words *dissent* and *dissident,* both of which started to be used around the sixteenth century, are semantically related, though they have different etymological roots. *Dissident* "derives from 'dissidēre' (dis+sidēre)—to sit or settle oneself apart, and by extension, to be out of alignment, hence to disagree, differ, be at variance," while *dissent* "derives from 'dissentīre' (dis+sentīre)—to feel or think in a different way, hence to differ in opinion, to disagree."[3] The figures I discuss in the pages of this book both sat apart from and felt differently from many of those in the wider society around them, though since they were peaceful people they remained in fellowship with each other. They were often at variance with, and dissented from, received opinion, but their views also were often strongly held in the communities out of which they emerged. They were willing to accept the social and political consequences accompanying principles that were sometimes unpopular more widely. Some of them had strong commitments to religious freedom and to ideas of liberty, derived from a long history of political thought and action, and looked to historical traditions and precedence to reinforce their behavior and remind them of other principled acts of bravery.

Relatedly, since many of them held ethical principles that found expression in political acts, they also behaved in a *dissident* manner, often making enemies or at least opponents as they pursued the causes they supported. This was particularly the case when their ethical principles were at variance with the law. Some undertook acts of civil disobedience such as tax resistance, accepting imprisonment as a consequence. Following the logic of this etymology, one might describe them as dissidents, though the word now has distinct connotations that do not invariably apply to them. Some of the figures in this book used the language of benevolence while acting in radical ways. Girls and women were empowered within Quakerism, encouraged to take on preaching roles or to become involved in social justice activities. International peace activism, along with what Julie Holcomb calls the moral commerce of free produce activism, was foundational to the lives of many Quakers and was closely connected to other reform movements. I will explore the relationality of such activities, amplifying Holcomb's argument that commitments to boycotting slave labor "create diverse, biracial networks that simultaneously divided and united their efforts as they worked to reorganize the transatlantic economy on an ethical basis."[4]

Highly aware of participating in groups with a long-standing and principled commitment to challenging convention, they were often open to becoming the allies of other marginal figures and were willing to take on unpopular causes. These figures included, most particularly, free and enslaved Blacks who were committed to abolition. Cross-racial, cross-class, and cross-gender friendships and other forms of alliance created a labile, shifting, and extensive social network, or fellowship, across and within the Atlantic world. This transcended the operations of the nation-state and reached out beyond ports, cities, and towns into the hinterlands. At times it brought together figures who learned of each other through sources as varied as local talk, a variety of print sources (including powerful local newspapers), correspondence, and even the medium of chance face-to-face encounters. Antislavery was often organized and tactical, but it also relied on happenstance and opportunism. It changed and developed over time, and as Manisha Sinha has persuasively argued, it was an integrated and radical social movement foundationally underpinned by the actions of enslaved themselves.[5]

Key participants in the meeting that evening included some who make a brief appearance here but will not be discussed further. Still, since they are a part of the background of the wider story the book addresses, I will introduce them now, along with some further details that help locate them more fully. They include the meeting's chair, the mayor of Leeds, Sir Peter Fairbairn, a self-made engineer who had become wealthy through the manufacture of flax- and wool-spinning machines. Queen Victoria and Prince Albert had stayed in his home in Leeds the previous autumn when they opened the town hall. His first announcement was that Lord Londesborough (who had been a Whig member of parliament) had sent his apologies due to "a severe attack of influenza."

Though this was an inauspicious start to the evening, neither harsh weather nor illness had put off Edward Baines, who was connected to many of the leading male citizens of Leeds, most of whom had contributed to (and benefited from) the rapid rise in the city's fortunes. He had been educated at a dissenting academy in Manchester and would go on to become one of the founders of the Leeds Literary and Philosophical Society, which had offered doughty support to the campaign to build the new town hall. An influential antislavery voice, Baines had attended the World Anti-Slavery Convention in London in 1840, and like several of the most prominent attendees he had a network of interlocutors stretching across the Atlantic. He edited an influential local newspaper, the *Leeds Mercury*, whose stories were frequently copied and circulated on both sides of the Atlantic.

His father (also Edward Baines) had purchased the *Leeds Mercury* in 1801, with the backing of a progressive group of dissenters, including John Marshall, a leading textiles manufacturer who had died in 1845 after amassing a fortune. Along with many of the city's successful industrialists, Marshall was inspired by the intellectual currents of the period. He was personally fascinated by Egyptology, and his celebrated factory, Temple Works in Holbeck, South Leeds, was designed to resemble the Temple of Edfu at Horus. Constructed from 1836 to 1840, it was thought to contain the largest single room in the world. Outwardly, the design was ancient, but in other ways it had innovations, as befitting a building in a city that wanted to show it was on the rise. For instance, the ingenious design of the chimney made it resemble an obelisk, and even more ingeniously, grass was grown on the flat roof to keep the mill's humidity constant (and the flax workable). This created the issue of how to manage the growth of the grass, and technology came to the rescue. A hydraulic lift hauled sheep up to the roof so that the level of the grass could be maintained by grazing. This brilliant though risky solution meant the sheep were close to another of the factory's state-of-the-art features, the huge glass skylights that dotted the same roof, harnessing the natural light and helping the machine workers below. But sheep and skylights are a risky combination, something revealed when an unfortunate animal stumbled into (and then through) a skylight, with disastrous consequences. The stunning building is currently derelict, though the British Library plans to develop it to serve readers in the North of England, something that would delight Marshall.

He was one of the many Yorkshire dissenters shaping the development of nineteenth-century Leeds. A Unitarian, he had attended Mill Hill Unitarian Chapel, like the Leeds-born Joseph Priestley, who fled to Philadelphia in 1794 and established the first Unitarian church in the United States there before dying in 1804. Having established his wealth, Marshall turned to social causes also in the spirit of the time, founding a mechanics' institute and a school, to extend educational opportunities to workers and their children.

A key figure for the Anti-Slavery Society, and for this book, was Wilson Armistead, a Quaker merchant whose flax and mustard business was also based in Holbeck. He was committed to antislavery and various forms of philanthropy, and any account of nineteenth-century antislavery in Leeds must have him at its center. Nine years before the meeting, he had traveled to the United States, combining business with visits to family members, networking with abolitionists, and fact-finding about slavery. Having crossed the Atlantic, he stayed in Boston just before the passing of the Fugitive Slave Law. There he met many abolitionists, including Ellen and William Craft, who had emancipated themselves from enslavement in Georgia. The couple would go on to stay with him and his family in Leeds on the night of the 1851 census, when they were on the abolitionist lecture circuit with William Wells Brown. This prompted an extraordinary moment of what I call guerrilla inscription, when they were both entered in the U.K. census as fugitive slaves as part of a concerted campaign against the new law.

Armistead was clearly inspired by his meetings with Black freedom seekers, especially the Crafts, and his antislavery work developed even further after his experiences in the United States. Traveling south from Boston he had visited Philadelphia, the Quaker city, whose inhabitants included a long-standing community of free Blacks. At the time of the December meeting in Leeds he was putting the finishing touches on a book about Anthony Benezet, the Philadelphia-based Quaker abolitionist whom he held in the highest regard. He was an avid correspondent, and he personally circulated news of Leeds antislavery activities to his many interlocutors on both sides of the Atlantic.

A bookish individual, Armistead was a keen admirer of libraries and the opportunities they represented for personal development, as was true of other figures I discuss in this book. In this way as in many others he was a man of his time and place. He was a member of the Leeds Library on Commercial Street, a private subscription institution that had been founded in 1768 and was well used by the local bourgeoisie, much like Newcastle's Lit & Phil or the Library Company of Philadelphia. But the politics of knowledge production has always been a thorny matter. As this book acknowledges, institutions such as libraries have complex relationships to the histories they enable us to tell, as well as to those their collections effectively silence. One of the opening notices in the report he read out at the meeting drew attention to the existence of an antislavery library, accessible to all members of the Leeds Young Men's Anti-Slavery Society, "by which they can make themselves acquainted with every argument and means used for the abolition of slavery." He gave no additional details, but his announcement reveals his faith in the possibilities inherent in encounters with print, something animating his prolific writing career.

In some ways, though certainly not all, the December meeting is emblematic of the occasions in which British antislavery activists encountered each other in the public sphere. Such meetings were covered by local newspapers and then these descriptions were copied and reproduced in newspapers nationally and internationally. Since newspapers are relatively durable and accessible, details of occasions like this make their way into historical accounts of antislavery, including into this book. The consequence, as we well know, is that reports about such events are key to our understanding of particular moments in history. Yet, at the same time, the stories we tell about the past remain partial and need to be supplemented by other forms of historiography and evidence.

In recognition of that paradox, let us explore what focusing on this well-publicized event threatens to occlude. It is highly probable that all the local attendees (like the speakers) in Leeds that cold December evening were white men, though of course antislavery has never been the sole preserve of white men. The advocates of antislavery at this meeting were allies of the most significant and radical activists of all, namely freedom-seeking Blacks who resisted and challenged their enslavers and the exigencies of white supremacy on a daily basis. It is well documented that Leeds was a key location for visits by Black abolitionist lecturers, including William Allen, Henry "Box" Brown, William Wells Brown, Ellen and William Craft, Alexander Crummell, Martin Delany, Frederick Douglass, James W. C. Pennington, Sarah Parker Remond, Moses Roper, Samuel Ringgold Ward, and James Watkins.[6] Some of the evening's attendees at the town hall had certainly attended these lectures, and in this way they heard vivid firsthand testimony about slavery.

Locally, too, the picture of who was involved in campaigning was more complex and varied than was represented by the meeting. There were no women and children there, for instance, though six years earlier, in February 1853, the Leeds Anti-Slavery Association had been founded, admitting both women and men as equal members. This was largely due to the work of two Garrisonian abolitionists, the American Sarah Pugh (raised as a Quaker, though she eventually became a Unitarian) and the Leeds-based Unitarian Harriet Lupton. Pugh was well known as a long-standing member of the Philadelphia Female Anti-Slavery Society, and she had also been a delegate to the World Anti-Slavery Convention and author of a protest against its treatment of women delegates. She deepened her transatlantic alliances when she lectured in England for about seventeen months, starting in 1851. She had close personal relationships with a number of Black abolitionists and was committed to working in an intersectional manner. She had participated in the famous meeting of the Anti-Slavery Convention of American Women in 1838, when a proslavery mob set fire to Pennsylvania Hall. The women had exited the building two by two, Black women and white women linking arms in pairs as they left in peaceful solidarity.

To signal its progressive commitment to gender equality, the Leeds Anti-Slavery Association adapted the well-known Wedgwood emblem "Am I not a

man and a brother?" and added "Am I not a woman and a sister?," along with
an image of an enslaved woman, just as the Birmingham Ladies' Negroes'
Friend Society had in 1826.[7] In doing this, it used an emblem reproducing a
highly problematic image recently described as "notorious for its emblematic
portrayal of a mute, deindividualized, servile, and supplicant slave" aiming to
solicit "affective moral engagement by calling into question the widely un-
disputed humanity of enslaved people."[8] Its use signaled the discriminatory
attitudes of many of those who considered themselves to hold progressive
antislavery beliefs, at precisely the moment at which the association sought
to represent an emerging and welcome egalitarian consensus. Mary Armistead was the association's librarian, and her husband, Wilson Armistead,
was its president, part of an interdenominational committee in which women
outnumbered men. Despite this, Clare Midgley argues, the association was
male-dominated in practice, replicating patterns from households and wider
society.[9]

The newly formed association hosted Harriet Beecher Stowe when she
visited the city in 1853. In consequence of the huge popularity of *Uncle Tom's
Cabin,* selected scenes from the novel were adapted and performed in Leeds's
theaters around and beyond that period. On 19 April 1853, the program advertised on the Princess Theatre's playbill included *The Slave Hunt or, The Fate of
St. Clair and the Happy Days of Uncle Tom,* though the theater's commitment
was to ticket sales rather than antiracism, as its description of the performers
and its emphasis on sensation and sentimentalism make clear.[10] The presence
of (often illustrated) playbills advertising this kind of popular performance
at this and other theaters, including the Theatre Royal, made U.S. slavery a
visible part of the daily life of the city of Leeds and its inhabitants, albeit in
highly mediated ways.

Living and working in an industrial city that relied on international trade
made local people aware of the impact of markets, as regular financial crises
showed them just how vulnerable they were to an increasingly interconnected
global economy. The nearby cotton mills in Lancashire were reliant on slave-
produced raw materials, as mill workers in Yorkshire also knew. Just a few
years later, at a meeting in Manchester's Free Trade Hall in December 1862,
Lancashire mill workers and middle-class activists passed a motion support-
ing abolition and the blockade of slave-produced cotton, despite the fact that

many of the workers were aware that they would become virtually destitute in consequence. Long-standing antislavery had developed into unequivocal abolition and was part of a spectrum of closely linked international campaigns for social justice and political equality. They understood that their resistance to a system that relied on unfree labor was part of a principled and radical commitment to challenging the status quo, one which insisted on the international recognition of civil liberties and labor rights. Their ethical and political championing of the blockade was a logical development of the earlier campaigns for sugar abstention and ongoing campaigning for free produce.

And here we encounter an irony. The cotton mills of Lancashire produced huge quantities of cloth that would go on to be made into clothing and other goods that eventually themselves became rags. These rags, produced from slave-grown cotton, were then used in the production of paper in the period before rags were gradually replaced by wood pulp in the paper manufacturing process. Thus, even as early activists outlined the importance of abstaining from the sugar that came from the labor of the enslaved, their words may well have been circulating on paper that was itself the product of enslavement.

Antislavery was certainly not just the preserve of self-selected groups like the one that met in Leeds that cold December evening. Slavery was discussed and debated in chapels and churches as well as newspapers, and doubtless also in homes, pubs, and streets, among trade unionists and others. Given the all-male status of the meeting, we might try to imagine the whereabouts of the local antislavery women and children. Some of them might have been sitting at home elsewhere in Leeds, possibly reflecting upon Wilson Armistead's recent letter about Harpers Ferry, published in the *Leeds Mercury*.[11] He argued that though he personally deplored violence, he imagined that the radical abolitionist John Brown was actuated by deeply held beliefs and was undoubtedly doing what he thought to be right when he attacked the U.S. arsenal. Armistead warned, correctly, that the United States was on the brink of disaster unless slavery was abolished. Given his deep knowledge of the history of antislavery, he would have been able to take the long view of its progress through the early campaign for abolition onward, recognizing that Harpers Ferry marked a transformative moment in the argument for how abolition might be achieved.

Immediately beneath his letter was one titled "The Dog Nuisance." Its proximity to a letter about Harpers Ferry shows the mixture of local and global in the pages of newspapers. The writer explains that the male-owned out-of-control dogs in the vicinity of Woodhouse Cliff and Woodhouse Ridge in Headingley, North Leeds, had particular consequences for the lives of women. They were being forced to spend increasing time in their homes to avoid the rampaging animals. While thus constrained, some of these women may have sewn antislavery objects such as pincushions to be sold in antislavery bazaars. Sarah Pugh had been very active in promoting this labor in Philadelphia, and British women had responded with enthusiasm. Some might have written to other antislavery women or men—possibly to family members who had emigrated to the United States and wrote home asking for news. Some, wearily putting children to bed and struggling to keep warm, may have been comparing their own hard lives with the imagined lives of those held in slavery across the Atlantic. They might have complained about the dogs, the long winter nights, or any number of other pressing issues. Some of them might have previously attended meetings at the Woodhouse Mechanics Institute, where Black lecturers such as the Crafts urged them to support abolition and might have been discussing these and other events taking place outside of their homes. Perhaps here or elsewhere in the city, children of reading age and with access to books, like Mary and Wilson Armistead's son Joseph, may have been fascinated by George Catlin's *Letters and Notes on the Manners, Customs and Condition of the North American Indians* (1842).[12]

Moving beyond the city, about one hundred miles further north in Newcastle upon Tyne, the Quaker activist Anna Richardson was perhaps corresponding across the Atlantic with the American abolitionist printer William Shreve Bailey as she prepared her tract for juveniles, *Little Laura, the Kentucky Abolitionist* (1859), describing the life and death of his daughter, Laura Bailey. He had also experienced the impact of the violent aftermath of Harpers Ferry and had been threatened and attacked by a proslavery mob in consequence. Perhaps some of the children staying at home that December night had encountered one of the free labor tracts circulated by Anna and her husband, Henry, asking them not to purchase or consume items produced by the work of the enslaved and encouraging them to become what Michaël Roy calls "young abolitionists."[13] The couple had first met at Ackworth School, which had a significant impact on the foundation of Westtown School in Pennsylvania, the institution attended by a young Sarah Pugh. Such transatlantic connections were strong and lasting and will recur throughout this book.

Two former Ackworth scholars, Hannah Hoyle and Joseph Sharp, had separately emigrated to the United States from West Yorkshire, married in Ohio, and raised their family in Philadelphia. Active in antislavery there, they kept in regular contact with family members in Leeds—and who knows, perhaps that very evening their family in Yorkshire, like other local families, was reminiscing about loved ones living in the United States. Sharp was a keen reader of poetry; a favorite writer was William Cowper, well known and admired by Quakers for his abolitionist principles. Others that evening may have been reading the abolitionist poetry of British poets such as Cowper or Anna Laetitia Barbauld, both popular with dissenters, or of the American Quaker poet James Greenleaf Whittier. They might even have been reading the work of the abolitionist James Montgomery, for many years the radical editor of the Sheffield *Iris,* who had been sent for his education to Fulneck Moravian Settlement, just outside of Leeds.

His parents were Moravian missionaries to Barbados and Tobago, tasked with converting the enslaved without encouraging them to rebel against their enslavers. Moravian missionaries mainly kept to the church's official policy, while also emphasizing the spiritual equality of Blacks and whites. British Moravians were closely tied to the earlier phases of abolition, and West Yorkshire played an important part in this history. Indeed, Moravians were a more familiar part of the British religious and abolitionist landscape than they are today. Restoring them to our understanding of the cultural, religious, and social landscape of Britain allows us to change the way we think about the past.[14]

It is more difficult to trace some of these stories than others. Reflecting on both together enables us to create a fuller picture of the relationship between public antislavery and the way antislavery was embedded in daily life. I have sought to reimagine this vital but more resistant world of the everyday by focusing on (for instance) what can be reimagined through reading of conversations captured in correspondence, or reflecting on what children were being taught in schools and how it prompted them to seek out knowledge for themselves. A spectrum of connected activities encompassing free produce campaigning, sugar boycotts, and peace activism thread their way throughout this book, reminding us that social reform movements are interconnected and operate together.

Campaigning brought together individuals on both sides of the Atlantic, sometimes using existing networks established via trade and by religious affiliations, especially to the Society of Friends. Indeed, as we know, alliances forged out of progressive religious and political commitments to dissent enabled a set of expansive connections within the Atlantic world. These emerged from local proximities and sympathies, combining an optimistic commitment to social justice and education with a radical global vision of the possibility of a better future. Dissenters played a crucial role in British antislavery, the provision of educational facilities and training, scientific discovery and invention, architectural innovation, and advances in medicine.[15] Though they often were excluded from certain kinds of public office, some developed rewarding lives through close connections with institutions such as the schools they founded in the period. A number of those schools educated girls as well as boys, and though their curriculum was invariably gendered, access to formal education transformed the young lives of their pupils.

In addition, libraries and reading rooms were critical to the activities of many individuals. They were spaces where the local encountered the global through collections of books that allowed their members to imagine the possibility of distinct kinds of geographies, systems, and worlds beyond their immediate environs. Libraries were also physical locations of sociability where like-minded individuals met, providing sanctuaries for those who faced persecution elsewhere and enabling an array of meetings—sometimes chance, sometimes organized. Thomas Augst and Kenneth Carpenter have argued that libraries and related locations in which reading happens are both places for reflection and quiet and sites of personal, even revolutionary, transformation for readers on both sides of the Atlantic. Elizabeth McHenry, whose work restores lost and neglected knowledge about the importance of the reading practices of free Blacks in the North before the Civil War and of Black Americans after the war, writes that Black literary societies "furthered the evolution of a black public sphere and a politically conscious society."[16] Libraries exceed what is contained on their shelves. The interactions taking place within them, and the imagined other world they conjure up, are both resources of great value.

Libraries contain the possibility of extraordinary liberatory power but they can also be the product of troubling histories. Sean Moore has revealed that while some colonists were agitating for abolition, early American libraries were building their collections using money made from the slave trade. Marshaling considerable evidence to make his case, he writes that libraries "stood at the nexus of two major branches of transatlantic commerce: the book trade and the slave trade." Meanwhile, Ellen Gruber Garvey has demonstrated the importance of antislavery reading rooms to the Black community in New York and Rochester in the 1830s and 1840s.[17] Libraries need further investigation if we are better to understand their role in redressing the democratic deficit experienced by dissenters such as those investigated here, and even more particularly, by the enslaved individuals whose rights were abrogated by the system of slavery and by free Blacks who also fought against white supremacists.

To signify both sides of cultural, political, and social work of the library, as both location and collection, I want to think about the library as *unquiet* rather than quiet.[18] The meanings of the word *unquiet* all encompass elements of what we see throughout this book, namely a sense of restlessness and activity, an absence of quietness, and the production or creation of disquiet. In other words, though libraries are superficially spaces or places of silence—or more precisely are locations in which a temporary silence or a cultivated quietness becomes the condition within which work can take place—what that silence ultimately produces is something unquiet. Written texts are not silent; they are containers of ideas and words, speech, and discussions of all kinds. The print public sphere is fundamentally a social sphere, as a helpful respondent reminded me at a conference, while libraries are also social and even sociable locations. They were key sites of activism, debate, learning, and network building in the mid-nineteenth century. In discussion groups, correspondence, and conversation stemming from library membership, dissenters and others promoted egalitarianism and peaceful cooperation both locally and across national boundaries. Alliances forged out of progressivism enabled a set of expansive connections across the Atlantic world. These emerged from local proximities and combined an optimistic commitment to social justice with a transatlantic connectedness in a revolutionary era.

Such unquiet libraries, together with the reading that goes on in them, can produce powerful and transformative actions, which includes writing books. Furthermore, libraries are memory-keepers of stories only they can tell. Yet it is worth reiterating that libraries exclude as well as include. Their exclusivity extends from issues about uneven and unequal access (or which readers are allowed access to their collections) to ones about content (or which works are contained there in the first place). Finally, libraries are increasingly threatened with closure or have been closed, and the practice of banning books is on the rise.

The destruction of libraries and their collections has been a key weapon for these who wish to assert control, dominate the sources upon which knowledge production relies, and silence dissent. Library scholarship reminds us that curatorial and archival practices are never neutral and have a key role in determining whose voices are contained and preserved, creating what Alberto Manguel, the one-time director of the National Library of Argentina, has called "a shadow library of absences."[19] McHenry reminds us about what such a loss entails, noting that in general "the words African Americans did write were not valued by libraries, museums, archives, or other institutions charged with the responsibility of preserving literary and cultural material."[20] While such shadow libraries are important locations of antislavery, so are methodologies that seek to compensate for both what is not in the library and what is not in the archive. Productive methodologies for developing our understandings of the past include a set of strategies adopted by scholars to combat this and move beyond silence and absence into possibility and narrative. By invoking the unquiet as a category of investigation, I reimagine the contemporary scholarly relationship to archival material and what it speaks to, thus opening up dialogues that emphasize the "speakerliness" of archival material rather than what might otherwise get framed as long-standing silence.

This takes us to the distinction between libraries and archives. Richard Ovenden, Bodley's librarian at the University of Oxford, has given a simple yet telling definition:

Libraries are accumulations of knowledge, built up one book at a time, often with great strategic purpose, while archives document directly the actions and decision-making processes of institutions and administrations, even of governments. Libraries often hold some of this material as well . . . but archives are by their nature full of material, often mundane in its character, not intended to be read by a mass audience. But where libraries deal with ideas, ambitions, discoveries and imaginings, archives detail the routine but vital stuff of everyday life: land ownership, imports and exports, the minutes of committees and taxes. Lists are often an important feature: whether they are lists of citizens recorded in a census, or lists of immigrants arriving on a boat, archives are at the heart of history; recording the implementation of the ideas and thoughts that may be captured in a book.

The flip side of this, of course, is that the significance of books and archival material is recognised not only by those who wish to protect knowledge, but also by those who wish to destroy it.[21]

The "routine but vital stuff of everyday life" is as crucial to the stories recounted here as the accumulated knowledge contained in scholarly works—texts that are often highly valorized. Important, too, is the issue of just how much never makes its way into the archive or library and how scholars manage this ethical and epistemological challenge. Powerful models of how to combine archival findings with imaginative interpretive modes have been produced by Saidiya Hartman, who in multiple works has pioneered methodologies of combining archives with imaginative retellings to create narratives that would otherwise be lost to us. In seeking to reimagine the lives and experiences of some of the figures I focus on here, I have learned from her work, along with that of other scholars, including Antonio Bly, Marisa J. Fuentes, Eric Gardner, Simon Newman, Ann Laura Stoler, and Michel-Rolph Trouillot, all of whom have developed a range of creative ways to manage archival absences and silences.[22]

Quietness and unquietness, silence and noise, all are probed within the pages of this book, and all have a great deal to say if we pause to listen. Such listening includes paying attention to the referenced and catalogued (to use library terms) personal information, experiences, and memories that people carry with them, which can be accessed at times of need just like the contents of a physical or material library or an archive. Print enabled the circulation of important information, which boosted and supported (and sometimes supplanted) other forms of circulation and transmission of information. But it was also reliant upon, and vitally sustained by, embodiment. Embodied subjects were responsible not just for the content of books, newspapers, and other items but also for the production of ink, paper, and print. The long and expert processes out of which rags or paper pulp were produced, and the skills and intelligence that led to the preparation of the pages on which print was reproduced, were forms of knowing that people carried with them. It was body knowledge rather than book knowledge, often communicated orally and face-to-face, and it is vital to the story told here.

People who know how to remain quiet, or who are constrained to behave quietly, also possess radical potential that can produce unquiet consequences. Anthony Benezet, a quiet man and library philanthropist, framed his interventions on slavery and injustice in relation to sound. In a letter on the slave trade to the Quaker abolitionist Richard Shackleton dated 6 June 1772, he asked rhetorically, "Can we be both *silent* and *innocent* spectators?"[23] He used networks of printers, booksellers, libraries, purchasers, and readers to disseminate his writings and create textual unquietness. He also relied upon friends and acquaintances to carry letters and printed texts across the Atlantic to petition for change. Crucially, though, his writing was vitally connected both to his immersion in the holdings of the Library Company of Philadelphia and to his long-standing interactions with the Black community.

Library collections make it possible to understand the textual history of the abolitionist beliefs of prominent figures like Benezet. Yet it is also important to imagine the ways in which the conversations with figures with firsthand experience of enslavement and racism profoundly shaped his intellectual and ethical landscape, a fact he acknowledged. It is harder to trace this because of gaps and silences in the archive that often overlook the quotidian and day-to-day. Yet all of us engaged in academic research know just how important casual remarks and everyday encounters can be in shaping our work. How often can we capture that on the page itself? At best we can only hope to suggest our varied debts in our "Acknowledgments" section.

When it comes to Benezet, it is certainly true that print was an important source for him, but his arguments were fortified and given life by these vital personal interactions. His interlocutors were living libraries with invaluable experiences and testimonies and inventive ways of gathering vital intelligence.[24] Their knowledge and acts of resistance were as foundational to him as the books he read, shaping his intellectual formation. As Manisha Sinha has argued, the "actions of slave rebels and runaways, black writers and community leaders, did not lie outside of but shaped abolition and its goals."[25] Understanding abolition as a radical social movement, as Sinha asks us to do, means acknowledging the importance of the relations between the many stories of human interaction and movement that can be discovered through the holdings of the libraries in which scholars undertake research, in conjunction with those that still remain outside of their boundaries.

At least two of the men attending the Leeds meeting in December 1858 had traveled to the United States and had their commitment to antislavery reinforced by their experiences. George Howard, 7th Earl of Carlisle, told the attendees of the Leeds Young Men's Anti-Slavery Society of the powerful impact of travel, saying that he "had been in America, and he was certain that no person having the feelings of a Christian could fail to be shocked at such pictures of slavery as would daily meet his observation in Maryland and Virginia," words that met with applause.[26] Meanwhile, Wilson Armistead's experience of visiting the United States was personally transformational. He met a number of inspirational Black individuals and came back to England a changed man. This geographic travel further shaped both men's commitment to abolition. They figuratively journeyed to a different political position as their abstract sympathy for the imagined figure repeatedly described paternalistically by phrases such as "the poor slave" moved toward righteous anger on behalf of fugitives who included personal friends and interlocutors. Abolition, citizenship, and equality for all could be the only acceptable outcomes.

Yet antislavery was also fostered in many other locations and ways. Tasking itself with investigating where, when, and how antislavery happened, the present book pays particular attention to print culture, material culture, and the materiality of print. It examines objects, including embroidered samplers and the sewn antislavery workbags and other items, that not only provided regular reminders of antislavery but also raised money to support campaigning. It thus reflects upon the written and the sewn, and the productive ways they could be brought together. Enslaved and free women on both sides of the Atlantic used their sewing skills to produce antislavery samplers, to petition against injustice, to purchase their freedom and support themselves financially, to create the disguises enabling them to escape enslavement, to build community with like-minded women, and even to prove family relationships. Seeking to capture antislavery's many forms, I focus both on well-known figures from history and on those whose stories are stubborn and resistant, because they were not lived out in the public domain.

A transatlantic connectedness continued in the period I examine, despite a dominant wider political culture sometimes encouraging hostility and national separation. Reflecting on outward-looking and transatlantic models of personal relationships from history offers the opportunity to conceive of inclusive models of community, challenge, and care. This demonstrates the importance of communities that flourish outside the formal limits of the nation-state, refusing its coercive strictures. Certain kinds of connectedness can thrive even in times of extremity. To understand this, I bring together insights from several areas of historical, literary, and cultural studies that have each produced distinguished scholarship, particularly histories of print, material culture studies, transatlantic literary studies, and the study of transatlantic abolition. These enable an analysis of the formation of distinctive transatlantic relationships created through personal interactions and to the exchange of ideas and objects.

This book seeks to fulfill novel intersectional approaches to the study of archival material, to the libraries and other repositories that hold it, and to the stories that may be uncovered through microhistory, group biography, and material culture studies, combined with detailed readings of carefully historicized literary and cultural texts. In doing this, it builds on key issues raised in recent scholarship, including that of literary and cultural scholars. Ellen Gruber Garvey has probed the limitations of the current shape of the archive, and Jared Hickman has argued that further historicizing the field offers ways of reorienting the discipline. Sandra Gustafson has asked how scholars create "interpretive methodologies for reading works that do not match current critical conceptions of the literary or fit into critical narratives that have been laboriously pieced together over the last few decades."[27]

Increasing disciplinary self-reflexivity and flexibility have been evidenced by models of critical investigation, including but not limited to American Studies, Black Atlantic studies, postcolonial studies, transatlantic literary and cultural studies, and hemispheric studies. Recent transatlantic and transnational turns in literary and historical studies have led to new methodologies for understanding the complexities of the past. This has often focused on studying patterns of communication and flows of capital and culture, people and objects, and people as objects. However, the category of national identity itself has sometimes remained in place, only slightly troubled by a changing emphasis on interconnections.

The ways in which a scholarly emphasis on Anglophone cultural and political traditions has influenced our understandings of cultures of the transatlantic has been challenged in recent years.[28] A growing body of work on the significance and impact of the extensive Moravian missionary networks has drawn attention to the kinds of discoveries still possible in their extensive archives, much of which is written in German. Though Moravians were often described as religious dissenters, they did not see themselves in this way, instead insisting that they belonged to an ancient episcopal church. At the same time, many of their communal practices were outside of the mainstream, meaning that they were happy to be dissidents, or at variance with wider society, while also being in fellowship both with avowed dissenters and with members of the established church. Moreover, though British abolitionists relied on Moravians as allies and important sources of knowledge, the Moravian position on slavery was complex, as I have already suggested. Including Moravians in the story this book tells builds on existing discussions of transatlantic antislavery, creating a fuller picture of the contingencies of key alliances.

With the understanding that Yorkshire is at the heart of the transatlantic and transnational work undertaken in these pages, I return to the account of the December 1858 meeting of the Leeds Young Men's Anti-Slavery Society. The evening included several speeches met by repeated applause and cries of "Hear, hear!" that must have echoed around the town hall. Though we do not know the sound of many of the participants' voices, we can imagine them by reading of their cheers and occasional outbursts of laughter, and note the noise produced by their repeated outbursts of applause. They are a physical presence, though only recorded as sound on the printed page of a newspaper, itself an ephemeral form. In a long address, the Earl of Carlisle recollected that he remembered how nervous he was the first time he gave a public speech, which by coincidence had also been in Leeds. "In the first moments of silence and nervousness he was much cheered by hearing someone in the centre of the crowd cry out—'Good, lad.'" This was met by the applause of a local audience who appreciated a down-to-earth Yorkshire comment. They also enjoyed hearing him invoke the antislavery contributions of men with a Yorkshire connection, such as William Wilberforce, laughing at William Cobbett's comments that it was the "fuss" made about slavery by the "'crack-skull' county of York" that really galvanized campaigning.

He ended his address with a description of the powerful recent work of Charles Babbage, which reflected on sound itself. In *The Ninth Bridgewater Treatise* (1838), Babbage had made an argument about the way sound travels. He explained that though a voice is only audible for a certain distance from its source, it is carried in the air by what he termed particles, continuing even when inaudible to the human ear. He claimed that it took twenty hours for a sound (such as that uttered by a human voice) to make its way around the world. Further, and even more radically, he explained that all sounds remain in existence in perpetuity. Citing this powerful claim, the earl told his appreciative audience,

There was a sublime notion connected with the laws of sound, which he believed Mr. Babbage had most impressively mentioned in one of his works, namely, that all sound whatever, even the mildest word which escaped their lips, was never wholly lost, but was so impelled by the ululations of the air, or whatever the medium might be, as to leave its impress through all space and during all time. Such a notion seemed to invest their utterances with new and undreamt of responsibilities. (Hear, hear.) Even the very youngest person had been startled by the marvellous effects of electric communication; and he asked them only to figure to themselves that, by a chain of connections and sympathies, even more to be relied on than the great Atlantic Cable which still lay submerged at the bottom of the deep, they were, from the Town Hall of Leeds, wafting that night, across the mighty ocean to those rugged steeps once trod by the Pilgrim fathers,—to those wide plains where Washington unfurled the standard of independence, or (to present the exact reverse picture) to the rice swamp, the sugar plantation, and the slave mart, where the slave still toiled and bled, and was sold afresh—that they were wafting from this real land of liberty to the still subsisting home of slavery the accents of their sympathies with the abolitionists, their pity for the slave, their allegiance to the undying cause of freedom. (The noble lord resumed his seat amid loud cheers.)[29]

He invoked an image of antislavery and abolitionist clamor and noise permeating all parts of the United States without regard for human distinctions of class or race. The noisy cheering with which his comments were met was undoubtedly envisaged as contributing to this invisible but always present soundscape. Though he focused on the movement of sound from an antislavery meeting in Leeds across the Atlantic, his audience would have understood that sounds and voices traveled the other way too. They worked together, and separately, to create a vocal and polyglot mélange. In this manner there was a kind of antislavery call and response among people whose lives were hugely different but who all shared a desire to abolish slavery. The way he imagines sound traveling and remaining for all time has a profound materiality, conjuring up a rich sonic world. Indeed, in a resonant passage Babbage suggested that since voices are never lost, even if they are not written down and remembered, "The air itself is one vast library, on whose pages are for ever written all that man has ever said or woman whispered."[30] Sounds from the past, present and future reverberate as "ululations of the air," hovering in our midst. If we listen hard enough, we can surely hear the echoes of this acoustic world, an unquietness worth hearing.

I

Sewing the Seeds of Antislavery

ACKWORTH SAMPLERS IN THE ATLANTIC WORLD

On 5 October 1780, eight-year-old Eliza Beavington, a Quaker from Chipping Campden, Gloucestershire, started her life as one of the first scholars (as they were termed) at Ackworth School, near Pontefract in West Yorkshire. The school had been founded by the Society of Friends in October 1779 and aimed to provide an education for the children of Friends who were "not in affluence."[1] She attended the school for two years, after which her existence is unrecorded until 30 September 1784, when she was readmitted to Ackworth together with her cousin Thomas Beavington (also from Chipping Campden), who was two years her junior.[2] The school's records show that both Beavingtons left in 1786. Thomas returned to Ackworth eleven years later, now as the school's reading master. He departed after a year, returning yet again in 1814, when he had a further trial in the same role because the boys' reading was causing concern.[3] But after two further years as reading master he was given notice to leave due to inadequate performance of his duties, departing permanently in 1817.[4] As Ackworth's detailed records reveal, then, the two Beavingtons had a connection to the school spanning four decades.

Neither Eliza nor Thomas Beavington led a particularly remarkable existence. Indeed, both might be described as what the eighteenth-century poet Thomas Gray famously calls the "unhonour'd Dead," who pass through the world leaving little impact. The fathers of both Beavingtons were tanners, a skilled and respected occupation, though poorly paid and known for its stench and gore. The work of both mothers is unrecorded, suggesting their labor was directed to the household and its associated economies, the kind of unwaged activities that are not fully documented or always even recognized as work.

As a consequence of Thomas's gender, his textual imprint is slightly more substantial than that of his cousin Eliza. This means that something of his life can be pieced together, at least until he ended his connection with Ackworth as a middle-aged man. In contrast, beyond census and other public records, there is negligible trace of Eliza Beavington after she eventually left Ackworth aged fourteen. We know she married Edward Hopkins on 3 March 1803, by which time she was thirty-one, quite old by the standards of her day. Beyond this, she vanished back into obscurity and cannot easily be found. After leaving school she returned to the family home, where she used her newly learned skills to help with domestic tasks, perhaps passing even into domestic service as did other scholars of this early period.

One important material artifact enables her to be restored to the historical record in a more personal manner. Her most tangible legacy is an embroidered inscription sampler.[5] It is sewn in black thread on an undyed linen background and was produced during her second period at Ackworth. She finished work on it in 1785, when she was thirteen. Its text consists of a religious verse titled "Resignation the Duty of Man," the words offset by a decorative border. The sampler speaks forcefully and poignantly across the years, bringing Eliza to life once more. More than that, though, by calling to mind the sense of an embodied presence, it carries a powerful affective load. Examining the delicate sampler, now nearly two and a half centuries old, I see a finished object displayed in a picture frame and protected by glass. But in order to understand it, I imagine it in medias res, in the very process of being created and pored over, laboriously, over many hours, by a schoolgirl in Yorkshire at the end of the eighteenth century.

Eliza would first have encountered the piece of linen she was to transform by her work and would have been given a needle and thread with which to accomplish this task. Slowly, holding it in her young hands, she painstakingly completed her stitches, and as she did so, she spelled out the didactic message of the chosen text, while who knows what thoughts went through her head. Were they of resignation and duty, rebellion and escape, or of something else entirely? In the absence of evidence or testimony such as a personal diary, memoir, or letters, it is impossible to say for sure.

However, her sampler is revealing in broader ways and can be used to piece together a larger set of connected and dynamic transatlantic stories about gender, educational training, opportunities, and social class in the period between the end of the eighteenth century and the middle of the nineteenth. Material objects such as samplers give us access to realms of meaning and representation that were particular to women's lives. They offer ways of thinking about elements of the past that often evade scrutiny.[6] It is possible to find out more about sampler-making practices and patterns, as well as the behaviors of girls and women as they sewed, and (in some cases) the provenances of samplers and the ways they, like Eliza's sampler, were handed down over time through families or into the hands of collectors.

For the past seven decades Eliza's sampler has been hidden in plain sight, carefully protected from direct sunlight on one of the less prominent walls in the various houses within which it has been passed down since 1785, now including my own. I know something of its history as I am one of her descendants. The sampler currently hangs on the wall opposite my writing desk—still carefully kept out of the sun. At some point the sampler was given to my paternal grandmother by her parents, and she in turn displayed it in the English home she moved to after many years of living abroad. When she died, it was passed to my father, who also was living abroad with his own young family, including me. It therefore spent frequent periods in storage, only unpacked and displayed sporadically when we were back in England. This preserved it, but also ensured that it was overlooked, rather like what can happen to some of the archived material with which this book engages, safely looked after and containing important and as yet untold stories.

By the time we resettled in England and the sampler was returned to yet another wall, it had been defamiliarized by its long absence and seemed, at least to me, like a very old-fashioned and dull object. Books and print were always more exciting than embroidery to someone brought up in the late twentieth century. The sampler's message of dutiful resignation also was positively distasteful to a teenage girl, whose budding feminism and avowed atheism resisted any such injunction.[7] The first line is a capitalized title, "RESIGNATION, THE DUTY OF MAN," followed by six stanzas, opening with "Transient is human Life, all Flesh as Grass, / The Goodliness of Man but as a Flower: / Fine Gold must through the fervid Furnace pass, / Through

RESIGNATION, THE DUTY OF MAN.

Transient is human Life all Flesh as Grafs,
The Goodlinefs of Man but as a Flower:
Fine Gold muft through the fervid Furnace pafs,
Through Death we Immortality explore.

Through Judgment muft Deliverance be known
From vile affections and their wrathful Sting,
True peace pertains to Righteoufnefs alone,
That flows thro' Faith from Lifes eternal Spring.

Should Man to Glory call'd and endlefs peace,
Bewail his momentary adverfe doom,
Or in deep thankful Refignation, kifs,
The Rod that promps him on his Journey Home

Unfearchable the Providence of God,
By boafted Wifdom of the Son of Duft;
Lo! Virtue feels oppreffions iron Rod,
And impious Spirits triumph o'er the Juft.

Shall hence a self-conceited Reptile dare,
The omnifcient Rulers Equity arraign?
Say here thy Wrath is fit, thy Bounty there,
Good to promote and evil to reftrain!

Believing Souls unfeignedly can say,
"Not mine, but thy all perfect Will be done,
If beft this bitter Cup shou'd pafs away,
Or be endur'd, to thee not me is known."

ELIZA BEAVINGTON ACKWORTH SCHOOL 1785.

Eliza Beavington sampler.
Owned by the author and photographed by Lee Dalley.

Death we Immortality explore." Death leads to eternity and is not to be feared, though life itself will doubtless produce hardships. The third stanza turns to the familiar theme of resignation to the will of God: "Should Man to Glory call'd and endless peace, / Bewail his momentary adverse doom, / Or in deep thankful Resignation, kiss, / The Rod that promps [*sic*] him on his Journey Home." I am ashamed to admit that perhaps if it had it been brightly colored or had featured some of the fascinating decorative patterns of later Ackworth samplers, it might have caught my attention.

Now, years later, a combination of the scholarly turn to material studies and the sampler's connection to Ackworth and to myself has made me look at it with more interest, excitement, and emotion. It is an ostensibly mundane object that tells a remarkable story about a moment in the history of the Society of Friends and of its relationship to both the quotidian and the globally significant. When I look at Eliza's sampler, I am also examining a remnant of a family history of which I have limited knowledge, part of the material of a larger story I have been stitching together for several years. The surface of Eliza's sampler is marred by several small stains, the product of its age and fragility. My grandfather framed it, and it stays behind glass to protect it from any external elements that might cause damage. Grateful to those who enabled this survival, I remain committed to continue with its preservation and to keep pursuing the stories it can reveal. As I hold this sampler in my hands, I find myself thinking of Jonathan Senchye's powerful description of encountering the materiality of the archive:

> Who has not been moved in some way by being present with an object in an archive? A person we care about very deeply for one reason or another moved their hands over this paper in the creation of this manuscript, and it is possible to lay our hand there too. My eyes are struck by the bite of very black type on astonishingly white rag paper; my fingers move on the bumpy echo of eighteenth-century type pressed through to the recto of a sheet. I wonder about the enslaved African American man who I know printed this sheet and place my hands where his were.[8]

Eliza Beavington's sampler offers itself up as an object that enables me to "be present" with it and to seek to understand it on its own terms. This chapter will take up the generous gift of its invitation. With all of this in mind, I use her sampler to start a consideration of sampler-making and sewing in the transatlantic world. I will examine the relationship between cultures of print and sewing, and the oral and scribal, reflecting on the movements of texts across and between books, diaries, letters, sewn objects, and speech. Sampler-making can teach us a great deal about how cultural, intellectual, and social exchanges took place, and by examining samplers we can see how patterns, methods, practices, and ideas circulated. I seek to reimagine the mis-en-scène of creation as well as to discuss the afterlife of completed samplers.

To do this I focus on a few samplers, largely sewn at Ackworth, to understand more about the ways in which contemporaries understood samplers as carriers of significant values.[9] Though I touch briefly on the act of sewing itself, my argument is focused on what inscription and antislavery samplers reveal about how a pioneering Quaker School in West Yorkshire shaped the lives and prospects of its girl scholars. The education offered at the school contributed to shaping a dissenting culture in which the values of Friends, including a commitment to antislavery, were reinforced. At the same time, it speaks to a set of contexts that take us way beyond a remote school in the North of England and has implications for the many women who understood what it meant to work with needles and textiles. Girls and women, in conditions of either freedom or enslavement, knew the invaluable and inventive possibilities of their sewing, the second focus of the chapter.[10] Sewing women used their skills for petitions or protests, or to support themselves or their families in enslavement, or to manufacture clothing that would enable them to emancipate themselves. Sewing is a creative act, and we will see that some sampler-makers made subtle alterations to the familiar texts they sewed, thus amending their meanings and creating new interpretations of those texts.

Ackworth samplers started to incorporate antislavery messages in about the second decade of the nineteenth century, in the period around the United Kingdom's Slavery Abolition Act (1833). Anna (Atkins) Richardson, who left the school in 1819, went on to become a formidable antislavery activist around this time. She was born in Chipping Norton, a small market town about seventeen miles from Chipping Campden, where Eliza and Thomas Beavington originated. She started at Ackworth in 1817 and left in July 1819, doubtless having sewed a sampler while there, though its current whereabouts (if it has survived) are unknown. While at the school she met her future husband, Henry Richardson of Newcastle, who was from a close-knit and well-to-do family. His father, George, described by Anna in 1852 as a "venerable" man and "an old and long tried friend of the negro," was well respected and widely known within the community as a solid Friend and active campaigner.[11] Anna Richardson's own parents, Esther (Millard) Atkins and Samuel Atkins, were also committed to social justice, especially to peace and to antislavery. Anna's activities in the public domain were profoundly connected to the communities in which she was nurtured, including that of Ackworth.

In contrast, neither Eliza Beavington nor the other sampler-makers I discuss went on to have public lives. For this reason, it is difficult to know what they hoped for or what they thought about some of the pressing matters of the day. However, by positioning them within what can be discovered about their families and communities, it is possible to build a rich context within which their lives can be imagined and recreated. This kind of contextualization is enabled by examining census records, commonplace books, correspondence, diaries, memoirs, and ships' manifests. Some of the sampler-makers are known at only one remove, their existences and experiences glimpsed when they are mentioned in letters or listed on records. On occasions, when they can only be found in passing references, they must be imagined in relation to others. They are also vividly present through the samplers that offer testimony to their lives and activities and record crucial information such as their names, ages, and schools.

The individuals I focus on here participated in activities that helped build and sustain their varied communities; they are both in and out of the archive. In seeking to reimagine them I have reflected on the work of scholars who have offered a range of ways to manage silences creatively. At times, without definitive proof of what demonstrably is the case, I have aimed to be sensitive to probability. Mathematicians have a useful phrase, "almost surely," for assumptions where probability cannot be absolutely determined but nonetheless there is near certainty. Its semantic formulation points to the fact that even in a discipline governed by proofs there is a vital and important understanding that there is sometimes a gap between the almost and the surely. Of course, my focus is on human subjects and the patchy record of their lives, which all too frequently destabilizes the empirical or evidence-based forms of knowledge production that are the basis for historical inquiry. In those instances, I rely on that which is almost surely the case.

Throughout the book, and especially in this chapter, I have tried to avoid reproducing a hierarchy in which print trumps other sources. Wherever possible, I have paid attention to letters and reported conversations to supplement and extend print and create a generative reimagining of the worlds within which the individuals I discuss moved and made their lives. Such sources are like the bodily gestures accompanying speech acts, giving life to them and enabling an experience of what is being said that transforms the words themselves into something more performative and grounded in the body. When thinking about how to manage these varied sources and forms, I have found Mary Kelley's comments regarding networks of Black Philadelphian abolitionists especially insightful. She writes, "We understand oral performance, scribal writing, and print publication not as a series of separate and autonomous acts but, instead, as a series of continuously intersecting and mutually reinforcing habits."[12] As we will see, this observation about intersectional forms of communication is helpful when studying many of the figures associated with Ackworth School.

ANTISLAVERY READING AT ACKWORTH AND BEYOND

A letter written in 1838 by Anna's sister-in-law Rachel Richardson, four years after the death of her sister Rebecca, brings together Kelley's trinity of oral performance, scribal writing, and print. Remembering walks they had taken together, Rachel notes, "One walk in particular seems so fresh in my recollection when our beloved departed one repeated Barbauld's beautiful hymn . . . I think I was never more struck with its beauty."[13] This touching letter exemplifies Kelley's understanding of the ways in which modes of communication and expression work together. In addition, it suggests the kinds of poetry to which young scholars were exposed, and learned by heart, while revealing the way kinship networks were sustained by correspondence. Finally, it tells us of the kind of leisure habits the sisters enjoyed. All of this is contained within a few lines of a letter that was probably read aloud or shared with a wider group with a connection to the sender.

I want to explore, briefly, what Rachel's letter reveals. Barbauld's *Hymns in Prose for Children* (1781) was a collected series of short numbered pieces, or "hymns," designed to be memorized and recited aloud. They focused on nature and its relationship to God, in particular, inviting readers to imagine themselves in the world depicted for them. At Ackworth, reading was taught by a process in which small groups read in unison aloud in front of the reading mistress or master, "paragraph by paragraph, all standing so remote from her, as to render a proper exertion of their voices necessary, by which they are inured to read audibly."[14] We can imagine the considerable impact of hearing one of these hymns read aloud in an environment in which access to books remained limited and silence was both encouraged and sometimes required. When Rebecca recited the hymn on a walk with her sisters, she was reproducing and adapting early performative and pedagogic experience.

Barbauld was well known as an educator and writer and from 1774 to 1785 ran the highly regarded dissenting school, the Palgrave Academy in Suffolk, with her husband. Her father had been a teacher at the famous Warrington Academy, a key dissenting institution, where Joseph Priestley also taught. In hymn 8, Barbauld describes forms of social groups, from the family to the nation, arguing that all are part of "God's family." Juxtaposing an image of an enslaved woman who sits weeping with her ill child with that of a powerful monarch, she argues that God is aware of them both:

> Negro woman, who sittest pining in captivity, and weepest over thy sick child; though no one seeth thee, God seeth thee; though no one pitieth thee, God pitieth thee: raise thy voice, forlorn and abandoned one; call upon him from amidst thy bonds, for assuredly he will hear thee.
>
> Monarch, that rulest over an hundred states; whose frown is terrible as death, and whose armies cover the land, boast not thyself as though there were none above thee:—God is above thee; his powerful arm is always over thee; and if thou doest ill, assuredly he will punish thee.[15]

The juxtaposition of particular individuals, here a Black woman and a monarch, and broader message, here of God's sympathy or punishment, is typical of the *Hymns*. By the 1790s Barbauld was an active abolitionist. Her bold poem "Epistle to William Wilberforce Esq. on the Rejection of the Bill for Abolishing the Slave Trade" (1791) attacked both the British Parliament and society's moral contagion. She described slaveholders and those who supported them as tyrants and predicted an inevitable cataclysm, writing,

> In Britain's senate, Misery's pangs give birth
> To jests unseemly, and to horrid mirth—
> Forbear!—thy virtues but provoke our doom,
> And swell th' account of vengeance yet to come;
> For, not unmark'd in Heaven's impartial plan,
> Shall man, proud worm, contemn his fellow-man?
> And injur'd Afric, by herself redrest,
> Darts her own serpents at her Tyrant's breast.[16]

Rachel Richardson's admiration for Barbauld was shared on both sides of the Atlantic. Her work was widely quoted, appearing in edited antislavery collections as well as on embroidered samplers. Indeed, a sampler sewn in 1793 by Mary D'Silver, a Black schoolgirl at the Bray Associates Negro School in Philadelphia, contains four lines from Barbauld's "The Mouse's Petition" (1773). The mouse argues against having its liberty taken away and appeals for compassion and liberty based on justice. The original reads "The well-taught philosophic mind, / To all compassion gives; / Casts round the world an equal eye / And feels for all that lives," but D'Silver's sampler contains a subtle but powerful change. The word *all* is replaced by the word *each*, so the last line of the stanza reads "And feels for each that lives." Since D'Silver was only eight when the sampler was completed, it may be that her unknown teacher suggested the substitution for a political reason, to emphasize the equality of her Black pupil to white sampler-makers. Perhaps it was simply an error. Yet other young abolitionists were creatively reworking texts. James Anthony, a pupil at the New York Manumission Society's African Free School demonstrated this in 1816 when he adapted Hannah More's poem "Slavery" (1788) for the particular context of his public recitation.[17]

It is ironic though revealing that D'Silver herself, like many other Black figures from history, remains so enigmatic and unknowable, subsumed within the generality "all" rather than the singularity of "each," the very word she herself sewed.[18] Her sampler ended up in England, suggesting that it may have been produced to be sold to raise money for the school, again emphasizing the possibility of deliberation in the word choice.[19] It was almost surely a considered change, a creative act of literary and sewn remaking. Her work is a fine example not just of the transformation of print into stitching but also of Barbauld's use of the petition, a familiar form of protest that I will discuss later in the chapter. The sampler was recently included in the *Black Founders: The Forten Family of Philadelphia* exhibition at the Museum of the American Revolution in Philadelphia. The exhibition also included samplers sewn in 1817 and 1822 by two important future Black abolitionists, the eleven-year-old Margaretta Forten and six-year-old Mary Forten.

Material culture artifacts such as samplers contribute to our understanding of the lives and works of girls and women who are otherwise hidden from history. Ackworth samplers provide evidence of the way the school's curriculum adapted over time, for instance. As the school slowly became more outward looking, its girl scholars displayed a growing awareness of the culture of antislavery and abolition. It is evident that some of this came through the circulation of news as it filtered into letters and conversation, while some came through print. For example, in 1803, Enoch Lewis, who was teaching at Ackworth's sister school, Westtown School in Pennsylvania, challenged a group of slave catchers who had come to the village of Westtown and forcibly captured a Black man who had settled there. The unnamed man was only released on condition of the payment of $400, some of which was immediately raised; the rest was loaned to him by Lewis.[20] We can speculate that the story of Lewis's encounters reached Ackworth scholars because of the connections between the school and Friends on either side of the Atlantic. But what we know for sure is that in Lewis's household, the New Garden School (another of the schools with which he was associated), and Westtown School, the poetry of William Cowper, with its support for abolition, was highly regarded, as it was at Ackworth. From this we can also trace the transatlantic literary culture within which the ethical and literary sensibilities of its diverse readers developed. Cowper's poems from the 1780s were well known and widely read among Quakers on both sides of the Atlantic, including Alice Jackson of Pennsylvania, who would go on to marry Enoch Lewis. Prior to her marriage she lived on a Pennsylvania farm, and though her numerous activities included spinning and other domestic tasks, she also had time for reading. Her son later described the family's reading as follows,

> The books to which they had access, if not numerous, supplied wholesome, mental nutriment, and contained nothing that would injure the morals or vitiate the taste of the reader. While they included the best of the writings of Barclay and Penn, with many Friends' Journals of less value, except as incitements to pious reflections and feelings, they also included works of the highest reputation in English literature, but no novels of any grade. Works of fiction, with which Paradise Lost and Pope's Translation of Homer were not classed, were rigorously excluded from the family library, being, according to the approved nomenclature of Friends, "pernicious." Addison, Young, Grey, [sic] Thomson and Cowper were among her favorite authors. She delighted particularly in The Task, and her literary taste was formed mainly on similar models.[21]

When she worked with her husband at the New Garden School, Alice encouraged the pupils to read to her, one recalling, "She frequently gave to me the privilege of reading to her in the evening the poetry of Cowper, for which we felt a common admiration, both for the beauty of thought and diction, and the general excellence of the sentiments."[22] Both anecdotes give a sense of the kinds of texts considered appropriate as well as the ways in which reading events took place. The experience of reading poetry aloud to a sympathetic adult listener was of great significance to her young pupil.

John Sharp's reading of Cowper as he crossed the Atlantic was transformative, as I will outline in more detail later in the chapter. Cowper was also of importance to another reader, Harriet Jacobs; Philip Gould reminds us that her famous image of the "loophole of retreat" (the roof space where she hid to make herself both unseen and unheard) is derived from Cowper's The Task.[23] Cowper's readers were united across the color line, reminding us of W. E. B. Du Bois's famous observation, "I sit with Shakespeare and he winces not." Ackworth scholars were familiar with Quaker abolitionist writing such as Elias Hicks's Observations on the Slavery of Africans and Their Descendants, and on the Use of the Produce of Their Labour, first published in 1811 but reissued in 1814 and 1823.[24] In March 1826, thirty-three girls in the school's west wing petitioned the school's superintendent, Robert Whitaker, asking him for more information about the condition of enslaved Blacks, writing, "The juvenile inhabitants of the 'West Wing' respectfully request the company of Robert Whitaker . . . for the purpose of telling them something further respecting the suffering of the poor Slaves: they feel greatly interested on their behalf, and would be very happy to do anything in their power to alleviate their sufferings."[25]

Whitaker replied promptly, thanking them for their invitation and proposing a meeting time. Over a few days, he visited the girls and talked to them about a range of topics and texts, including the work of Cowper. He obviously understood that poetry could perform a vital educational function. He also took pains to discuss the writing and personal example of Anthony Benezet, whose educational work with Blacks was admired by many Friends. In addition, several meetings were then held at the school, with teachers relaying to the scholars "such information . . . as they thought would give them a just idea of Slavery—and all its attendant evils." The discussions, reading, and sewing of the girl scholars were all operating together to develop their understanding and independence. In addition, some of their emerging knowledge, leadership, and self-confidence doubtless came from access to print, where they would have encountered reports of a burgeoning culture of British and U.S. petitions, including female-driven petitions. They were becoming young abolitionists.

PETITIONING FOR CHANGE

Petitioning drew on popular and local forms of protest, harnessing them to wider concerns. It encompassed a wide range of causes, from personal grievances to collective issues. Female petitions were being made through sewn protests in the period of the Ackworth petition to Whitaker, as the tragic case of Mary Frances Heaton exemplifies. Heaton was from a well-off family in Yorkshire, but after her father became bankrupt, she went to London to earn her living as a teacher. She returned to Doncaster to care for him in his last illness and remained there after his death. From 1834 to 1835, she gave twice-weekly music lessons to the daughters of an Anglican vicar. When he did not give her the wages they had agreed upon, she disputed with him publicly, verbally protesting his behavior in his own church.

The weight of the establishment was brought to bear upon her solitary female voice. She was taken to court and then committed to the West Riding Pauper Lunatic Asylum in Wakefield (about ten miles from Ackworth). There she was subjected to brutal medical interventions and attempted escape. After a few years, she seems finally to have broken down and accepted her fate, behaving in a docile manner, unlike her earlier demeanor. Abandoned by her family, she remained locked up for the rest of her life, dying after about four decades of incarceration. But she retained her sense of the injustice meted out to her, using her sewing skills to produce many sewn inscription samplers in which she complained about her treatment.

Though her lengthy and poignant petitions were unsuccessful, they give lasting attestation to her experience and courage. Her creative and resourceful use of her skills was not unusual, though the content of, and contexts for, her sewn complaints is particularly striking. She clearly understood existing forms of protest, overtly using the conventional form of the humble petition in a highly unconventional format, such as creating a sewn sampler addressed to Queen Victoria. In it she asserts, "Our Most Gracious Sovereign The Queen Victoria Is most respectfully petitioned to affix her Royal Seal to this sampler in token of approbation thereof." Refusing to be seen and not heard, she produced impassioned and angry protest as she challenged her unfair fate. Her samplers are unequivocal about her ongoing outrage, as this extract from another sampler shows:

In its blackest, most heart sickening, most confirmed, most important, most unequivocal, and most extraordinary form, whereby the world is reduced to a blank, and the brevity of human life the only consolation the heart can ever know, such its dire effects. . . . The office of "Mayor of Doncaster," was filled in 1837 by a fellow for whose crimes the punishment awarded to the assassin of Henry 4 wou'd not be disproportioned, and I solemnly believe that the British Government will be of the opinion shou'd I live to relate my story. Having purposely & distinctly remarked in the presence of half a dozen persons including the Mayor that I wished the vicar would submit to arbitration, my claim against him for music lessons given to his daurs [sic] regularly twice a week during the years 1834–1835.[26]

Other women who petitioned against their treatment around the same period included Elizey Price from Kingswinford, near Dudley in the West Midlands. In 1845 she "complained of the 'cruel proceedings' by which she had been taken into custody by local constables and experienced 'great inconvenience and expense and endured much suffering' in a petition she signed with her mark."[27] The Ackworth petition took a different form, but the girls positioned themselves as humble petitioners making a request to a powerful figure, the customary form of petitioning.

Abolitionists in Britain and the United States had adopted the well-established practice of petitioning early in their campaigns. Petitions in the United States included one organized in Boston in 1787 by Prince Hall, in which free Blacks campaigned for improvements to the education provided for Black children.[28] The unsuccessful petition was followed by three further petitions the following year, all demanding an end to the slave trade. The first was partly organized by Hall and was presented to the Massachusetts General Court, the second came from the New England Yearly Meeting of Friends, while the third was signed by Boston's clergymen and others.[29]

The girls may also have heard of the petition of the well-known Quaker Paul Cuffee, who, together with his brother John, refused to pay taxes because free Blacks were not able to vote in Massachusetts. They subsequently went on to petition to end taxation without representation, and though this was unsuccessful, it paved the way, in 1783, to the granting of votes to all free males in Massachusetts. Cuffee, who had built a business for himself as a mariner, became well known in Britain when his vessel *The Traveller* docked at Liverpool with a free Black crew. An extract from the *Edinburgh Review* discussing this extraordinary and pioneering achievement prefaced his 1811 work *Memoir of Captain Paul Cuffee, a Man of Color*, published in book form in Britain after initially appearing in the *Liverpool Mercury*.[30]

Other significant petitions included an abolitionist petition produced in 1783 by the London Yearly Meeting's Meeting for Sufferings, signed by 273 Quakers and subsequently presented to the House of Commons. At the same time, twenty-three male Friends formed the Committee on the Slave Trade, and a more informal group, composed of men who were able to mobilize their transatlantic networks, was also formed. They included the Pennsylvania-born William Dillwyn, a former student of Benezet, and Thomas Knowles, whose wife, Mary Morris Knowles, was a supporter of women's education and a highly regarded needlework artist.[31] Within a brief time following the 1783 petition, there was a significant expansion of the number of petitions (including antislavery petitions) presented to the House of Commons.[32] Indeed, a particular impetus for the Ackworth girls' petition was the extraordinary quantity of petitions—almost eight hundred in total—produced in Britain between 1823, when the London Anti-Slavery Society was formed, and 1824, when it held its first meeting.[33]

The girls' handwritten petition was produced within a developing culture of juvenile antislavery activism and widespread debates about Britain's continued involvement with slavery even after the 1807 Slave Trade Act. Like other Quaker schools, Ackworth held a Gala Day to mark the passing of the 1833 Slavery Abolition Act. Ackworth's event included an address by the Quaker radical and former scholar John Bright (connected to the Richardsons through marriage). When Frederick Douglass visited England on his first tour (1845–1847), he regularly stayed in the Rochdale home of Bright, who was at the start of his illustrious career as a member of Parliament. Bright was also one of the contributors to the fund for Douglass's manumission. In nearby Bradford, the Eastbrook school ended its celebrations of the day with a collection of twenty shillings to help "the black population in the colonies." The *Bradford Observer*'s account of this event positioned the children as what Kathryn Gleadle and Ryan Hanley call "active recipients of the antislavery message." Gleadle and Hanley give many instances of the development of juvenile antislavery principles, including sugar abstention, through "peer-to-peer socialisation of young people."[34]

All of this suggests an atmosphere within the school in which its young scholars were increasingly participating in the abolitionist and antislavery debates going on in the wider culture. The gradual emergence of sewn antislavery motifs on Ackworth samplers is linked to these changes, and as I have shown, the girls' petition shows a familiarity with forms of political activity shaping public life, especially antislavery. It reveals the way the girls appropriated the model of emulation that was also the very basis of sewing samplers.[35] Such emulation (of the petitioning taking place elsewhere and of the iconography characterizing the campaign against slavery) provides evidence of the positive enactment of a desire for participation in the wider world. Further, the girls understood that their samplers could have a relation to a culture of abolition and antislavery that scholars often conceive of as largely shaped by, and articulated within, print. To start to explore this, I now turn to the importance placed on sewing and sampler-making in female education.

SAMPLER-MAKING AND SEWING IN AND BEYOND ACKWORTH

Pioneering scholarship on schoolgirls' samplers has often focused on the way American and British schools taught practices and designs from a long European tradition. The increasing focus on Black women's needle skills and their relationship to legacies of African textile traditions has provided an important corrective. Additionally, economic historians and others are paying new attention to the ways Black women used sewing to improve their life situations or had their skills and labor used by slaveholders. Focusing on the work of Black schoolgirls, Kelli Racine Barnes has argued that the "quiet activism revealed in their embroideries continued with the formation of their families and the support they gave their communities," while Karol Weaver shows the ways enslaved women seamstresses capitalized on their skills and negotiated favorable positions for themselves, "fashioning freedom" as she puts it.[36] A woman's sewing could be used to support herself and her family, keeping poverty at bay, or even, in the case of enslaved women, to purchase or otherwise attain freedom. Barnes cites the case of two enslaved women in South Carolina who used their skills to work within the free Black community to save money and finance their escape from enslavement.[37] A particularly audacious example of emancipatory sewing took place when Ellen Craft made the trousers she wore when she disguised herself as "Mr. Johnson" and together with William Craft escaped from enslavement, assisted by a combination of her now well-known disguise, pale skin tone, and acting skills. She then supported herself by her "work with her needle" when in Boston.[38]

Sewing was a vital, though frequently undervalued, element of the entire system of enslavement, as Alexandra Finley has argued. By examining records advertising the sewing skills of enslaved women, she shows the ways in which slaveholders argued that skilled women could be sold for more than their peers. In addition, she demonstrates the complex entanglement of different forms of labor, moving away from an abstract to an embodied idea of the market, noting, "In the clothing industry, the invisible hand of the market was actually a very visible, tired, and female hand whose freedom depended on the meaning attached to its particular hue."[39] But she also notes the ways in which this labor has been rendered invisible over time, both by the absence of records and by the domestic ideology that rendered their work as an expected form of activity that did not need to be noted: "Lack of material does not mean lack of significance; the nature of these women's labor obstructed its broader survival in the records. Everything from the construction of the archive to the construction of a sentence pastoralizes these women's labor as much as the sentimental fiction and prescriptive literature of the antebellum era."[40]

Despite her reminder that such labor was difficult and tiring, leading to strained eyes and sore hands, more positive emotions could also be a powerful element of the sewing process. It could bring together love and politics, along with a desire for longevity and anticipation of the power of memory-making. This was undoubtedly what prompted an enslaved woman named Rose to act in South Carolina in the 1850s, when her daughter Ashley was about to be sold away. She packed her precious daughter a cotton bag with a few items, knowing they would never see each other again. As Tiya Miles writes in her beautiful book *All That She Carried*, "Rose couldn't know how things would turn out, but she held fast to a vision. She saw her daughter alive and provided for her into the future, a radical imagining for a Black mother in the 1850s."

In 1921, Ashley's granddaughter Ruth Middleton, at that time living in Philadelphia, embroidered the history of the gift and the love of a mother for her daughter on to the sack, which had somehow been kept by a bereft girl and preserved over time. She sewed the words "My great grandmother Rose / mother of Ashley gave her this sack when / she was sold at age 9 in South Carolina / it held a tattered dress 3 handfulls of / pecans a braid of Roses hair. Told her / It be filled with my Love always / she never saw her again / Ashley is my grandmother / Ruth Middleton / 1921." Summarizing the relationship between the three women and the importance of Ruth Middleton's embroidered words, Miles writes, "Without Ruth, there would be no record. Without her record, there would be no history. Ruth's act of creation mirrored that of her great-grandmother Rose. Through her embroidery, Ruth ensured that the valiance of discounted women would be recalled and embraced as a treasured inheritance."[41] Rose gave her daughter an extraordinary gift—the gift of love. She added an assurance that it would survive against the odds and in the most difficult and traumatic circumstances. Her great-granddaughter lovingly preserved this in her stitching about seventy years later.

Around the time Rose gave Ashley her loving gift, a Black woman from North Carolina, sewed three Black dolls for Edith, Imogen, and Lillian Willis, the white children of her employers. The dolls made by that woman, Harriet Jacobs, were carefully looked after and passed down through the family as treasured objects of memory and friendship. It seems highly likely that Jacobs also sewed a doll for her much-loved daughter, Louisa, who herself developed lifelong relationships with the Willis family. The three dolls she gave to the Willis girls have recently been exhibited at the New-York Historical Society's powerful exhibition of Black dolls, where they were joined by abolitionist Black dolls that were not sentimental objects in any conventional way. The dolls included disturbing and realistic details such as slave collars, bespeaking the powerful assertion that antislavery began at home and that juveniles could also be abolitionists, though the ideology of the period suggested they should be seen but not heard.[42]

Samplers—like some of these dolls—offered the physical sites on which antislavery beliefs could be represented by the incorporation of features such as those I have described. Additionally, the act of sewing itself enabled a kind of early feminism and solidarity with like-minded women. Occasions on which women gathered to sew could be important to community formation, conversation, and cohesion. While this could undoubtedly be conservative, maintaining gendered roles and the status quo, it might also help develop more radical talk. Many of these conversations have not been formally recorded, though they can sometimes be reconstituted from the fragments, snippets, and scraps noted in letters, diaries, and women's fiction.

Over time, Ackworth School became extremely well known for its sampler-making, and due to the survival of numbers of Ackworth samplers, the distinctive medallion patterns associated with the school have had their wider significance amplified. Despite this, there is no consensus about how or why these patterns first appeared, though from the 1790s onward they traveled across the Atlantic, into American schools.[43] One probable reason for this transatlantic migration was the influence of charismatic American visitors to the school who visited and then returned to the United States, such as Rebecca Jones, who had attended Ann Marsh's well-known school in Philadelphia.[44] While such incomplete knowledge is a useful reminder about how much we still must learn about sewing more broadly, it also reminds us is that people are carriers of ideas, and that these spread widely and in multiple ways that are not obviously measurable.

TAKING ANTISLAVERY INTO THEIR OWN HANDS

Eliza Beavington sewed her sampler during the early phase of the Industrial Revolution. Her work is therefore positioned during an important moment of global change. Though it provides physical evidence of how an individual was spending her time as she made a transition from girlhood into woman-hood, it also speaks to a historical period in which a significant step into a recognizable modernity was taking place. In the decades that followed, there was a wholesale change in the labor market, in associated modes of work, and (on an even larger scale) in what Immanuel Wallerstein has termed the "world system." Sewing would remain a core element of female education, taught to girls either at home, in schools, or even in classes held in churches and chapels.[45]

Mechanization would gradually alter women's relationships to sewn objects. The production of handcrafted work remained important within female education and activity, but the mass production of cloth and sewn goods led to wide availability of ready-made clothes and then to the emergence of the department store and of shopping as a leisure pursuit. Eventually, sampler-work was often regarded as an arcane remnant of a previous age, and the work of sewing itself was also increasingly devalued in a world of easily reproduced cheap clothing. Still, women understood that sewing remained a crucial skill, and the occasions on which women sewed alone or in groups could be highly valued by them. As I have shown, sewing could be a way into economic security, self-emancipation, and expressing love, though it was often also a form of drudgery.

At the other end of the spectrum, fine sewing and embroidery, like other forms of domestic handicraft, were regarded as forms of refined feminine accomplishment, though sewn objects were invariably categorized as craft rather than as the products of an inventive or imaginative art. The emergence of a transatlantic ideology of domesticity in the mid-nineteenth century meant that domestic accomplishments were important acquirements for middle-class girls and women.[46] Embroidered samplers demonstrated the kind of skill that was valued by the prospective suitors of wealthier girls and women, and by those who helped them make their matches. In both cases, albeit differently, samplers could be what Maureen Daly Goggin has called a "material CV."[47]

Along with changes to the status of sewing, the Industrial Revolution also brought with it another transformation, made possible by the invention of new paper manufacturing processes. As we know, paper had traditionally been made from rags (of cotton as well as linen, the very material on which Beavington's sampler was sewn). Women were encouraged to collect rags in their ragbags, and the relationship of domestic work to the production of paper was playfully discussed in three poems by the American poet Lydia Sigourney, an abolitionist and activist for Native American rights. "To a Shred of Linen," "To a Fragment of Silk," and "To a Fragment of Cotton" all reflect upon the processes of production as well as the role of gendered domesticity. In "To a Shred of Linen," Sigourney takes her reader through the process by which flax is grown and made into linen cloth and paper. In this way she celebrates both sewing and writing, as well as the way poetry and print lead to posterity.

The rag paper manufacturing process was costly, and in consequence books and other paper items were often expensive. All of this changed when paper began to be manufactured from wood pulp, which was cheaper and more widely available. By the 1840s, this new way of producing paper had become established, though it would really start to flourish in the 1860s.[48] As fiber extracted from wood replaced fiber made from rags, costs were reduced. The increase in the production and availability of books and newspapers changed the cultural, economic, social, and political landscape. It contributed to the huge expansion of print, and together with the invention of writing implements such as the pencil and fountain pen, it transformed the world of education and the life experiences of those being educated. As we will see, its impacts were felt within the community of scholars who attended Ackworth.

But this should also remind us that prior to this period the relative scarcity of books meant that print was only one of the ways in which antislavery ideas were being disseminated.

In the early years of the school, its young scholars were kept from knowledge of the wider world, receiving a guarded education—that is, one that guarded children from outside influence. However, while maintaining its distinctive identity, the school slowly looked outward toward wider society and to events taking place beyond its confines. Understanding the early story of Ackworth involves tracing a web of friendships, professional contacts, and beliefs extending across the Atlantic. This reveals that the school's closely knit rural community was nonetheless at the heart of a transnational network. Friends' long-standing commitment to social justice issues such as antislavery and peace meant that Ackworth scholars were exposed to geopolitical contexts.

Due to its easy reproducibility, print eventually became the dominant form in which antislavery arguments were articulated and circulated in the public realm. Print made it possible to share copious amounts of valuable information readily within, and beyond, the Atlantic world. Printed texts were crucially supplemented by a huge amount of scribal writing in the form of letters, diary entries, memoirs, and petitions. These give evidence for the importance of meetings, discussion groups, lectures, and conversations, not all of which can be accessed in the manner of print. As Mary Kelley puts it in a slightly different context, "With all the books, pamphlets, and newspapers cascading from the presses on both sides of the Atlantic, it is not surprising that scholars have privileged print. Early nineteenth-century Americans did not. For them, no single approach to reading and writing prevailed."[49] This was also true of their British counterparts, who likewise operated at the intersection between the printed, sewn, oral, and scribal. Texts and objects, recovered conversations, and glimpses of daily life all offer an extension of the antislavery archives. They allow us to listen in and discover more about communities of friends and interlocutors whose writing did not make it into the print public realm but who nonetheless had keen passions, ideas, and arguments. Letters were often lent to readers who were not their original recipients, or copied or read aloud to others. In this manner they had a circulation that exceeded that of a single addressee—frequently, they were not thought of as a private form.

In addition to these kinds of textual production, material artifacts, including sewn antislavery objects, were also circulating. Sewing was an acceptable mode of women's cultural and material production. It was also something a girl or woman might quite literally take into her own hands and control. But the apparent docility and silence often associated with the act of sewing frequently hid the active minds and activist agendas of the women who sewed. An early training in needle crafts resulted in girls and women having access to a distinctive, powerful, albeit frequently underrated form of political campaigning and community formation. The creation of antislavery samplers involved considerable agency. It was linked to the development of a self-conscious desire for knowledge about slavery and a desire to contribute to transatlantic protest.

Evidence of this can be found in antislavery samplers themselves. Antislavery messages and iconography can be found on these samplers and many other sewn objects (such as pin balls and workbags made from free produce cotton) crafted by antislavery women. These were produced for use or display within their own homes or to be sold at antislavery fairs. Between 1825 and 1827, nearly all of the £400 the Birmingham Ladies' Negros' Friends Society (whose treasurer, Elizabeth Heyrick, had made her name through her campaign for abstention from slave-produced sugar) spent on producing antislavery print came from selling handmade workbags.[50] The bags were used to store needlework and embroidery, as well as printed tracts placed inside of them for distribution to purchasers. Print and sewing thus came together in a productive conjunction. Female antislavery sewing labor supported antislavery print and aided its Atlantic distribution. Likewise, older models of the direct exchange of goods underpinning economic interaction (including the antislavery bazaar) sat alongside emerging market models (such as mass printing) developing within a mechanized industrial era.

THE FOUNDING OF ACKWORTH SCHOOL

The founding of Ackworth School was a significant development in the educational provision for English Friends. Leading the campaign for the establishment of a Quaker school in England was John Fothergill, the Yorkshire-born Quaker, physician, philanthropist, and plant collector. He was remarkably well connected on both sides of the Atlantic and had many American friends and correspondents. These included Benjamin Franklin; William Logan; Benjamin Rush; Benjamin Waterhouse, the physician and cofounder of Harvard Medical School, with whom Fothergill had worked in London; James Pemberton, the politician and president of the Pennsylvania Abolition Society; and John Morgan, the eminent physician responsible for the foundation of the University of Pennsylvania School of Medicine.[51] Fothergill's transatlantic connectedness suggests his vision and ambition, elements which were at the basis of his desire to offer Friends' children a secure, practical, and academic education. The issue of education was also being actively debated within the large Quaker community in Pennsylvania. How could Friends provide guarded schools for their children? The situation was particularly complex in the new republic, since debates about a guarded education clashed with the pressing issue of educating future citizens whose chief loyalty was to the nation.[52]

The situation of Quakers in England was different but also complicated. Many English Friends did not want their children to attend church schools, for reasons of conscience. Pledging allegiance to the established church and the Crown was antithetical to Friends' beliefs. While wealthier English Friends had access to other forms of educational provision such as private tutors, the education of the children of those with less money was suffering. Ackworth opened within this important juncture, in consequence of a larger transatlantic conversation about the future direction of the Society of Friends.

The site on which the school was located had previously been used as an extension of the London Foundling Hospital, founded in 1745 after extensive and energetic lobbying by Thomas Coram. The Dorset-born sailor and shipwright had made his fortune while living in the English colonies. When he returned to London as a wealthy man, he was shocked by the situation of the poor, and especially by the plight of abandoned children. He used his extensive connections and powers of persuasion to gather sufficient funds to open the hospital. It was awarded a government grant subject to an agreement that it would never turn a child away. But given the extent of need, it quickly became overwhelmed.

To manage this crisis, the hospital opened additional locations in England, including the Ackworth Hospital in West Yorkshire, which operated from 1757 to 1773, when the withdrawal of the charity's government funding led to its closure. This was fortuitous timing for Fothergill, who was on the lookout for a suitable location for the new school he was planning. Five years later the site, with its recently completed buildings, was purchased by the Society of Friends. The families of scholars paid eight guineas a year, and scholars were expected to contribute to the running of the school. Their labor was gendered; boys often performed manual work, while the girls were given training in "housewifery and useful needlework" to prepare them for their adult lives and for domestic labor. They also brought in earnings through the sale of their needlework.[53]

The foundation of Ackworth was followed with great interest by American Friends, including Owen Biddle, who had long participated in the campaign for a guarded education for the children of American Friends. Once Ackworth opened, he asked several American Public Friends to visit Ackworth and collect information to help plan similar institutions in the United States.[54] The Philadelphia minister William Savery visited the school on his ministry to Europe (1796–1799). While in England, he met Hannah More, William Wilberforce, and Elizabeth Fry and traveled throughout Britain, Ireland, and Germany, visiting Friends and cementing transatlantic relationships. Doubtless he talked about Ackworth to Fry, who herself visited the school in August 1799, "took part in the examination of the children in their various exercises," and met Thomas Scattergood and Elizabeth Coggeshall.[55] Scattergood was a Philadelphia Quaker who spent six years in England and learned from the model William Tuke had established for the treatment of the mentally ill at the Retreat in York. Though he had planned to teach at Westtown on his return to the United States, he instead focused on establishing the Friends Hospital in Philadelphia. Coggeshall was an American Quaker minister who visited Europe on two separate occasions, traveling extensively to Quaker meetings. Writing in 1790 and echoing the model of Ackworth, Biddle proposed that in any planned school "the girls make and mend their own apparel, the boys [sic] linen, and the house linen; and do such needle work, as may be sent to be executed in the house; also wash and get up their own small linen."[56] When Westtown School was founded in Pennsylvania in 1799, it closely followed Ackworth's model, including in this regard. Appropriate pedagogical texts were suggested, including *Lessons for Youth,*

Selected for the Use of Ackworth and other Schools (1798). Other Friends' schools were being opened in the United States, including Nine Partners School in New York, which benefited from generous contributions from the United Kingdom. This included £350 from Lindley Murray, the Pennsylvania-born lawyer and grammarian who had relocated to York in 1789. His books on grammar were widely used in Quaker schools, and he redirected the money he earned to philanthropic work.

Meanwhile, Ackworth's curriculum was gradually developing, and the daily activities of scholars were changing in turn as the school evolved. By the start of 1800, the amount of time the girls spent on sewing and knitting was limited to allow a new focus on spelling, reading, and writing. This necessitated the introduction of appropriate reading matter, something which caused disputes between the London Committee and the more conservative Country Committee, who together oversaw the school. The London Committee proposed Anna Laetitia Barbauld's *Hymns in Prose for Children* (1781), but the Country Committee initially determined that Barbauld's work was inappropriate for the Ackworth scholars—though it is not clear why—instead suggesting *The Rational Dame: or Hints towards Supplying the Prattle for Children* (1795) by Ellenor Fenn, who wrote prolifically under the pseudonym "Mrs. Lovechild." Fenn's popular work was influenced by Barbauld, whom she may well have known.[57] Eventually, this decision was reversed, and Barbauld's work became popular with scholars, as we have seen.

The shift into a culture in which poetry became acceptable is exemplified by an incident that took place in 1848. The school's current superintendent, Thomas Pumphrey, was a keen amateur poet and even authored a long poem titled "Ackworth" in the album of George Pollard, a scholar who was about to emigrate to Canada. Written in the imagined voice of the young future emigrant himself, it describes the ways that memories of Ackworth, or "archives of mind," will sustain him through any future difficulties. The final stanza is an affirmation of loving connectivity:

> The Atlantic divides us, but can it estrange
> The heart of affection that turns to you still?
> No, my love for my kindred and friends cannot change
> Or the colds of a Canada winter e'er chill![58]

The shift in the school in favor of wider reading had been fermenting over a long period. By 1793, some fourteen years after it was founded, the school's limited collection of printed texts was expanded to include a work titled *Collection of Debates on the Slave Trade*. Just three years later the school created a library encompassing literary texts, including poetry. This started a gradual process of reimagining the reading matter thought suitable for scholars, which in turn opened them up to the intellectual currents shaping life outside of Ackworth.[59]

The pace of change at the school was slow, though steady. Important developments in the first decade of the nineteenth century included the introduction of John Evans's *An Epitome of Geography*, along with several maps, suggesting the way the school was gradually becoming more outward looking, encouraging its young scholars to imagine what lay outside the boundaries of their own experience. Lindley Murray's *Spelling Book with Reading Lessons* was introduced, and three hundred copies of Joseph Donbavand's *Studies in Penmanship* (produced while he was a writing master at the school) were also purchased for use by scholars.[60]

A direct and rapid consequence of the changes introduced in the late 1790s and early 1800s can be seen by comparing their impact on two sisters who were educated at the school just before, and after, this new focus on writing and spelling. Margaret Wood, a scholar from 1794 to 1797, wrote in what Sandra Stanley Holton calls "a plain, if serviceable, hand." Her punctuation was "erratic, and her spelling sometimes unsure." But her youngest sister, Martha, who started at the school in 1797, used "an elaborate copperplate script" and could "make proper use of punctuation and adopt conventional English usage."[61] Knowing how to spell accurately and produce a more sophisticated form of writing was now considered more appropriate than having a more rudimentary grasp of both, suggesting that the school's ethos was evolving.

Overall, the school was increasingly focused on developing new skills in its scholars by means of a more challenging academic curriculum. Although this would continue, and deepen, in the subsequent decades, Enoch Lewis from Westtown found the ethos of Ackworth frustratingly underambitious and limited. He reported that shortly after Westtown opened, he was visited by a patron member of the Ackworth school committee. He wrote, "It was manifest that he regarded it [Ackworth] as a model, perfect in all its parts."[62] When Lewis asked whether the scholars were taught mathematics or Greek and Latin, the visitor replied in the negative, leading to a heated exchange about what constituted an appropriate education.

Around the same time, Ackworth also accepted increasing numbers of international scholars from Australia, Russia, and the United States, who doubtless brought innovative ideas with them. Records show that Alexander Swain from Nantucket attended Ackworth from 1801 to 1805, while Frances and Rebecca Eddy from Philadelphia attended from 1804 (or 1805) to 1809 and 1811, respectively. International visitors would also have changed the tenor of school life. The school's visitors book from 1796 to 1804 notes that Samuel Elam, from Rhode Island, visited the school in December 1796. The following year, there was a visit from William Byfinch[?] from Barbados, and two years later, from Joseph Teesdale of Boston.[63] Later visitors books reveal a similar pattern, showing that the remote rural location of the school did not prevent it from being a modest nexus of international activity. International visitors included, in 1832, Elizabeth Shillito of Jamaica, while Samuel Rhoads was one of several visitors from Philadelphia, part of a pattern of visitors from the United States in the 1830s. In the following decade, Rhoads would visit former Ackworth scholars Anna and Henry Richardson in Newcastle.

Intriguingly, too, in 1797, two leading members of the Moravian Church, Ignatius Traneker and his wife, Catherine, visited from Fulneck Moravian Settlement, about twenty miles away. The groups had long-standing connections, despite doctrinal and other differences. The silence favored by Friends' religious services, for instance, was very unlike the Moravian emphasis on music. Still, Ackworth and Fulneck were founded within a few years of each other, and the two groups maintained a friendly mutual interest.[64]

SEWING TIME

Throughout this period of change, girl scholars continued to work on their samplers. Embroidered samplers often have lasted well, some becoming collector's items. Many were originally displayed in households, and as time went on and their makers died, they became objects of memory, handed down through the generations. Samplers often reproduced affectionate tokens of friendship or family genealogies, reminding later generations of the history of their creator. In these instances, both the process of sampler-making and the content of the sampler were important constitutive elements of the final object. It can be less easy to track the moments within which sewing took place—the how, where, and when of acts of sewing, or what might be called sewing time. This had many variables. Girls and women might work on their samplers alone or in groups; likewise, they might sew in silence or talk, or while listening to a text being read aloud. The importance, even power, of silence should not be underestimated. It was certainly understood by women who were accustomed to being ignored.

Elizabeth Freeman, the first enslaved African American to file and win a freedom suit in Massachusetts, attributed her knowledge of the Bill of Rights to her determination to pay attention to what was going on around her while staying quiet herself. She explained that "when she was waiting at table, she heard gentlemen talking over the Bill of Rights and the new constitution of Massachusetts," and by "keeping still and minding things," she determined to seek her own rights.[65] The kinds of observations and knowledge acquired by those who seem invisible can be genuinely transformational; "keeping still and minding things" enabled Freeman to seek, and obtain, her emancipation.

Reflecting further on the conditions within which women produced their work, and the reading, conversation, or silence within which they carried out this labor, helps us recreate the conditions of production. However, it can be difficult to discover specific detail about how girls and women sewed or what they thought about as they worked. Once we do know more about sewing time, we can extrapolate further and understand its contribution to building female community and knowledge. The sampler becomes the object that represents frozen time, or includes a radical message, but it is also produced by hours of reflection and active work. Arguing that sewing could be "as radical an activity as petitioning," Deborah Van Broekhoeven's comments on American antislavery circles are also applicable to their British counterparts:

Anti-slavery woman [*sic*] sat month after month, for some year after year, in weekly sewing sessions, listening to Theodore Weld's *American Slavery As It Is*, tales from Lydia Maria Child's *The Oasis*, or stories from current issues of anti-slavery newspapers. The practice in most sewing circles of one member reading anti-slavery literature aloud while the other members sewed, knitted, braided, or pieced articles for an upcoming sale helps explain why abolitionists might attribute greater importance to sewing circles than to petitioning. In this context the social circle of abolitionists transformed the tiresome, mundane and normally private activity of needlework into the radical and public work of anti-slavery fairs.[66]

We lose sight of a great deal if we neglect to focus on the full contexts of women's sewing work in the nineteenth century. Novels, diaries, and journals are all invaluable sources for discovering more about how samplers and needlework were understood by contemporaries. On the one hand, sampler-making was thought to be a passive and feminine activity, producing docile domestic habits, while on the other, it was thought to produce the capacity for independence and potential rebellion. A short poem by Benjamin Latrobe captures the first of those perspectives. "Impromptu for My Juliana's Sampler" celebrates the experience of watching his young daughter dutifully sewing and his wife overseeing the activity. Latrobe, who was born in Fulneck, is better known as the preeminent American architect of the early national period than as the son of an Irish Moravian minister and his Pennsylvania-born wife. Yet he was both, and a proud father, as revealed in his short poem about sewing time. It was written in the United States after he emigrated there permanently in 1796, and it resonates with paternal pride and conjugal affection.

Watched by her Mother's glistening eye
Her needle Julie plied;
Uncounted flew the moments by,
While grew her sampler's pride.
The little hands with guileless art
That wove each lettered row,
While her bright eye, and playful heart
Still gladdened over the show.
When age shall dull that mother's eye
And all but love be fled
Then shall those hands with riper joy
Strew roses over her bed.[67]

In this revealing vignette, Latrobe interprets his daughter's sewing as a display of her innocent femininity and his wife's emotional watchfulness as an example of appropriate maternal activity. By referring to the "guileless art" with which the girl "wove each lettered row," he suggests that the proper place of a woman is in the home, pursuing appropriate duties. In contrast to the counting of stitches (girls were also taught counting through sewing), to which she assiduously attends, Juliana does not notice the passing of time, which flashes past "uncounted." This sense of temporality extends to the poem's reflection on the lives of mother and daughter. Juliana's "playful heart" will develop over her life and eventually, "with riper joy," the girl will live long enough even to "strew roses" over the deathbed of her mother. His daughter's needlework will freeze time, something which he knows can pass all too quickly. The sampler, like his poem, captures this moment and saves it, as time inexorably pushes on toward the deathbed scene.

This idealized depiction, with its celebration of a moment in his daughter's girlhood and anticipation of a long life for his wife, is highly revealing. Hidden within a piece of occasional verse is a significant but unacknowledged trauma. Latrobe longed for a settled and conventionally bourgeois family life after a childhood in which he was separated from his parents at an early age and brought up in the communal system of Moravians.[68] In this poem he celebrates having glimpsed its possibilities through his daughter's sampler-making.

Latrobe was first educated in Fulneck and then sent to Germany to be trained for the ministry. He had a lifelong desire for a close-knit home life and broke with the church when he was still young. Settling in London, he married Lydia Sellon, who died in childbirth, leaving two surviving children. A devastated Latrobe emigrated to the United States and subsequently married Mary Elizabeth Hazlehurst in Philadelphia in 1800. One year later the couple had their first child, whom they called Juliana. But she only survived for a few weeks, her death adding to his distress. The Juliana of the poem, also born in the United States, was therefore the second of his daughters to have been given that name. She would eventually fulfill the hopes expressed in the poem by outliving both her parents and dying in old age.

Sitting and sewing could certainly allow girls and women the opportunity for independent and autonomous reflection while they simultaneously engaged in feminine behavior. The novelist Louisa May Alcott, a keen abolitionist, described sewing as a useful form of moneymaking. Though it did not pay highly, it allowed her to engage in highly productive silent reflection. Some twelve years before publishing *Little Women* (1868), she wrote in her journal, "Sewing won't make my fortune, but I can plan my stories while I work, and then scribble 'em down on Sundays."[69] The labor with her needle that she undertook to sustain her daily life gave her the opportunity to plan. In this way, she put herself in a position to become a best-selling writer who eventually earned enough to support herself and others using her pen. At this point she no longer needed to sew, but sewing had served its purpose. Alcott rescued her family from the financial crises brought upon them by her father, Bronson Alcott. Sewing time allowed her to generate the ideas for her fiction, and she was not the only writer who embraced the possibilities of sewing. Harriet Martineau, a keen abolitionist who had been brought up in a dissenting family in England, combined sewing with writing in a comparable manner when her family experienced financial distress.

The creation of samplers was often an important part of the girlhood of middle- and upper-class women on both sides of the Atlantic, though by the midcentury period this had changed. Still, in a discussion of American samplers, David Stinebeck has claimed that the sampler "may, in fact, be the best artefact of all to gauge the values of the American middle class as it comes into being, both before the Revolutionary War and in the new nation."[70] The sense of the growing unfamiliarity of sampler work during a period in which print increasingly dominated is captured well in a midcentury American novel by Julia C. R. Dorr in which a young girl, Bessie, is depicted sewing. Bessie's struggles with her sampler are extensively tracked. At one point she almost burns it, out of sheer frustration, after several hours of unsuccessful work. Dorr's description of diverse kinds of samplers—containing alphabets, decorative and symbolic pictures, genealogies, and so on—instructs her readers that samplers could take many forms and that they contained representational and pictorial devices with discernible meanings. One passage suggests the way in which such objects could end up being displayed in a kind of isolated splendor, placed in a part of the home restricted to special occasions.

She was learning to form letters with her needle; in other words she was making a sampler. This last word may possibly puzzle some of our younger readers; for in these days of indelible ink, the good, old-fashioned sampler upon which the maidens of the olden time were wont to exercise their ingenuity, has fallen somewhat into disrepute. But if they have not forgotten their last visit to their grandmother, they may possibly remember that upon the wall of the best parlor there hung a square bit of canvas, neatly framed, and protected by a glass. All the letters of the alphabet were wrought thereon, in divers forms, and stitches, and sizes; and there was perhaps a weeping willow there, also, drooping over a young lady whose white dress was not at all tumbled, or disarranged, or soiled by her position upon the grass. And there were family names, and dates of births and of deaths, and at the bottom their grandmother's maiden name in full, as a mute witness that all the above was her work.[71]

The genial and patronizing tone of the narrator reminds "some of our younger readers" about the place of the "good, old-fashioned sampler upon which the maidens of the olden time were wont to exercise their ingenuity" in the history of previous generations of women. In an era of mass-produced books and writing—"these days of indelible ink"—the sampler seems old-fashioned, even quaint. Though it is displayed in the "best parlor," it is represented as if it is a relic of a long-gone period in which the embroiderer herself was literally muted.

The narrator's tone might have changed if she was made aware of the fact that such an enumeration of "family names, and dates of births and of deaths" could have a crucial role in U.S. legal history. Several families of Revolutionary War veterans seeking pensions used early American samplers as evidence of relationships. The government accepted the samplers as legal proof of consanguinity and awarded pensions accordingly.[72] Sampler-makers and those who valued samplers knew that they could be far more than trivial distractions, something this example makes particularly clear.

Yet samplers have many enemies, including clothes moths, damp, mildew, fire, water, exposure to the elements, and shoddy materials that lead to their early decay. Others include fashion and taste, as Dorr's novel suggests.

Many of the sewn objects that were so painstakingly produced by women were subsequently disregarded. Sometimes they were seen as trifles and became lost or discarded when moving house or following a death. However, as we have seen, samplers or other sewn objects are often treasured objects, circulated and displayed as part of a sentimental economy that connects women and preserves time. Esther Sleepe's sampler became a lasting memorial after her premature death. Her daughter, the novelist Fanny Burney, displayed it together with a handwritten label explaining its history—which also, though indirectly, acknowledged her devastating bereavement.[73] The sampler was sewn by Sleepe when Burney was eight years old, two years before her mother's death, and it became one of Burney's most precious possessions.

Samplers such as this contain the spirit or personality of the person whose hand produced them. While they can be key resources of memory and female history, they can also be valuable artifacts for those who love the stories they tell or can be made to impart. Some of these include elements of radical autonomy, for a girl or woman skilled with her needle might produce works that challenge or stand up against accepted orthodoxies, using her needle for messages of her own choice. In this context, the connections between *sewing* and its homonym *sowing,* are important, as suggested in this chapter's title. Sewing and sowing each name very distinct activities; sewing frequently takes place inside, while seated, but sowing is associated with being outside and physically more mobile—standing or bending. Thus, they require distinct kinds of energy and levels of activity, different skills and knowledge.

Yet the two are also foundationally connected at the level of sound. Some sewn objects are designed to sow ideas—to plant seeds in the minds of those who sewed them as well as of those who encounter them. This act of sowing did not simply stop at the point at which the last stitch was sewn and the needle put down. At that point, objects such as samplers or workbags started a new life as they circulated and were displayed or otherwise used. They were simultaneously valued examples of personal craft and items of accomplishment, and sometimes beauty. As they often incorporated didactic texts or commentary, they could also be highly legible. Finally, we should note that women's sewing skills have long been directed toward wider protest movements such as peace, suffrage, temperance, and trade unions. Women have traditionally made the embroidered banners that were displayed in protest meetings and marches and bolstered political campaigns for suffrage, early feminism, and antislavery.[74]

Many antislavery samplers used extracts from literary texts, as we can see in the sampler of Mary Ann West, who was brought up within British antislavery circles. In 1828, age just nine, she sewed a long-inscription sampler titled "Liberty and Slavery" that comprised more than a thousand words from Laurence Sterne's *A Sentimental Journey* (1768). Sterne, who corresponded with Oluadah Equiano and Ignatius Sancho, was known for his abolitionist beliefs. Indeed, Sancho wrote to him in 1766 urging him to lend his writing skills to abolition.

West's selected text describes a moment in the novel just after the famous scene in which the protagonist hears a voice repeating "I can't get out!" Searching for the source of this distressing cry, he finds that it is coming from a starling trapped in a cage. After failing to free the bird, he reflects upon the "bitter draught" of slavery. In reproducing this lengthy extract, West was articulating a powerful message at a critical point of antislavery campaigning, just prior to the passing of the 1833 Slavery Abolition Act.[75] Hector St. John de Crèvecoeur had picked up on a similar image of distress in letter 9 of *Letters from an American Farmer* (1792). In a section titled "A Melancholy Scene," he depicts an encounter with an enslaved man who is being subjected to brutal torture—suspended from a tree in a kind of cage, where he is being pecked at by birds of prey, attacked by insects, and left to die. He cannot get out or protect himself, and he asks the narrator to kill him and save him from a miserable and agonizing existence. Like Sterne, Crèvecoeur encourages his readers to understand slavery as a system that entraps its victims, exposing them to brutality and torture and depriving them of liberty.

Clearly, an array of sewn antislavery products, including samplers, was being produced in substantial numbers on both sides of the Atlantic, in homes and schools, both by individuals working alone and within antislavery sewing circles. Several Ackworth samplers will be discussed in more detail later in the chapter. But first I will outline the development of sampler-making at the school, starting with Beavington's sampler.

THE RESIGNATION OF ELIZA BEAVINGTON

It is probably not possible to discover where Eliza Beavington's sampler was during the first years of its existence, though it probably remained in her family home until her marriage, passing with her to her marital home. Unlike the families of wealthier Quakers, hers was not a memorializing family, and those who might have access to this knowledge are no longer alive. The sampler preserves her in history as a thirteen-year-old girl whose life chances were improved by virtue of spending a brief period at an emerging school. Although she only had access to a circumscribed education, it was one that she would not otherwise have had at all. Hers was a dissenting life that was respectable (at best) rather than genteel, and neither especially poor nor notably prosperous.

Beavington's sampler directs attention to a young provincial English dissenter whose existence seems to have been without major incident. The sampler is one of six remarkably similar inscription pieces produced in the school in the 1780s, all of which contain lengthy extracts, including didactic religious verses. They suggest the importance placed upon the acquisition of some level of literacy and of familiarity with appropriate religious sentiment. One of their distinctive features is the decorative borders surrounding the inscription. These included bellflowers, a motif often associated with American samplers.[76]

The border of Beavington's sampler is more elaborate than any of the group to which it belongs. Like many other elements of her life, the reason for her additional embellishment remains something about which it is only possible to speculate, though it does intimate an element of autonomy. The decorative bellflower edging—in contrast to the edging on other samplers—is in direct tension with the serious message of the text, which emphasizes dutiful resignation. This illustrates incongruous elements at play in the sampler, and indeed in the girl herself. She had an imaginative or creative side that even the austerity of Ackworth could not quash. She may have wanted more than the limited life offered by the routine activities with which she had to engage—after all, she had sufficient proficiency to manage this level of decorative detail. Indeed, she may have already produced other samplers and wanted to experiment with designs of additional complexity.[77] Though it is impossible to determine why her sampler stands out in the manner it does, we can instead try to imagine the probable impact of an Ackworth education on this young female Friend from the Cotswolds. By understanding more about her sampler and the probable conditions of its production, we can fill out existing understanding about the juvenile education and activities of female Friends on both sides of the Atlantic.

While the earliest samplers produced at the school were inscription pieces sewn in black thread, by the 1790s samplers were increasingly elaborate and decorative.[78] A cluster of rectangular samplers sewn by girl scholars between 1785 and 1787 all bear a resemblance to Beavington's work, suggesting some kind of shared endeavor. It is reasonable to suppose that she would have sat with the other girls who were producing samplers and worked her sampler alongside them, quite possibly discussing stitching, progress, and texts. Therefore, we know that she would have been familiar with Sarah Johnson, a scholar from Crake in the Lake District, who attended Ackworth from 1784 to 1785 and completed a sampler titled "An Evening Thought" in 1785. Its subject is the passing from day into the evening, something compared with life's inexorable movement toward death. The final line ends emphatically with the words "Resign'd and peaceful let me bow my Head, / And Heaven enjoy when number'd with the dead." The words suggest tranquil acceptance and heavenly reward, for death was not something devout Friends feared. Since the school's records showed that several scholars died of infectious diseases and other causes while at Ackworth, the lesson was particularly apt. In addition, the invocation of acceptance or resignation was an element shared with Beavington's sampler and widely acknowledged as a key Quaker virtue.

Beavington would also have known Benjamina Rickman, a Londoner from Westminster who spent five years at Ackworth, leaving the school in 1785, and produced a sampler titled "A Meditation on the Dew." The passage she sewed opens with a description of the way in which, at the end of each day, "this penetrating, invisible Moisture, embalms each Herb, and Flower, and Fruit, that grows." This might initially sound like a work of natural history, but students of the Old Testament would have quickly recognized its allegorical character. Reflecting upon the dew that gently saturates plants, allowing them to flourish, it reveals the moment at which God reveals his covenant with Israel and tells Hosea, "I will be as Dew unto Israel!" There is evidence of a touching human imperfection in the way she worked her sampler. For instance, lines 13–14 should read "The Lord says by Hosea his Prophet, / 'I will be as Dew unto Israel.' Heavenly Dew!" However, she omitted the space after the comma, an indication that she was not yet wholly proficient with her needle. A pattern of repeat flower heads on three sides frames the centered text, along with three larger flower heads. Her name and that of the school appear underneath the passage.

The text Rickman sewed was well known by Friends, who used it in a variety of contexts, sometimes with slight variations. For example, after Thomas Pumphrey was recorded as a Quaker minister, his father, Samuel, wrote to him with advice about his future life, writing that now that he had married Rachel Richardson he would benefit from the example of his "new parent," George Richardson. Reflecting on the young couple he adds, "I pray in an especial manner, that you will be blessed with the dew of Heaven."[79] Wilson Armistead reprinted the same text in the second series of *Select Miscellanies, Chiefly Illustrative of the History, Christian Principles and Sufferings, of The Society of Friends* (1851). In a reflection on the miscellany as a textual genre, he notes, "Remarkable incidents and striking passages . . . selected and perused in their detached form, are calculated to impress the mind of the reader with a sense of the truths they are intended to illustrate, and may possibly make a deeper impression on some than a studied and lengthened address."[80]

Presumably, he believed that the words he reproduced, almost identical to the text sewed by Rickman, was one of these "striking passages." Sampler texts might equally "make a deeper impression in some than a studied and lengthened address." In a slight variant, the extract reproduced by Armistead contains the final words "Let all remember that God is a spirit, and seeketh such to worship him, who worship in spirit and in truth." Immediately after the passage is a poem simply titled "The Dew," signed "R. S." and dated "Glasgow 2 month [February] 1839." Its unnamed Quaker author used the prose as the starting point for a poetic variation on the well-known passage, giving its words yet another iteration.

But it is in the work of Susanna Smith from Waddington in Lancashire, a scholar from 1783 to 1787, that we find the closest connection to the work of Beavington. Both girls sewed the same text, though Smith completed hers in 1786, a year after Beavington finished her sampler. There are subtle differences in the way they set the titles and attribution. The most significant are in the framing borders and decorative detail: while Smith sewed a simple line of bellflowers around her verse, Beavington embellished her framing borders. Both texts were based on Isaiah 40:6: "The voice said, 'Cry.' And he said, 'What shall I cry?' All flesh is grass, and all the goodliness thereof is as the flower of the field." Interpretations of the meaning of this passage depend on the way in which translations relate to the Hebrew or the subsequent Greek. It seems most likely that the text questions human commitment to the covenant with Israel; God has been faithful to his word, but his people's commitment has been transient, just like the flowers of the field, which fade away. As the girls sewed their texts into the material in front of them, they would undoubtedly have reflected on the varied meanings of the words they carefully stitched.

Many scholars came from families with an overt commitment to antislavery, and by the 1820s onward the school was actively encouraging debate. The emergence of antislavery symbols in Ackworth samplers corresponded to the period in which the school purchased texts about slavery and became increasingly involved with the outside world. These two elements, coming together when the poetry of Barbauld entered the school, changed the school's culture.

Two Ackworth samplers from the 1830s show the way in which girl scholars were now using abolitionist iconography.[81] An incomplete and undated sampler reproduces the motif of a kneeling image of a chained figure, widely familiar as the seal of the Society for the Abolition of the Slave Trade. A second undated Ackworth sampler, probably sewn by Jane Stickney, is now part of the collection at York Castle Museum. She was admitted to the school in 1829 and died there of inflammatory fever two years later. Her unfinished sampler clearly reveals a familiarity with the iconography of contemporary antislavery. It is composed of medallions and octagons, with half-medallions and octagons decorating its edges. The initials CT are embroidered within one of the medallions, while another contains the words "Peace to my friend." The name Stickney is sewn slightly off-center and to the left, while diagonally above that is the well-known kneeling image of a chained enslaved figure. Like the other Ackworth antislavery samplers, it includes multiple elements.

Several of Jane Stickney's siblings also attended Ackworth, including her sister Mary, a scholar from 1824 to 1827, who eventually became a mistress at Ackworth in 1841. By that time, paper was starting to be made from wood pulp rather than rags, but Mary Stickney's Ackworth arithmetic book from 1826 contains a torn page carefully repaired with stitching, reminding us not just of how skills can be adapted for multiple uses but also of the importance of sewing to bookbinding.[82] Another sister, Esther, subsequently worked as a governess in the household of Rachel Priestman of Newcastle. She remained in the Priestman household for nearly thirteen years and may well have encountered fugitives from slavery who stayed there as they passed through Newcastle.[83] Jonathan Priestman's active engagement with abolition stemmed from his early meeting with Olaudah Equiano in Newcastle, as he announced publicly in 1847 in his welcome to Frederick Douglass, who was lecturing there.[84]

Esther Stickney's presence can be traced through the memoirs, letters, and diaries of the Newcastle Friends (discussed in the chapter 2), allowing us to piece together connections between Ackworth, antislavery, sewing, and women. In January 1832, she participated in an essay meeting at the house of Margaret Bragg, along with leading Newcastle Friends including Ellen Richardson, the sister-in-law of Anna Richardson. The female sewing meeting of between twenty and thirty women also gathered for three hours a week to sew clothing for the poor, and they may well have used their skills to make antislavery objects.[85] All of this exemplifies the highly connected local contexts for transatlantic community formation and for debates about antislavery and abolition. These early proximities certainly had a significant impact on the lives of Quakers who emigrated to the United States, as well as of those who remained at home.

THE ATLANTIC MIGRATION
OF HANNAH HOYLE AND JOHN SHARP

Some Ackworth samplers remained within the United Kingdom, while others traveled abroad with their creators. A number ended up in the United States and were bequeathed to museums, making them available for study. At the point of deposit, family members and museum curators often pieced together the histories of the girls who sewed them, revealing fascinating stories of migration and settlement. Alongside this physical movement, it is sometimes possible to trace the ways these girls and women reframed their existing beliefs, including antislavery, within the distinctive contexts of the place to which they had relocated.

One of these sampler-makers was Hannah Hoyle, who was born on 1 November 1795 in West Yorkshire and attended Ackworth from 1808 to 1810. She later emigrated to the United States and married another Ackworth scholar, John Sharp, who had moved there separately. Three samplers sewn by Hoyle reveal that she was a sampler-maker even before she attended Ackworth. Her descendants recently donated the samplers to the Philadelphia Museum of Art. I will close the chapter with an account of what I have been able to discover about Hoyle, Sharp, and the samplers through a combination of research and the assistance of Celia Wolfe, the archivist at Ackworth School, and Jane Alden Stevens, one of Hoyle's descendants.

The first sampler, completed in 1806, when Hoyle was eleven, is a simple and attractive piece comprising a four-line verse and below it the figures of Adam and Eve. Running from top to bottom are a set of identical images on each side of the sampler—a lion, a perching bird, decorative flowers, and a girl or woman holding up a stick for her tiny dog. Collectively, the figures simultaneously evoke the heraldic and the domestic or everyday. No additional information has survived about its production, about the identity of Elin Williamson, whose name is at the bottom left on the sampler, opposite that of Hoyle.

The second of the trio is more complex in design terms and suggests not just the advances Hoyle had made in the three years that had passed between the two samplers but also the impact of Ackworth. It uses the medallion motifs characteristic of many Ackworth samplers, combining these with the date and various inscriptions. They include the words "A Token of Love," while another states "HH to JH" (perhaps indicating her father, John Hoyle), and yet another "to HW," whose identity remains unknown.

The final one is a simpler inscription piece that most resembles Eliza Beavington's sampler. It is sewn in black thread and contains lines titled "Solitude" surrounded by a simpler and striking plaque-like circular border. The smallest of the three, it is signed and dated at the bottom and corresponds to other samplers using the same text and style.

The language of the text emphasizes a sense of the divine that is distinct from the language of Eliza Beavington's sampler. However, the idea of resig-

"Sampler," 1806, by Hannah Hoyle (1795–1870).
Philadelphia Museum of Art: Gift of Jane Alden Stevens, William Croll Stevens,
Ann Howe Stevens, and Nancy Dunbar Stevens, 2020, 2020-26-1.

nation to one's duty was certainly familiar to the Yorkshire-born John Sharp, who had attended Ackworth shortly after Eliza, from 1801 to 1803. In the very first letter he wrote to his brother Joseph from the United States, he urged Joseph to join him: "Adversity may be both our Lots, this is the best country, we may weep at our lot but it shall be in *resignation*, no misconduct shall tarnish truth & virtuous intentions. I am already persuaded, it is rather our *duty* to try the world, rather than shun it; for we always calculate on evils to come, greater than we feel them when they are at hand" (emphasis added).[86] On 9 July 1817, after living in Philadelphia for two years, he married Hannah

"Sampler," 1809, by Hannah Hoyle (1795–1870).
Philadelphia Museum of Art: Gift of Jane Alden Stevens, William Croll Stevens,
Ann Howe Stevens, and Nancy Dunbar Stevens, 2020, 2020-26-2.

Hoyle, who had traveled from Liverpool in 1815 on the brig *Hercules* with eleven other members of her family.[87]

Beyond Hannah's samplers, it is difficult to trace her, but we can track the couple's life together in the letters John Sharp routinely wrote to friends, family, and business contacts in England. His extant archive, split between the West Yorkshire Archives and the Historical Society of Pennsylvania, reveals how transatlantic kinship and business networks were maintained. Correspondence and miscellaneous items such as his commonplace book and various printed records about his business affairs reveal something of

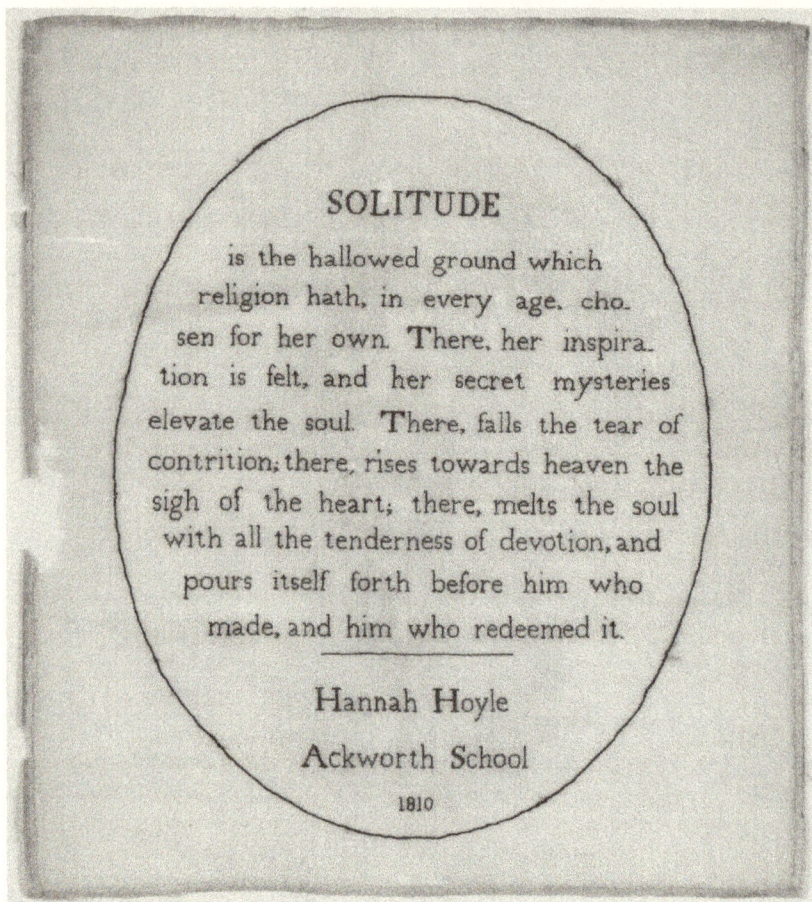

SOLITUDE

is the hallowed ground which
religion hath, in every age, chosen for her own. There, her inspiration is felt, and her secret mysteries
elevate the soul. There, falls the tear of
contrition; there, rises towards heaven the
sigh of the heart; there, melts the soul
with all the tenderness of devotion, and
pours itself forth before him who
made, and him who redeemed it.

Hannah Hoyle

Ackworth School

1810

"Sampler," 1810, by Hannah Hoyle (1795–1870).
Philadelphia Museum of Art: Gift of Jane Alden Stevens, William Croll Stevens,
Ann Howe Stevens, and Nancy Dunbar Stevens, 2020, 2020-26-3.

the story behind his emigration. At the same time, they are revealing about his religious and ethical beliefs and his reading practices. This all helps to clarify the ways in which Ackworth shaped the American life he embarked upon in 1815.

In the spring of that year, Sharp returned to his family home in Yorkshire and announced that he had decided "either be a man or a mouse." Because he was a man, he stated, he was going to emigrate to the United States. He left

Liverpool on 18 April 1815, disembarking in New York at about midday on 12 June. Four days later he set off for Philadelphia, arriving on 17 June, by which point he was "very ill." Having recovered, he found himself immediately delighted with the city. He reported, "It has a grand appearance at the first and the more I see the better I like it. I will be bound to say there are more benevolent, literary & commercial institutions in this city and on a larger scale for the magnitude of the place than any town the old country can boast of. The people have every appearance of wealth and prosperity. The black people are numerous and seem to be much above, in point of enjoyment, the lower class of people in England."

Immediately below this, he announces that he has accepted a job as a bookkeeper and occasional laborer in a "wholesale hardware store." This gave him "emply [*sic*] during the hot weather when I cannot go in the country in search of other objects and gives me a speedy insight into business here." Two days later, he writes with understandable satisfaction, "This day I entered into the employ of Isaac Smedley & Co. after being out of any employ that brought in a penny for 3 months to a day."

On 30 September 1815, he wrote to his brother urging him to come to Philadelphia. He tells him that he has met the Hoyle family, noting their arduous transatlantic journey: "Our friend J. Hoyle and family have been in this city and a most dreadful time they had at sea, 101 days!!! And many trying circumstances, the limits of my paper will not admit to say much.—They will move into the state of Ohio in a few days, contrary to most of their friends' advice and my own regret. If I write again I may add many interesting tales about them, or the pleasure to tell thee face to face."[88] Perhaps his expression of regret is due to his separation from the woman he would marry two years later, but if so, he does not reveal this to his brother.

Sharp's letters, despite the "limits" he mentions, convinced several close family members (including his brother) to join him in Philadelphia, where he remained for the rest of his life with his wife, now Hannah Sharp, and their children. They lived on South Second Street, where the family business was also located. It was a busy commercial area, and in its immediate vicinity were many Black churches, businesses, and households, including the home of the wealthy and powerful Forten family.

Sharp's papers make it possible to understand how the Yorkshire antislavery culture merged with his experience of living in Philadelphia. He was certainly familiar with antislavery arguments from a young age. In 1806, three years after leaving Ackworth, he made a careful loose-leaf copy of William Cowper's extremely popular and widely circulated "The Negro's Complaint" (1788). This may have functioned as both an exercise in handwriting and an opportunity to reflect on what Wilson Armistead would later term a "striking passage." Reproduced on the cover of William Fox's *Address to the People of Great Britain on the Propriety of Refraining from the Use of West India Sugar and Rum* (1791),[89] the poem was widely reprinted, and inspired responses such as Frances Ellen Watkins Harper's poem "The Slave Mother" (1854), set to music and sung.[90] Cowper's poem uses the voice of an enslaved man to argue for his rights, concluding in a demand that enslavers should show their own humanity rather than questioning the humanity of those they enslave:

> Slaves of gold, whose sordid dealings
> Tarnish all your boasted powers,
> Prove that you have human feelings,
> Ere you proudly question ours!

The fact that Sharp copied the work is evidence of his early exposure to poetry and antislavery and their mutually sustaining contexts. It obviously resonated with him, for in 1810 he made a second copy of the poem in his commonplace book.

His deep admiration for Cowper is evident in a remarkable journal entry in which he describes his response to reading the first three books of Cowper's *The Task* as he crossed the Atlantic.[91] Read within the overall journal, it appears that his epiphanic encounter with this work during a period of seasickness made him not only a deeper and more sensitive reader but also a more reflective writer. A series of early comments he notes prior to his reading of *The Task* describe his days as characterized by sameness. He writes,

> 4 mo. 12 Employed as yesterday with the same effect
> 4 mo. 13 Attended meeting
> 4 mo. 14 Nothing partic—
> 4 mo. 15 Ditto

These entries are striking, though not because of their revelation about particular activity. Instead, what is interesting is that they are devoid of any detail and appear to have been written in haste, without much thought. In contrast, five entries later everything changes when he reads *The Task*. His onboard experience is dull, but his reading is transformational. After a note covering 19–30 April and indicating that for this period he has been "dreadfully ill" with seasickness, he writes to describe its impact. By this time, his illness has settled, and in an entry on 11 May he describes his earlier ordeal before noting what followed. He writes, "During the whole of my indisposition sound sleep has been a stranger to my eyes. Yet in every situation I felt resigned and in the line of duty."[92] Once again, his language reveals the extent to which his Quaker upbringing governed his behavior. He then goes on to describe what he calls "seasons of mental enjoyment which words have no name for," continuing,

> One night after reading the three first books of Cowper's Task, I went to bed, slumbered for a few hours, and waking could sleep no longer. For why? Being absorbed in the most profound and poetical reverie, eclipsing anything I had ever known, was it possible I could forgo. At the same time my heart was as soft as the muse it cherished. Tears of feeling too would have been their course. I have usually been a stranger to seasons of this kind, often regretting the long, hard and callous state of my soul, quereing [*sic*] could sin be the cause? Though not without regret in the retrospect of some parts of my conduct, I never felt the sting of remorse. Ever after my resolution to undertake this journey, I have felt satisfied of being in the way of duty. In life or Death I seem resigned. Death seems to have lost his terrors and the prayer of my heart is that it—not a delusion of the enemy.

Reading *The Task* initially led to an emotional and spiritual crisis, which resolved itself, leaving him with a feeling of peace and acceptance. What he calls "the long, hard and callous state of my soul" was changed by his encounter with a blank verse poem that encompassed (among many other subjects) a critique of slavery and reflections on religion and despotism.

It is a powerful reflection on the impact of a literary text. His writing becomes more expansive and detailed, though this may (more prosaically) be ascribed to his recovery from seasickness. Though it is probable that the vessel he was traveling on had a ship's library from which he could access reading matter, he also had a personal library to which he could turn throughout the voyage. He certainly seems to have been a keen reader, for on 30 May, after a "violent relapse" of seasickness that had started four days earlier, he was well enough to read Robert Barclay's *An Apology for the True Christian Divinity* (1676), a key Quaker text.

It is likely that Cowper and Barclay, both writers approved of by Friends, would have been part of Sharp's own library. He was also familiar with the work of Anthony Benezet, and at some point made a copy of a letter Benezet wrote to John Pemberton in 1783 discussing educational training and the abolition of slavery. His commonplace book also contains an extract from Benezet's *Remarks on the Slave Trade* and extracts from various antislavery publications, all carefully copied.

It is unsurprising, then, that in 1836, now married, settled in business and raising a family in Philadelphia, the Yorkshire-born former Ackworth scholar became a member of the Pennsylvania Society for Promoting the Abolition of Slavery. Benezet and others, chiefly Quakers, had founded the society in 1784. Hannah Hoyle would certainly have known of the racially integrated Philadelphia Female Anti-Slavery Society, founded in 1833 by a group of women that included Charlotte, Margaretta, Sarah, and Harriet Forten; Angelina Grimké; Lucretia Mott; and Sarah Pugh. Two decades later, Pugh would cofound the Leeds Anti-Slavery Association.

It is possible that Hoyle became a member of the Quaker-dominated Philadelphia Female Anti-Slavery Society, and even that the couple's children participated in related juvenile groups, though I have not been able to trace any firm evidence. Had she joined, she may well have contributed to its meetings, petitions, and fundraising activities. Its main fundraising was the annual fair selling items produced by women's antislavery sewing circles. While the reach of the Philadelphia circles was initially local, this changed rapidly. By 1845, it had expanded from two to twenty "nearby areas" and beyond, to Boston and Nantucket and even Leeds and Paris.[93]

Thus, it is reasonable to speculate that Hoyle may have used her sewing skills to participate in the Philadelphia circle and encouraged her female relatives in Yorkshire to contribute. The Forten sisters were skilled sampler-makers, whose work shows evidence of Quaker influence. Hoyle's letters have not survived, but Sharp family members on both sides of the Atlantic kept up a lively correspondence in which they discussed family matters, and they clearly saw it as an important way of maintaining transatlantic connectedness. Their correspondence was driven by the sense of obligation inculcated from a young age. A letter dated 23 December 1841 from Priscilla Walker, Benjamin Walker, and Rachel Walker to Cousin Rachel (probably Rachel Sharp) in Philadelphia updates her on recent events back in Yorkshire. Priscilla writes that they are not going to the United States, implying that the family had been contemplating emigration. One family member had now been an Ackworth scholar for three years, while others were visiting from Canada. A lovely two-line rhyming addition from Rachel Walker, written carefully in a childish hand, simply states:

> Though so very parted by sea
> I think it my duty to write to thee.[94]

The word *very* carries a particular poignancy in this short piece; though semantically unnecessary, its emotional load emphasizes the extent of the family's transatlantic separation. Yet this "very parted" family, and others like it, remained very connected. In the letters they sent across the ocean they exchanged information, newspaper clippings, and other items of interest, but also quite possibly sewn objects. An envelope posted in Leeds in 1852 and addressed to J. W. Sharp on South Second Street contains a few words written in list form on the inside of the envelope: "Main Liquor Law / Whose a Slave / Moral [comment unreadable]."[95] In a period in which paper remained a valuable commodity, writing on available scraps was not unusual. Might these words be shorthand for a speech or sermon being listened to or planned? A lesson in ethics of some kind, however informal? Notes from something being read and reflected upon? What should we make of the grammatical error of "Whose" rather than "Who's"? Such jotting or musings on the inside of an envelope sent from Leeds to Philadelphia might have been further developed in the letters crisscrossing the Atlantic and keeping a geographically divided community in touch with thoughts and activities.

As we know, women from British antislavery circles produced handcrafted items that were then sold in antislavery fairs in the United States. The long-standing relationship between Friends and their extensive commercial connections enabled this to take place with some ease. The girls and women who created abolitionist objects for homes on both sides of the Atlantic were effectively transforming larger abstract discursive formations into slogans, texts, or images that could be displayed within domestic interiors. They used the medium of tangible articles such as embroidered samplers, pincushions, and other handcrafted ware to display antislavery sentiments. In this way they were decorating intimate spaces with items intended to inculcate messages but also were demonstrating that the home had always been a political site. Further, they were showing that girls and women could, and should, participate in antislavery. One woman who took this lesson to heart was Anna Richardson, to whom I now turn.

2

A Tireless Laborer

REAPPRAISING ANNA RICHARDSON

Around 1855, G. M. Gillett visited George Richardson's grocery in Newcastle. While there, she purchased a piece of paisley cloth with an accompanying label stating, "Made by escaped slaves, work which Friends in the United States organised." Half a century later she passed on to her daughter this gift that was, as Bronwen Everill points out, "a piece of family history, but also, by the twentieth century, a point of family pride, an heirloom handed down from mother to daughter and, in 1927, from daughter to the Quaker archives."[1] Like the samplers of Eliza Beavington and Hannah Hoyle, and Ashley's sack, the small piece of cloth gained affective value due to its connection to the history of a family, and to relationships between women. In addition, the carefully saved scrap is significant for the story I am telling here. It connects us to two Ackworth scholars, Anna and Henry Richardson, and to their extensive activism, encompassing correspondence, tract writing, attending and organizing meetings, and working with allies.

In his 1848 free produce tract *A Revolution of the Spindles, for the Overthrow of American Slavery,* Henry uses a Quaker term, arguing, "Our watchword ought to be '*No commercial union with slaveholders*'" (his emphasis). He does not mention that his own grocery shop at 48 Cloth Market stocked free produce, but he does advise his readers that if they want to purchase free produce goods, they need to make their voices heard. The only way to make such goods easily available is to take action. He urges his readers to take matters into their own hands:

Ask for them. Already are these untainted fabrics to be found in the most respectable shops of several of our large towns. Ask for them always—ask for them everywhere, and we shall be much mistaken if they do not make their appearance. But to be sure they are genuine, buy them of tradesmen on whom you can rely. Ask to see the certificate which generally accompanies these goods, or look for the free-labour stamp which marks their origin. Remember the manufacturers will not make them, not will the shopkeepers keep them unless there be a demand. . . . The spinning jennies of Manchester, with their everlasting twirl, are twisting and drawing closer to the bonds of the Negro; and that so soon as the manufacturers are induced to substitute free grown cotton for the blood-stained fibre, will every revolution of their machines be twisting and strengthening that cord, which is destined to bind the monster of slavery; and which, with God's blessing, at no distant time, if the friends of freedom would unite in the effort, might be found even strong enough to drag the tyrant from his throne.[2]

In these highly charged and emotive terms, Henry urged his readers to become what we now call ethical consumers. He drew attention to the connection between the purchasing habits of individuals and households, patterns of demand and supply, and the period's larger reform movements. While abolitionist lecturers were displaying chains and shackles, he shows that cotton thread is just as powerful as those other means of violent restraint.

Anna and Henry Richardson were at the forefront of the British arm of free produce campaigning, focusing on the origins of material goods, especially food and textiles. They produced several other powerful pamphlets and organized displays of free produce goods in Newcastle and Gateshead.[3] They were also vital participants in several other linked reform movements. Their beliefs were forged in their respective childhoods and the ideas inculcated to them in their daily lives about ethical and social responsibility. Though the couple worked closely together, I particularly focus on reimagining the cultural and social contexts of Anna's political work to understand what made her into such an energetic activist. Her strong religious sensibility undoubtedly governed her labor, but I turn more to the emotional, intellectual, and interpersonal currents shaping her life, and to the networks within which she operated. This adds nuance to the extensive work scholars have already undertaken on the transatlantic impact of Quakers.

Within a few years of each other, Anna Richardson and Eliza Beavington had both traveled from the Cotswolds to West Yorkshire to attend Ackworth School. When Anna entered the school at the age of just eleven, she encountered a group of individuals who would go on to have a profound influence on her development, including her future husband. She attended from 1817 to 1819, and Henry from 1818 to 1820, meaning the pair overlapped for a year. He came from a powerful and well-off family of tanners with deep connections throughout the North of England. His father, George Richardson, highly regarded for his ministry, ran a grocery store that was managed by his wife, Eleanor, during his absences as a traveling minister.[4] The family business was the precursor of Pumphrey's Coffee of Newcastle, which still thrives today, though the original premises is now a bar, something that would horrify the teetotal Richardsons.

Following their marriage in 1833, Anna and Henry settled at 5 Summerhill Grove, Newcastle, a substantial terraced house in a quiet square. They had a long, happy, and childless marriage, though Henry suffered from ill health that eventually confined him to a wheelchair after a stroke. Their home was in close proximity to the homes of other members of the tight-knit community of Newcastle Friends. The couple contributed very fully to the familial, social, and reform activities of this group, whose expansive family, business, religious, and political networks extended across the English Channel and the Atlantic. Unlike several of their local circle, they never visited the United States.

Rachel Priestman of Newcastle spent 1843 to 1844 engaged in public ministry in the United States, where she met Ann and Samuel Rhoads, keen abolitionists and supporters of free produce (also known as free labor or free labor produce). The Rhoads subsequently stayed in her home in Newcastle when they visited the United Kingdom, and there they met Anna and Henry. Ann Rhoads was already familiar with Anna by reputation, noting in her journal that Anna's "interest and exertions on behalf of the slave is well known."[5] They all became lifelong correspondents and friends, and Anna frequently entrusted Samuel with sums of money to help fugitives.[6] She also participated in a transatlantic speaking and writing commons, with the couple's home and business the center of transatlantic operations. They hosted American visitors to Newcastle, while their letters, along with financial contributions, tracts, and other items crisscrossed the Atlantic, building campaigns, solidarities, and friendships. The artist William Bell Scott, with whom she formed an unlikely friendship, mentioned that she was never seen without her "inseparable bag of letters."[7] Famously, Frederick Douglass stayed in the Richardsons' house during his first visit to Britain and Ireland, and it was there that Anna and her sister-in-law Ellen lobbied for his manumission. It may also have been there that he first met Julia Griffiths.[8] Anna's wholesale embrace of the range of networking possibilities offered by the intersection of print, conversation, and letter writing allowed her to operate with considerable success within activist circles on both sides of the Atlantic.

Though many elements of her activism are now increasingly well known, a good deal of work remains to be done to do justice to her legacy and to understand its relationship to the interlinked communities within which she moved. In particular, the importance of her early home life and her education at Ackworth need further investigation to understand the extent to which she moved to Newcastle already primed for a life of daily undertakings of committed labor. These involved public and private acts ranging from letter-writing and proselytizing, to cajoling, editing and publishing, hospitality, and conversation. Searching through archives, public records, and the writings of her wider circle has produced fruitful revelations about her experiences, enabling a reappraisal of her activist life.

Anna lived a life made up of what William Still described as "unwearied labours" on behalf of "the wants of the oppressed in various directions."[9] She participated in many of the reform causes and forms of benevolence embraced by middle-class dissenters, such as prison visiting, temperance, educational provision, free produce, peace, and abolition. She corresponded with well-known abolitionists and other reformers and assisted the enslaved in their efforts to achieve self-emancipation by fundraising, publicity drives, and acts of personal generosity. Like today's community organizers and activists, she saw these as part of a broader and connected spectrum rather than as discrete or atomized areas of activity. Rather unfairly though, her reputation is mainly due to her successful role in seeking Douglass's manumission.

Anna Richardson. From Emma Pumphrey and Thomas Pumphrey,
Henry and Anna Richardson in Memoriam, 1892.

Copyright © 2024 Britain Yearly Meeting of the Society of Friends (Quakers).

Anna and Henry Richardson. From Emma Pumphrey and Thomas Pumphrey, *Henry and Anna Richardson in Memoriam,* 1892.

Copyright © 2024 Britain Yearly Meeting of the Society of Friends (Quakers).

Following her lead, this chapter will focus on their relational quality of her activities, linking them to key elements of her biography as well as to her immediate community. I will start my discussion with her *Annual Monitor* obituary, which speaks not just to the values of her own long life, which spanned almost a century, but to those of other late nineteenth-century Friends looking back on an admired member of the community. Importantly, it includes quotations from what it describes as autobiographical "reminiscences, penned in her old age for the benefit of relatives in Canada and elsewhere."[10] Unfortunately, they have only survived in tantalizingly brief extracts quoted in the obituary and in a short and little-known memorial book published by Emma and Thomas Pumphrey in 1892, which also contains several photographs that have not been reproduced until now. Some of her prolific correspondence, chiefly regarding slavery, was published in the nineteenth century, as were several juvenile antislavery tracts. Many of her letters remain scattered in archives on both sides of the Atlantic.

Turning first to discuss her childhood, and then to her adult life in Newcastle, I situate her within the wider transatlantic sphere of the Society of Friends to understand how, and why, she developed her interests. I investigate her varied modes of campaigning, including editorial work, letter writing, face-to-face meetings, tract writing, and what can best be described as the drudgery of political campaigning. Combining her own words with those of activist allies, friends, and family, I also draw upon existing work on Quaker women's antislavery labor.[11] I end the chapter with a consideration of the particular significance of two little-known pamphlets, aimed at juvenile readers. The first, *Who Are the Slaveholders? A Moral Drawn from "Uncle Tom's Cabin," Respectfully Submitted to Readers of that Work* (1852[?]), is set in rural England and suggests to its young readers that they can become ethical consumers, like the children it depicts. Starting as a didactic tale, it ends as a shopping advice manual and includes a highly practical list of products that householders could purchase if they want to avoid slave-produced goods. The second, titled *Little Laura, the Kentucky Abolitionist* (1859), uses the example of a girl named Laura Bailey to persuade "the young friends of the slave" of the importance of developing abolitionist principles.

EARLY LIFE IN CHIPPING NORTON

Anna Atkins was born on 5 January 1806 to a family of moderate means. Her father, Samuel Atkins, was a meal man (a dealer in meal), and her mother, Esther (Millard) Atkins, directed her labor to the household. Samuel's early death in 1821 left Esther, "a saintly woman—one who resorted much to earnest prayer for herself and her family," to bring up their children alone.[12] In later life Anna wrote, "When I think of my mother . . . and remember the various times in circumstances of extreme distress under which I have seen her leave the family circle with a pale and almost agonized countenance, and return to it from her private retirement in half an hour bright and cheerful, it is difficult now, as it was then, to resist the imperative conviction that God had comforted her. No mental struggle, no mastery over nature's feelings, could possibly have effected the change."[13]

Her recollection of her early life reveals the way in which her political and ethical beliefs, especially regarding peace and abolition, developed within the family home, and how "the seeds were there sown of that philanthropy which so remarkably characterised her in after days." These brief comments on her earliest years suggest that lessons taught to her at home were applied just outside of its doors, within and beyond the local community. This in turn helps to create a larger picture. She learned about global social justice issues while still a young child, an early introduction that would influence her throughout the rest of her long life. Her parents showed her that the home was not a sanctuary from the influences of outside world (as nineteenth-century domestic ideology would later insist). Instead, what went on outside its walls had an impact that required reflection and management. They taught her a set of religious ethics that influenced their consumer choices and had a significant impact on decisions regarding appropriate reading and behavior. Thinking back on the lasting influence of her parents, Richardson notes,

Perhaps my *Peace* sympathies were first awakened then (the time of Napoleon's wars), for I well remember that when there had been a great victory, the stage-coaches from London used to be adorned with laurel. One of them passed near our premises on its way to Worcester, and as we had plenty of evergreens, my father was asked for a fresh supply. But no; he did not wish to assist in giving any approval to slaughter and bloodshed. But in 1815, when the war was over, the good people of Chipping Norton were at liberty to have as many evergreens as they pleased for making wreaths and bowers in celebrations of Peace.[14]

Her father's death may have made the memory of his commitment to peace especially precious. He was clearly a man of strong principles who was unafraid to stand up for them in the period of the Napoleonic wars (1803–1815). His peaceful refusal was courageous, given the pressure produced by the xenophobic nationalism, especially the anti-French feeling, sweeping the country. Pacifists were vulnerable. In 1814, three members of the Ackworth staff were imprisoned in the Wakefield House of Correction for refusing to serve in the militia.[15] The (in)famous story of the Hartlepool monkey (an event that may or may not have its basis in truth) draws from that febrile moment. It goes like this: After a French vessel was shipwrecked off the coast of Hartlepool in the North East of England, the wreck's sole survivor was a monkey, dressed in French military uniform. The townspeople believed it to be a French sailor, accused it of spying, and subjected it to a trial, death sentence, and execution by hanging. The current inhabitants of Hartlepool are still known as "monkey hangers," and they cheerfully take pride in the dubious honor.

Elsewhere, fears of an invasion by Napoleon's forces were so great that fortified Martello towers were built along the English coast from Sussex to Kent (in the south), Essex to Suffolk (in the east), as well as in Ireland. But the anxiety about what would happen in the event of an invasion was also experienced further inland. A plan was made to move the gold at the Bank of England from London to the security of Worcester Cathedral. Had this happened, it would have traveled through, or near, Chipping Norton. Though the invasion never took place, Richardson doubtless returned to the memory of her father's steadfast pacifism throughout a life in which she consistently campaigned for peace.

In addition to describing her father's pacifist principles, Anna discusses a further lesson she learned at home, related to aiding the enslaved. She wrote, "Another early remembrance in connection with public subjects is, that *coloured* applicants for assistance were never to be turned away from our door without a little help; 'for, perhaps they might be slaves.'"[16] Richardson does not explain who these seekers for help might have been or even whether any appeared at the door, though they certainly would later in her life. Her words are simultaneously tentative ("perhaps they might") and definite ("be slaves"). What is unequivocal is the understanding that help should always be given, suggesting both general and explicit behavioral principles.

But how could the abstraction be enacted? What might the moment of the fugitive encounter, or moment at which the knock on the door or its equivalent took place, be like? Arguably, her long-standing work with figures such as Frederick Douglass and Henry Highland Garnet fulfilled this parental injunction. Metaphorically speaking, she was responding to the knock on the door. By the end of her long life, she had repeatedly helped fugitives from slavery in many ways, including by putting them up in her own home when they passed through Newcastle.

Beyond noting this important principle, it is worth pausing for a moment to reflect further upon the possibility that "*coloured* applicants for assistance" might appear at the door of a Friends' house in Chipping Norton. The distinctive clothing and speech codes of Friends (elements a guarded education sought to protect) were widely recognizable, including by fugitives who had learned how to decode the ciphers that enabled them in their quests for self-emancipation. Examples of this valuable knowledge being acknowledged are evident in ephemeral moments.

One is recounted in the journal that Anna Deborah Richardson, part of the wider Newcastle Richardson family, wrote about a trip she undertook in Ireland in August 1852.[17] A committed abolitionist, she was living in 6 Summerhill Grove in 1846 when Douglass stayed next door with Anna and Henry. She later met Harriet Beecher Stowe and her entourage when they stayed first with her maternal grandfather in Edinburgh and then in her parents' home in Newcastle. Her journal tells of a carriage journey in the west of Ireland, from Cork to Glengariff, taken on the advice of the abolitionist printer Richard Webb. She had "quite agreeable companions—a retired military office, who talked of the service he had seen in the Peninsular War; another gentleman, who covered us up with waterproofs; and a negro, who looked pleased and interested at every sound of a 'thou' or 'thee.'"[18] She suggests that he recognized the distinctiveness of Quaker speech, welcoming its implications.

Fragmentary details such as this are tantalizing and frustrating in equal measure. She says nothing more about this fellow traveler, though she would have known that Black antislavery lecturers, including Henry Highland Garnet, Charles L. Remond, Moses Roper, and James Watkins, all traveled throughout Ireland in the 1840s and 1850s. Douglass had toured Ireland in 1845, giving lectures and traveling across the same route.[19] Even sparse accounts of fleeting encounters challenge earlier understandings of a homogeneous British racial demographic. It is now well established that people of African origin lived in the ports and cities of Britain (especially London) and would have been a visible presence. More research is revealing that the Black experience in Britain is not just limited to urban spaces but also exists in rural locations, especially on or around transport routes.[20]

In Anna's childhood, a local Black presence likely comprised individuals enslaved by West Indian planters. Since Chipping Norton was on the stage-coach route from Worcester to London, it was a stopping point for travelers in the years before railways were built. One figure who might have stopped there was Jane Harry, the daughter of Charity Harry, a Jamaican woman, and Thomas Hibbert, a plantation holder whose own origins were in Manchester. Jane and her sister Mary were born in Jamaica, baptized as Anglicans, and sent to England for their education. Jane met Mary Morris Knowles, and supported and inspired by their friendship, became a Quaker. Thomas Knowles, a doctor and the husband of Mary Morris Knowles, was part of a transatlantically connected British-based Quaker group distributing and publishing abolitionist tracts and pamphlets.[21]

In 1782, Harry married Joseph Thresher, a Quaker physician, and moved from London to Worcester, where she died two years later, a few months after giving birth to their son. She had planned to return to Jamaica to free the enslaved individuals who had passed to her mother after her father's death, but this would be prevented by her own untimely death. Realizing that she would not be able to make the journey, she instructed her husband to make any necessary payments for the individuals' freedom once her mother had died.

In addition to Harry and other figures like her, there is also evidence of a Black presence in Moravian settlements, including Bristol but also East Tytherton, Wiltshire, about forty-five miles southwest of Chipping Norton and twenty-five miles east of Bristol, with its well-established commercial links to slavery. In the period of Anna's childhood, five formerly enslaved women from Antigua were living in East Tytherton. Leonora Casey Carr was the daughter of Fanny Loving, an enslaved woman, and a planter named George Carr. She was born in 1808 and came to England in 1817. In the same year, she, her sister Catherine, and her brothers Stephen and Edward were all manumitted.[22] Edward's full name, Edward Colston Carr, suggests a connection to the infamous slave trader Edward Colston, whose statue was toppled in Bristol in June 2020 during protests against the murder of George Floyd.

Transport hubs like Chipping Norton provided opportunities for static and mobile individuals to encounter each other; the world could come to the doorstep of someone who remained at home. Indeed, it was during a meeting of what Anna called "a few minutes' duration whilst the stage-coach was changing horses" in Chipping Norton that Henry became convinced that the girl he had come to love twelve years earlier at Ackworth had become the woman he now wished to marry.[23] More obviously, unexpected encounters can take place not just in vehicles such as stagecoaches, carriages, trains, and ships but also in liminal or interstitial sites such as railway stations. It is not surprising that so many nineteenth-century novelists, from Nathaniel Hawthorne and Edith Wharton to Leo Tolstoy, were fascinated with unexpected railway encounters.

The Leeds-based Quaker abolitionist Wilson Armistead and the Baptist minister Thomas H. Jones met by chance on a train in New England when Armistead was on a short visit to the United States. On 15 July 1850, the two men struck up a conversation when they traveled from Lynn to Boston, a route often taken by abolitionists. Armistead was visiting from Yorkshire and Jones had recently emancipated himself from enslavement in Wilmington, North Carolina. Armistead wore recognizable Quaker dress, which might have prompted Jones to hand (or more likely sell) him a copy of his newly published pamphlet, *The Experience of Thomas H. Jones, who was a Slave for Forty-Three Years* (1850). The meeting moved Armistead, who substantially reproduced the other man's narrative in the retrospective account of his visit he published in the *British Friend*. This resulted in the appearance of the only British edition of Jones's narrative, bringing his story to a sympathetic audience of Friends, something I have discussed elsewhere.[24]

Harriet Beecher Stowe famously drew wider public attention to Quaker recognizability in chapter 13 of *Uncle Tom's Cabin* (1852), "The Quaker Village." The idealized home of Rachel and Simeon Halliday is an Underground Railroad station where Eliza and George Harris and their son, Harry, are given sanctuary. In later life, Richardson was extremely familiar with the Underground Railroad, and William Still called her a figure

> whose generosity and benevolence knew no bounds; whose friendship devotion and liberality, were felt in all the principal stations of the Underground Rail Road; whose heart went out after the millions in fetters, the fleeing fugitive, the free, proscribed, the ignorant deprived of education, whose house was the home of the advocate of the slave from the United States, especially if he wore a colored skin or had been a slave. We would not venture to say how many of the enslaved this kind hand helped to purchase (Frederick Douglass and many others, being of the number.)[25]

Richardson was both pragmatic and uncomfortable about purchasing manumissions, something Garrisonians opposed. But faced with what her parents might have described as *"coloured* applicants for assistance," she always offered whatever "little help" she could manage. For instance, she raised funds in Newcastle to purchase the family of Henry Highland Garnet's adopted daughter, Stella Weims, though the campaign was messy and only partially successful.[26] In 1854, she and Ellen purchased the manumission of William Wells Brown after a campaigning process spanning the Atlantic. Their efforts opened at the Friends meeting house in Newcastle on 15 February and concluded in St. Louis in early July, with the exchange of the deed of emancipation.[27]

Four years later, she played a leading role in purchasing the manumission of two formerly enslaved women, Cornelia Williams Reed, whom she describes as Henry Highland Garnet's "bright young niece," and her mother, Dinah Williams.[28] James E. Crawford describes the assiduity of her commitment to the pair in an article in *The Liberator* drawing attention to a careful process. Anna received a request to help raise funds for Reed after she had raised $500 to purchase the freedom of Reed's mother. The request "was immediately responded to by an interesting and feeling letter . . . followed by others, and by an effort which resulted in the raising and sending to this country $481 through Mr. Lewis Tappan of New York. For this great assistance, we would return to our trans-Atlantic friends our heartfelt thanks and deepest gratitude."[29] A few years after Reed's manumission she married William B. Gould, formerly of Wilmington, North Carolina. His aunt was Rynar Jones, the second wife of Thomas H. Jones, the man Wilson Armistead had met by chance in 1850.[30]

This pattern of activity and generosity characterized Anna Richardson's long career. She was a shrewd and effective fundraiser, making sure she updated her correspondents about the activities of figures such as Douglass, Wells Brown, Reed, and others to maintain momentum and encourage antislavery. For instance, she acted as the British collector of subscriptions and contributions for *Frederick Douglass's Paper*, and distributed antislavery information, including a twelve-page tract titled *Anti-Slavery Memoranda*. She also sent regular updates titled *Monthly Illustrations of American Slavery* to newspaper editors to make antislavery copy readily available to them, adding editorial comments glossing some of the material she clipped from other sources.[31]

Another vital principal Anna learned from her childhood related to ethical consumption. Esther Atkins was a participant in the eighteenth-century abstention from slave-produced sugar. Years after her mother's death Anna asked, "Why did our dear mother take no sugar in her tea? Because it might be made by poor negroes who had been stolen from Africa." The campaign for sugar abstention was promoted by William Fox in his *Address to the People of Great Britain on the Propriety of Refraining from the Use of West India Sugar and Rum* (1791). This was quickly reprinted in Boston, New York, and Philadelphia. James Gilray published his caricature "Anti-Saccharrites, or John Bull and his family leaving off the use of sugar" in 1792, depicting King George, Queen Charlotte, and their family as sugar abstainers, albeit ones who do not much like the taste of unsweetened tea. In May 1792, the *New York Journal and Patriotic Register* copied an item from the British press noting that three hundred families in Worcester were abstaining from sugar, while the Philadelphia-based *Dunlap's Daily American Advertiser* (which had reprinted Fox's *Address)* claimed that more than twelve thousand people in Limerick were also abstainers.[32]

The campaign was boosted by the publication of Elizabeth Heyrick's *Immediate, not Gradual Abolition* (1824), an event of great significance to

Anna, who was to emerge as a firm supporter of the nineteenth-century free produce movement. First printed in England, Heyrick's pamphlet was then sent to Quaker abolitionists in Philadelphia, where it became an important stimulus for U.S. antislavery.[33] Thus, on both sides of the Atlantic a wide range of activists felt the impact of her work. Heyrick used the language of rights to articulate powerful claims based on social justice for the enslaved. Specifically, she recognized and championed the political rights and human dignity of all individuals, regardless of color. She argued that women could carry out key political interventions by being actively involved in consumer (thus economic) choices. Women were frequently responsible for managing household budgets and engaging in purchasing networks, and their involvement in sugar boycotts showed that they were familiar with the operations of global capitalism.

U.S. and British free produce groups found Heyrick's work a vital intellectual and political resource, echoing her arguments about using personal purchasing decisions to undermine the economic basis of enslavement. They argued that in this way the market for slave-produced goods would be fatally undermined. The pamphlet was reprinted in Benjamin Lundy's *Genius of Universal Emancipation* in 1825 and reissued in 1847 in the American free produce periodical the *Non-Slaveholder*. The latter was founded the previous year by its editors, Abraham L. Pennock, Samuel Rhoads, and George W. Taylor, further extending the reach of her arguments. Rhoads also gave an inscribed copy to Martin Delany the same year that he and his wife, Ann, first met Anna Richardson in Newcastle.

Heyrick's politics had their roots in the combined traditions of rational dissent within which she was raised, and female ministry and leadership which she embraced when she became a Quaker by convincement at the age of twenty-five. Her antislavery radicalism was marked by a distinctive edge, emphasizing political rights over feeling and benevolence. Heyrick was one of the founding members of the Birmingham Ladies' Society for the Relief of Negro Slaves in 1825, an avid writer of pamphlets, and a prison visitor. Her circle of Quaker friends extended to figures known to the Richardsons' circle, including the Tuke family, whom she met when she lived in York in 1802. Anna was connected to the Tukes by marriage but also through their shared interests in education and social causes. It is easy to see the connected ethos of the activities with which this group was engaged. William Tuke was a pioneer of mental health reform and founder of the York Retreat, an asylum for the insane. Unlike existing institutions, the York Retreat aimed to create an environment of tranquility and calm, in which patients were not restrained by chains or violently punished. His second wife, Esther Maud Tuke, founded the York School for Girls in Trinity Lane in 1785. Several family members were Quaker ministers and some of the couple's children attended Ackworth.[34]

By the time the young Anna Atkins arrived at Ackworth in 1817 the principles she had learned at home had been fully absorbed. They would continue to reverberate for the rest of her life, guiding her work and sustaining her through difficult personal situations. The environment at Ackworth was strict and the school was largely segregated, yet Henry admired, and grew to love, Anna there. Cousins and siblings were able to meet for outdoor walks after Sunday worship, and there was overlap between the Atkins and Richardson families, especially among the sisters.[35] Anna's sister Martha and Henry's sister Rachel both left Ackworth in the same year. Rachel remained involved with Ackworth, especially after her husband, Thomas Pumphrey, who was from Worcester, became its superintendent in December 1834, remaining in the post for twenty-seven years.[36]

Although Ellen Richardson left the school in 1822, her obituary reveals that Ackworth remained in her thoughts, rather negatively it seems, for she "often spoke of her school-days at Ackworth as a time of Spartan discipline."[37] When Anna moved to Newcastle, the pair deepened their relationship. Quakers encouraged careful fostering of close relationships between the family members of couples, especially their siblings. This helped to create tight-knit and attached kinship circles, connected by ties of family, religion, and business.[38] Evidence of the lasting quality of such relationships can be found in a letter Anna wrote to Ann Rhoads in October 1872. She told her that, "I am thankful to say that my dear Henry and I are still permitted to enjoy a comfortable show of health. Our surviving sister Ellen Richardson lives a little way from us and also our dear widowed cousin Jane Edward Richardson" (the mother of Anna Deborah, who had died after a prolonged illness).[39]

Anna settled into a married life that was busy but also materially comfortable. In the initial period of their marriage the couple chafed against some of what her obituary calls "the restraints at that time customary in the Society of Friends"—restrictions on reading as well as behavior.[40] She and Henry had sufficient wealth to be able to spend time outside of Newcastle, sometimes in the fishing village of Cullercoats, which Douglass visited while in the North East. A near neighbor was the abolitionist and journalist Harriet Martineau, who lived in Tynemouth between 1840 and 1845, recuperating from illness.

THE QUAKERS OF SUMMERHILL GROVE

The community of Friends who lived in and around Summerhill Grove had memorializing customs that make it possible to piece together details of their lives and beliefs. This allows us to have a better sense not just of public activities but also of the more intimate environments in which members of the community gathered. In a discussion of Margaret Wood (another Ackworth scholar), Sandra Stanley Holton suggests that Wood's journal and letters revealed a life of purpose and of dedication to her family and community. Holton draws attention to the multiple modes of recollection and history-making practiced by Newcastle Friends. Wood was well traveled, and after the death of her mother and sisters had spent 1831–1832 visiting family members who had settled in and around Philadelphia. Holton writes,

> The creation and maintenance of family memory among this circle was encouraged through oral storytelling and its written recording, through the passing on of houses, furniture, books and, most of all, of old diaries and letters . . . Almost two hundred years after her birth, subsequent generations of her kin might sit in her rocking chair, "very handsome, but high and severe," enjoy the sampler on "Industry" that she sewed as a pupil at Ackworth School, read her family chronicle, journal and letters, share recorded memories of her from those who had known her in life, and so learn from her cultural legacy.[41]

Anna's sampler has not survived, but doubtless the younger generation of Newcastle Friends would have encountered Ackworth samplers on the walls of the various houses they visited. They were a visible reminder of shared family history and faith, and a legacy of the childhoods of previous generations who were now middle-aged, elderly, or dead. If Anna Deborah Richardson is anything to judge by, however, these younger women were less willing than the previous generation to take up the needle.

Anna Deborah's indifference to sewing started early. Jane Richardson noted in her diary that her four-year-old daughter "improves in learning to read and spell. She puts up cleverly four or five maps and has some knowledge of the counties." By the age of five she was able to "read nicely, write tolerably, and has some general intelligence but an extreme dislike to all handicraft occupations." It seems unlikely that the spirited girl would have wanted to sew a sampler, though by the time she was seven Jane was able to write, "She has made some progress in reading and writing—a good deal in spelling and sewing, and is gaining a slight knowledge of geography."[42]

She did not follow the previous generation's path to Ackworth, though she certainly received a Quaker education. Anna Deborah was first educated locally, followed by a period at a school in Durham, before attending a strict school run by three Quaker women in Lewes, Sussex. She developed few ambitions to sew, though there was a single exception outlined in January 1860 in a letter to Kate O'Brien, thanking her for a pair of embroidered slippers. She marveled, "What a long, long, time it must have taken your dear tiny fingers to put in all those delicate stitches!" She confided, "I quite remember the time when I so disliked sitting still to sew more than half-an-hour at a time, that Papa promised me a watch when I had made six shirts for him . . . and I set to work, and in about three years—think of it, some of the poor slopwomen make a shirt in a day, and only get eightpence. I finished the task, and won the watch."[43]

Anna Deborah was committed to supporting women's education, a subject enthusiastically pursued by several women in her wider circle, including Emily Davies, who lived for a period in Gateshead, near Newcastle. They corresponded on a subject in which "she took the warmest interest"—the foundation of Girton College, Cambridge.[44] This pioneering institution would host Virginia Woolf in 1928, delivering the lecture which became "A Room of One's Own," in which she argued that women were rendered silent not due to inferiority but because the subjects and activities that interested them were considered insignificant by men.

Events taking place within the private houses of Newcastle Friends or in nearby public venues demonstrate the developing intellectual and social community creating sustaining contexts for antislavery. The establishment of a Book Society on 27 April 1826 resulted in serious discussions about appropriate reading. Novels were not the only texts regarded with suspicion. Charles Bragg proposed Aaron Smith's first-person captivity narrative, *The Atrocities of the Pirates* (1824). The popular work recounts the experiences of a young British sailor who was kidnapped by Cuban pirates in 1823 and then forced into piracy. Eventually escaping, he was arrested, brought back to England, and tried for piracy at the Old Bailey. Bragg's proposal was rejected by members, as were the works of Walter Scott.[45] Indeed, Anna Deborah would get into trouble at school in Lewes some years later when she quoted seemingly innocuous lines from Scott's poem *Marmion* describing the effect of the morning sun: "And tinged them with a lustre proud / Like that which streaks a thunder cloud."

The reading of the pupils at her school followed a familiar pattern. She was also encouraged to read Quaker biographies of William Allen, Stephen Grellett, and Elizabeth Fry, but she called them "Dreary works, which I used to devour for the sake of the thread of narrative which ran through them."[46] Novels were not acceptable, but the poetry of William Cowper, James Montgomery, and Henry Wadsworth Longfellow was considered appropriate for young readers—Anna Deborah was especially fond of Longfellow's poem "Evangeline." Longfellow not only made financial contributions to abolition but also hosted two well-known formerly enslaved men, Josiah Henson and Lunsford Lane, in his home in Cambridge, Massachusetts. Wilson Armistead doubtless knew this when he wrote to him on the headed paper of the Leeds Anti-Slavery Association in 1854 asking for a contribution to an antislavery collection he was compiling.[47]

The Book Society was so popular that a second was formed, but eventually both dwindled. Friends were increasingly able to access books and printed works in other ways. A key local resource was the library of the Literary and Philosophical Society, founded in 1793 (but only admitting women in 1804) as a mobile organization that hosted conversations and lectures. By 1825 it had a fixed location in a fine neoclassical building on Westgate Road, close to Anna and Henry's future home and the family grocery. It had a substantial library that was available to members, which some Friends utilized for the works they contributed to the meetings of the Essay Society, formed in the early 1830s. A letter from Sarah Richardson to her sister Susan Balk-will, dated 24 January 1832, gives a vignette of a Newcastle Essay Meeting attended by a large group:

> We attended at a short notice with an essay of sister Rebecca's on "Forti-tude." Sister Ann's a very good and pretty description of the neighbourhood of Keswick. Edward and Jane's [Anna Deborah's parents] two poems on the promised "Aurora"—Edward's much remarked upon as a very *original* metre, or no metre at all but irregular verse. Some of the other subjects were Con-tentment, on Prayer, on History, The Cholera, Friendship, Parting, The Grave, The Speedwell, The Holly Evergreen. A Magazine Ditty, by Joseph Watson, a very clever six-line verse on the events of the Past and the Coming Year. William Doeg's, a very long piece, good and clear, proving that great talents are not opposed to the possessor uniting amiable qualities, and that it is not merely to be affectionate that we are amiable, &c., &c.[48]

The wide-ranging combination of subjects was unlikely to have met with disapproval from more conservative Friends. These pieces focus on relatively conventional themes and only the "very *original* metre" of Edward Richard-son's poem, as Sarah Richardson archly calls it, attracts specific attention.

The society was so successful that in 1833 it issued a literary annual titled *The Aurora Borealis* (the "promised" publication noted in the quotation).[49] News of its appearance circulated widely, including as far afield as Philadel-phia, where John Sharp carefully clipped from a local paper and kept a notice about its appearance, evidence that he continued to keep up with news from English Friends long after settling in the United States.[50] Perhaps he even purchased a copy and circulated it to other immigrants, continuing a family practice of distributing periodicals and newspapers throughout their scat-tered circle. Had he done this, he would have encountered two contributions by Henry Richardson. One of them, written in December 1831, was titled "To a Boy, on Hearing Him Whistling in the Street 'The Bonnets of Blue,' during the Prevalence of the Cholera." Overall, the poem reads like a piece of kindly but firm chastisement (which it is) and contains at least one terrible rhyme.

But it does speak to a contemporary crisis: the first death from what would become a devastating outbreak of cholera emerged in Sunderland in October 1831. Two months later the disease had appeared in Newcastle, and by early in 1832 it had spread to Scotland before making its way across England. Henry would not yet have known of its terrible impact, but he expressed a solemn sense that his young addressee's cheerfulness was not to be encouraged. He admonishes the boy,

> Yes, indeed it is good to be wise,
> It is good to be honest and true;
> And the heart in which cheerfulness reigns, is a prize
> Surpassing the mines of Peru.
>
> But it is not a season for mirth,
> Nor should pleasure our moments employ,
> When the Angel of Pestilence walketh the earth,
> Commissioned to blast and destroy.
>
> Our neighbours around us are falling,
> By the arm of his vengeance laid low;
> And a voice from the tomb is impressively calling,
> "Be ye also ready to go!"
>
> Then can this be a time to rejoice?—
> Away with thy light-hearted rhymes,
> Or tune the soft notes of thy musical voice,
> To a strain more befitting the times.[51]

The "The Bonnets of Blue" was a well-known song expressing Jacobite sympathies. It celebrated and encouraged incursions into England by the Scottish laborers and farmers whose woolen bonnets protected them from the harsh northern weather. The fact that the song centers on the unstoppable movement of young men across the border would certainly seem sinister in the context of a rapidly spreading epidemic. A subsequent outbreak in 1853–

1854 led to the deaths of one hundred people a day in Newcastle. During this period Jane Richardson and other Quaker women visited those sick with cholera, despite the personal risk.[52]

Anna and Henry were married two years after the poem was published, on 4 July 1833, just before the Slavery Abolition Act passed into law. Henry worked at, and eventually took over, the grocery business. Anna immediately directed her energies to various kinds of philanthropic labor considered acceptable for female Friends. She was a keen supporter of educating working-class children who had little access to the advantages associated with literacy and numeracy. She offered wholehearted support, over many years, to Henry and Ellen, both of whom were involved in founding schools in and around Newcastle. Henry was closely connected to a boy's ragged school, to educate impoverished boys deprived of access to education or even sufficient food.[53]

Shortly after she left Ackworth, Ellen participated in the activities of the Royal Jubilee School for Girls in Newcastle, continuing her involvement until the school closed in 1884. She contributed to the teaching of reading and Scripture, and she published several educational and other texts, including one to assist scriptural study, titled *Communings with the Heart. Suggested by Passages in the Four Gospels. With aids to Self-Examination, and Prayers Compiled from Scripture* (1855). In addition, she was involved in the development of other schools, including one in Cullercoats.

When Henry Highland Garnet visited Newcastle in 1850 he spoke at two of the schools with which the Richardsons were involved, noting of the students that he "was struck with their strict attention, and their deep sympathy—but it was all accounted for, when I learned that their kind teachers, and their patrons make it a point to tell of the sorrows and the wrongs of my poor brethren."[54] Unlike the girls at Ackworth earlier in the century, the children attending these schools did not have to resort to a petition to be informed about slavery but were given firsthand testimony from a self-emancipated Black man whose abolitionism was reinforced by the curriculum of the New York African Free School, which he and James McCune Smith had both attended.[55] This must have been an extremely memorable experience for them and doubtless profoundly impacted their lives.

Following her marriage and relocation to the North East, Anna was involved in benevolent activities, something suggested by the following brief chronology. From 1834 onward, at the prompting of Elizabeth Fry, Anna undertook prison visiting. In 1839 she fundraised for Lutheran refugees from Prussia who were stopping off in Newcastle on their way to the United States. Six years later she went to see a group of Iowan and Ojibwe performers in Newcastle, part of the spectacle staged by George Catlin to encourage interest in his collection of portraits, known as the Indian Gallery. She organized the burial of one of their children in Newcastle, erecting a west-facing headstone that she subsequently tended.

She also was one of the key figures in collecting articles to be sent to the United States and sold at the Anti-Slavery Bazaar in Philadelphia in 1846, with contributors being advised that appropriate items included "Engravings of distinguished, religious, philanthropic or literary characters, drawings or models of their residences: simple implements, such as rulers or paperfolders, manufactured from articles belonging to them; autographs, new devices in worsted work, net worsted shawls, neck ties, papier maché articles, purses, needle-books, &c., &c."[56] Frederick Douglass noted, "Every stitch, every painting, embodied and shadowed forth a spirit of freedom and spoke of the power of English sympathy."[57]

Anna and Henry, who were devout in their religious beliefs, visited Paris in 1850 with two thousand presentation copies of the New Testament. Five years later they sent additional funding via Anna Deborah, and religious texts with other family members.[58] A few years later they distributed Chinese translations of biblical texts to Chinese sailors who had docked on the Tyne. Anna became a teetotaler around this time, and she and Henry went on to form temperance refreshment rooms in the autumn of 1853.

Her commitment extended beyond these kinds of reform activities, taking her into a transnational sphere within which her energy, intelligence, and generosity combined with her deeply felt religious beliefs made her into a formidable campaigner. She and Henry were becoming increasingly involved in the campaign for free produce, which was international by its very nature. Julie Holcomb argues that this was "the first consumer movement to transcend the boundaries of nation, gender, and race in an effort by reformers to change the conditions of production. Even when they acted locally, supporters embraced a global vision, mobilizing the boycott as a powerful material force that could transform the transatlantic marketplace."[59]

Though some scholars have questioned the long-term impact of free produce, the energy of its chief participants is widely acknowledged. Holcomb's description points toward the way the boycott harnessed economic and political understandings. Free produce campaigning showed the relationship between private and public acts. It enabled women to make purchasing decisions that revealed their understanding of the impact of choices made by households on the lives of individuals thousands of miles away. The interconnectedness made explicit by free produce campaigners showed the way in which multiple social causes were being mobilized by campaigners. Tracts circulated in Philadelphia urging Quakers to abstain from slave-produced goods, including one published in 1838 titled *An Address to the Members of the Religious Society of Friends, on the Propriety of Abstaining from the Use of the Produce of Slave Labour.* It used the examples of two leading Quaker American abolitionists, John Woolman, who also espoused tax resistance and other causes, and Elias Hicks. It urged Friends to "refrain from any participation in the crime of enslaving our fellow men."[60] The movement gained additional momentum in England due to the participation of the American reformer Elihu Burritt, known as the Learned Blacksmith. He capitalized on this moniker in his 1846 publication, wittily titled *Sparks from the Anvil.* It was published in Worcester, Massachusetts, by Henry J. Howland, who in 1857 would publish an edition of Thomas Jones's *Narrative.*

Burritt's interests in peace, temperance, and abolition had been honed in New England, where he was a lecturer and writer, and for a brief period, the editor of the American Peace Society's journal *The Advocate of Peace,* which he renamed *The Advocate of Peace and Universal Brotherhood.* After infighting within the Society, he left for England in 1846, initially staying with Joseph Sturge, the founder of the British and Foreign Anti-Slavery Society and the major organizer of the 1843 London Peace Congress.[61] Burritt in turn went on to organize the first International Peace Congress, which took place five years later in Brussels. Further congresses followed in Paris (1849), Frankfurt (1850), London (1851), Manchester (1852), and Edinburgh (1853). The novelist and peace campaigner Victor Hugo was so inspired by him that he made sure Burritt's work was circulated in France despite a repressive tax imposed by the French authorities to stop the circulation of radical texts.[62] Burritt also traveled widely within England, lecturing on peace and founding the League of

Universal Brotherhood to promote the use of free produce. He energetically gathered information and pursued connections. Writing from Exeter on 29 September 1849 to an unnamed recipient (the context suggest that this is a Philadelphia Friend), he asks for details of "all the facts necessary for a free exposition" of free produce.[63] He remained in Europe until 1853, galvanizing an existing set of groups and individuals with long-standing connections to social reform and social justice issues. Returning to England the following decade, he walked from London to Scotland, publishing *A Walk from London to John O'Groats* (1864), a book full of observations about the landscape and the communities with which he engaged.

Burritt was a prolific writer, and in addition to editing and publishing *The Advocate of Peace,* he produced a series of juvenile pamphlets called *Olive Leaflets.* He appears to have been a model of sorts for Anna and Henry, who became staunch supporters and in turn influenced his work. His twenty-nine-stanza poem "The Wall of Fire" depicts the experience of a German grandmother and her grandson under siege by the Cossacks. Though all their neighbors have taken up weapons, the grandmother, like her dead son, is an uncompromising pacifist. The first stanza states their pacifism:

To drive Napoleon from the throne,
Were battles fought and won,
Alas! How many lives were lost,
And how much evil done![64]

The frightened grandson then expresses his wish that his father was there to fight and protect them, but the grandmother insists that he would not have taken up arms, telling him, "Thy father's heart was full of peace, / And love to every one." The dead father's beliefs correspond to those of Samuel Atkins and other pacifist Quakers who refused to take up arms even when their own lives were at risk.

The poem appeared after Burritt and Anna first met, and it is worth speculating about whether Anna told him about her father's lasting influence. Burritt uncompromisingly defined laurel leaves as "wreaths of weeds or green leaves wound around the brows of a murderer who has girdled a vast country with a river of blood."[65] This would have resonated with Samuel Atkins, who refused to give laurel leaves to passengers in passing stagecoaches celebrating victory over the French.

Anna did not use such blunt language, though she noted that he did not want "to assist in giving any approval to slaughter and bloodshed." However, her ongoing support for Burritt and the causes they both believed in would be a significant element of her life. Following Burritt's arrival, she founded the Newcastle Ladies' Free Produce Association and actively argued for a boycott of slave-produced goods. By 1848 the association circulated "a forcible appeal" to encourage support for free produce, noting that though it is addressed to British readers, it is "equally applicable to the people of the free States of this Union; and we would earnestly commend it to their serious consideration."[66] The Richardsons encouraged the fugitive Henry Highland Garnet to cross the Atlantic and campaign for free produce. Then, from 1851 to 1854, Anna edited its periodical, *The Slave*.[67] Its circulation rose to between 2,500 and 3,000 copies per month. *The Slave* carried advertisements for free produce, including for products from the short-lived Cumberland Free Labour Gingham Company. In addition to selling goods to the Street Free Produce Store in Somerset, the company liaised with the Philadelphia Free Produce Association for cotton and a market for its goods.

Around twenty-six free produce associations were established during this period, and the couple were extremely active in creating organizational structures and fundraising to develop campaigning and to make free produce more widely available, including in the family's shop. Garnet attended the Paris Peace Congress along with Anna and Henry and several other activists from England, and the following year he attended the Frankfurt Peace Congress and participated in two antislavery meetings in the city. Returning to England, he stayed in 5 Summerhill Grove before lecturing throughout Britain. He gives a flavor of his experience in Newcastle in a letter published in the *Non-Slaveholder* in October 1850:

> This night at half past nine, I arrived in New Castle on the Tyne, [*sic*] and soon had the joy of entering the mansion of those laborious and untiring friends of the down-trodden bondsman, Henry and Anna H. Richardson. At once they made me feel at home, and immediately set themselves about making arrangements for our Free Labour campaign. You know the energy

of these dear friends. Leaf after leaf, covered with arguments and appeals in the behalf of the children of Africa, are scattered by their hands upon the winds of heaven. Not only does the anti-slavery cause receive their sympathy, but also the Bible, the missionary, and temperance causes, all are promoted by them.—Likewise the little children share their benevolence. Mrs. Richardson is at this moment busy in sending out letters for the appointment of meetings.[68]

Garnet's letter encompasses the hospitality and "energy" of a household whose inhabitants were active in an array of interlinked causes.

In June 1850 Anna published a circular encouraging women Friends who planned to attend the Yearly Meeting in London to participate in a free produce meeting.[69] The Richardsons continued to promote free produce, and Anna became increasingly involved with the Olive Leaf Circles, organized by women who sold items made of free produce and donated the proceeds to the League of Universal Brotherhood. Anna's involvement extended to editing a juvenile peace journal titled the *Olive Leaf* from 1844 to 1857. Meanwhile, Henry published a poem advocating peace, titled "The Church and the Camp," and edited the *Peace Advocate* from 1843 to 1851.[70]

Amid all this activity, in 1854 Henry suffered a stroke. Though this was a terrible blow, even this did not stop Anna's labor. In addition to caring for him, she wrote letters to her international network, clipped and circulated newspaper articles, edited periodicals, campaigned, and maintained her ties to her large local community and family. She wrote texts for juvenile audiences, to educate them about the ways they could contribute to antislavery and free produce. In October 1865 she was a signatory to an address sent from the Ladies' Anti-Slavery Society of Newcastle to its counterpart in Madrid. This was part of a wider campaign in which women antislavery activists in Birmingham, Edinburgh, Liverpool, London, Newcastle, and Paris all wrote in solidarity to the group in Spain to encourage them in their continuing work. Some of these letters were subsequently printed in the *Anti-Slavery Monthly Reporter*.[71] All of this suggests a life that was full of varying obligations and commitments to family, local community, and transatlantic campaigns. By the 1850s, this included tract-writing, which will be the focus of the rest of this chapter.

WHO ARE THE SLAVEHOLDERS?
A MORAL DRAWN FROM *UNCLE TOM'S CABIN*

Anna Richardson does not seem to have thought of herself as having literary abilities. In a letter to the educational and social reformer Mary Carpenter, who had asked her to contribute a piece for an edited collection for an antislavery bazaar, she writes, "I should have been glad my dear friend to have sent thee a better contribution but writing for pretty books has always been out of my line."[72] Many Friends shared her reservations about "pretty books." However, her letter suggests that her scruples were aesthetic rather than moral, for she certainly knew some literary texts by heart and toward the end of her life she often repeated them aloud, suggesting an enjoyment of poetry and recitation. Some doubtless reinforced her religious beliefs as she moved toward her death. A favorite was the lines written by the seventeenth-century hymnist and theologian Richard Baxter:

> Our knowledge of that life is small;
> The eye of faith is dim;
> But 'tis enough that Christ knows all,
> And we shall be with Him.

The four lines compare a myopic human existence with the vision and knowledge of a Christ whose presence comforts even those who experience fear or doubt.

Just as devotional pieces were acceptable to many Quakers, since they had an appropriate purpose, so were nonfiction forms such as tracts. The Richardsons' didactic tracts were part of the emerging genre of juvenile abolitionist writing that has been discussed extensively by Deborah De Rosa and Michaël Roy.[73] I turn first to *Who Are the Slaveholders? A Moral Drawn from* Uncle Tom's Cabin. This tract draws on the popularity of Stowe's best-selling 1852 novel in order to make the case for free produce, just under twenty years after the British Slavery Abolition Act.[74]

The text opens with a depiction of an idyllic and tranquil scene. The narrator asks readers to imagine "a pleasant country place, named Fernbrake, situated in one of England's midland counties." The setting elliptically acknowledges the influence of Elizabeth Heyrick, who hailed from Leicester-shire, though it also resembles Anna's memories of her childhood in nearby Chipping Norton. Additional details extend and deepen the depiction of a rural site that has little overt relation to global politics, or indeed to any geographic location beyond itself. Yet this sense of separation from wider concerns is immediately destabilized by a reference to Washington Irving's satirical *A History of New York* (1809). Since Irving expects his readers to understand that this description of New York is the unrealistic fantasy of an unreliable narrator, astute readers might rightly infer that Fernbrake also warrants closer inspection. The pastoral idyll of English village life might be more complex than the scene that initially meets the eye. The tract reveals the way in which slavery enters the rural English home, a pattern familiar to Anna from her parents' lessons during her childhood.

Bringing the reader into to the heart of the home and domestic life, the narrator describes the family circle of the Stanfields: "The time of our visit is the evening, soon after the tea-things have been dismissed." The family is quite prosperous, and their sitting room is comfortable; a "moderate fire" has been lit in the grate for additional comfort. Mr. Stanfield is in his armchair while Mrs. Stanfield and their "half a dozen happy-faced children, between the ages of four and fourteen" sit around a table, "occupied with various light handicrafts and amusement" as befits the bourgeois family at rest. For "several successive evenings" the older children had read aloud Stowe's "beautiful and affecting tale" to their siblings and parents. Her novel was the most successful example of the kind of Christian literature that would gradually make novel reading more acceptable to Friends. A lengthy passage describes their re-sponses to hearing the novel being read aloud.[75] "American slavery" is firmly relegated to a realm far from Fernbrake and is only (it seems) brought into the family through engagement with a literary text; slavery is quite literally brought home to them at the very moment of reading.

Beyond the vivid textual encounter (however moving—and indeed dra-matic), slavery does not appear to have a literal or economic connection to their household. However, the family remains troubled by what they have heard and are left with the question of how they should react to slavery's con-tinued existence. What are they to do? Their responses are vividly described. They had "laughed and wept, despaired and exulted, melted into tenderness, and burned with indignation." They had "trembled," "laughed," "sympathised [and] cried 'shame!'" Cataloging responses in detail, readers are told that members of the family had been "delighted" and "enraptured" and had "admired," "scouted," "marvelled," "rejoiced," "smiled," but also "shuddered," "wept," "melted," "mourned," "deprecated." This exhaustive (and exhausting) list starts with a rhetorical question: "Where is the Christian family that could stand the brunt of such an onset?" Such a family, it appears, cannot be imagined.

The list of their responses closes with the listeners riled up, their opposition to slavery made explicit. They "execrated," "thrilled," "agonised," and "boiled with indignation." Most particularly, the children express their pleasure that they are not slaveholders, something which lifts from them any sense of direct involvement in, or responsibility for, a system they believe to be located on the other side of the Atlantic. Their mother reassures them that though England had a long connection with slaveholding in the past, this is over. In fact, sailors now "bravely risk their lives in its suppression" while "Canada stands open to receive the hunted fugitives of American slavery, and secures them an asylum beyond the reaches of the Fugitive Slave-law . . . Thus, not only are we no slaveholders, but our influence is altogether on the side of the slave. We have renounced all connection with the accursed system; and surely this is a cause for thankfulness."[76] Mrs. Stanfield's comments show that she is like the "abolitionist mother-historian" figure of the period's U.S. juvenile texts.[77] She absolves the family from complicity in a system they feel they can safely abhor from a distance.

Yet Mr. Stanfield, while agreeing with his wife and children, offers an important corrective. He asks, "What if I could prove to you that we are all slaveholders?"[78] The children's expressions of innocent incredulity and fun at what they regard as a light-hearted comment contrasts with the growing sense of disquiet from Mrs. Stanfield. Meanwhile, Mr. Stanfield moves into an empirically based mode of argument, marshaling facts and details reminiscent of Henry's *A Revolution of the Spindles*.

He first asks whether it makes any difference whether the enslaved "work for us on our own premises or 4,000 miles away." Assured by his wife that it does not, he asks his son how many people live in the village. George's response shows a slightly improbable grasp of specific detail, telling his father that "at the last census we had a population exceeding a thousand, and if we reckon five people for each house, it will make rather more than 200 families." Deducing from this that such a population might have thirty "men, women and children" laboring in enslavement on behalf of the village, Mr. Stanfield launches into a detailed account of the kinds of violence meted out to the enslaved in South America and the United States. Enslaved workers on plantations produce the cotton, rice, and sugar that are being used within their own household. The family therefore unknowingly supports slavery, since consumers are implicated by their purchases. This observation challenges the comfortable generic expectations established in the earlier part of the narrative, moving away from its air of cozy domesticity and directly linking their comfort to the violence of enslavement. He discusses the economics of enslavement and the global system of finance, telling them, "So intimately are we connected with the cruel system, that the money value of a slave, in New Orleans, is said to be regulated on the Exchange of Liverpool: that is, when cotton rises rapidly in Liverpool, the price of slaves rises in America: when cotton falls, slaves fall . . . American slavery could not possibly exist without the support it derives from Britain." In other words, capitalism is foundationally reliant on slavery. This radical message moves the family away from their distanced benevolence, in which sympathy alone was sufficient, to one underwritten by a demand to take further action.

Moving on, Mr. Stanfield tells them there is unconscious and conscious support for slavery: "alas! there are Englishmen to be found, men, too, of high respectability and standing, who support the *slave-trade with their eyes open!*" He specifically notes the "chains manufactured for the purpose in Birmingham, or Wolverhampton," and a footnote indicates that items produced "expressly for the slave trade" in Birmingham had been shown to the author.[79] As further evidence of culpability, Mr. Stanfield cites cloth woven in Manchester and Glasgow and subsequently used for the clothing of the enslaved.[80] Most vividly, he describes the enslaved "writhing and gasping in the hold of a slave ship, fitted out by the aid of British capital, and landed, in the form of living skeletons, in Cuba or Brazil, to raise an article for the British market."[81] It is worth noting that he does not just focus on U.S. slavery but also draws attention to the inter-Atlantic realm of enslavement, and multiple footnotes citing abolitionist texts and authors and other sources back up his claims.[82]

He is then faced with his wife's mild, yet just, rebuke: "I wonder, my dear . . . that when you feel these things so deeply, you have never spoken of them before. You know I am always ready to carry out your wishes; and besides, I shall now consider it a matter of duty to do what I can to patronise free-labour." He replies that it is the power of reading and writing that has changed him: "The affecting exposure of slavery in Mrs. Stowe's book . . . has driven the subject home and compelled me to look at it seriously," suggesting an experience akin to that of the real John Sharp when he read William Cowper.[83]

Depicting a family's habits being changed by the experience of reading indicates a belief that reading can literally change lives. From now on, the entire family, from youngest to oldest, will do what she or he can to avoid slave-produced goods, becoming consumer activists, perhaps like readers of the tract. As the narrator notes, "From that day forward, there were stationed to keep watch over Mrs. Stanfield's table and wardrobe, six of those little cruisers, which, according to Elihu Burritt, if established in every family, would be more effectual for the suppression of slavery and the slave-trade than the largest squadron in the world."[84]

This tract draws from contemporary free produce arguments and wider abolitionist texts, but it is also indebted to the earlier phase of campaigning for sugar abstention and to juvenile tracts such as those written by Priscilla Wakefield and Amelia Opie. In particular, Wakefield's *Mental Improvement* (1794–1797), published on both sides of the Atlantic, depicted a series of conversations between Mr. and Mrs. Harcourt and their children. Number 10 focuses on sugar cultivation, before moving into a discussion of slavery and culminating, like *Who Are the Slaveholders?*, with the children pledging to abstain from sugar.[85]

To reinforce the relations between private behavior and public consequences, *Who Are the Slaveholders?* tried to make it easier for others to recognize (and avoid) slave-produced goods. It concludes with a full-page chart divided into three columns listing free produce, slave produce, and items of uncertain origin. Careful readers and consumers can change their activities and the lives not just of themselves but of others too. It concludes with a formal notice recommending that readers who want "a fuller exposition of anti-slavery and free-labour principles" can find them in *The Slave* (which Anna edited) and the Newcastle Anti-slavery Tracts. The tract directly addresses a juvenile audience, especially readers who have already encountered Stowe's novel. It suggests, albeit indirectly, that they will recognize and share the responses felt by the Stanfields as they heard *Uncle Tom's Cabin* being read aloud to them. In this way it also implies that they are ready for the lesson taught by Mr. Stanfield; in other words, such an experience will have prepared them for the consumer boycott it goes on to advocate. This lesson was further amplified in the next text I will discuss, which is simple, didactic, and to the point.

LITTLE LAURA, THE KENTUCKY ABOLITIONIST

The twelve pages of *Little Laura, the Kentucky Abolitionist* (1859) center on the short life of a real child named Laura Bailey, the daughter of William Shreve Bailey and Caroline Ann Withnall. Though we know little of Withnall, newspaper articles and correspondence allow us to know more about William Bailey's experiences as an abolitionist printer and editor. He was a working-class man whose abolitionist beliefs were the product of a fierce and unsentimental attachment to the rights of workers. In a piece titled "A Short Sketch of our Troubles in the Anti-Slavery Cause," he describes himself as originally working as "a cotton machinist and steam engine builder."[86] In 1839 he purchased a homestead in Newport, Kentucky, establishing a machine shop there.

In 1850 he published several articles in the newly established *Newport News*, arguing for immediate abolition. Its editor complained that the articles "were too radically liberal for a slave state" and persuaded Bailey to purchase the paper because it had been "injured" by Bailey's articles. Bailey writes that the "thought of an iron worker laying down the hammer and cold-chisel and forsaking the anvil and vice to take up the pen, was a wide reach from my former occupation; but I saw an independent press was needed to oust the overbearing tyranny of the *few* and show fair play to the *many*, and the mechanics and working-men of my acquaintance favoured the undertaking." Knowingly or not, his comments invoke Frances Vaughan's dedicatory poem prefacing Anna Weamys's *Continuation of Sir Philip Sidney's Arcadia* (1651), encouraging women to stop sewing and start writing, proclaiming, "Lay by your Needles Ladies, Take the Pen, / The onely difference 'twixt you and Men.'"[87]

Turning his back on his previous work by laying down his tools and metaphorically taking up the pen, Bailey bought the type and press and moved them to his machine shop, where he started a daily paper. This newspaper "gave the general news of the day, exposed the existing evils in the community and went on to encourage public improvements, industry, education &c. with now and then a good article, showing slavery to be the great curse of our general prosperity." It employed compositors, proofreaders and reporters, but opponents paid them to sabotage their own work, leaving it undone or badly performed. Withnall and her daughters learned how to set type to make sure the paper met its deadlines, just as Frederick Douglass's children worked on *The North Star.* But protests from male printers about girls and women doing this work led to the closure of the paper.

In August 1851, Bailey established the *Kentucky Weekly News,* which had a circulation of three hundred copies within just three months. Its success angered his opponents, who burned down the press and started an opposing paper. Borrowing money to purchase new equipment, and training a further two daughters in typesetting, Bailey continued printing the paper until 1858, after which he started a new publication, *The Free South.*

Bailey was a shrewd networker and money raiser, and Anna probably encountered his name and reputation through her American contacts. She was certainly corresponding with him and fundraising on his behalf by 1859, when she wrote *Little Laura,* and the decision to write the tract was made rapidly, in consequence of their correspondence.[88] In a series of letters written by Bailey to supporters on both sides of the Atlantic, he told them that attacks on his printing press were prompted by the paper's success.

His experience resembles the violence unleashed on Elijah Parish Lovejoy in 1837, who died when his printing press was attacked, an event which galvanized John Brown to spend the rest of his life fighting slavery. Lovejoy's murder also roused others, including juvenile antislavers. The Junior Anti-Slavery Society of Philadelphia condemned the murder in May 1838. In addition to collecting funds to support his widow, the society issued a statement pledging to "plead the cause of the suffering slave, and assert the duty of immediate emancipation undeterred by any threat or conduct of our opposers."[89] In a comparable manner, on 1 October 1859 the *Anti-Slavery Monthly Reporter* issued an appeal sent by the Newcastle and Gateshead Anti-Slavery

Society on Bailey's behalf, listing the Richardson grocery shop as one of the collecting points for contributions.[90] Also petitioning for funds, Bailey notes that after Harpers Ferry, "the most extravagant lies were told about me, as trying to excite slavers to rebellion; intending to seize the United States' barracks at this place, arm the Negroes, and commence war upon slaveholders. All these lies were told as profound secrets to the people by the tools of the slave-power. But these lies have already exploded, and the people are resuming their common sense again."[91] An article in the *Anti-Slavery Monthly Reporter* on 1 March 1860 updated readers about the current experiences of Bailey, "the editor and proprietor of *The Free South*—an antislavery newspaper published at Newport, in Kentucky, and on whose behalf we have inserted in our columns an appeal from anti-slavery friends in Newcastle." The appeal tells its readers that "he has lost upwards of three thousand dollars by damage done to his house and printing-stock by the mob which last attacked his premises."[92]

This U.K.-based money-raising drive continued when Bailey came to England and visited several leading abolitionists, including the Richardsons. In May 1861, shortly after he had visited Newcastle to deliver a public address (possibly staying in Summerhill Grove), a long piece titled "William Shreve Bailey" was published in the *Anti-Slavery Monthly Reporter*. It substantially reproduces his Newcastle address and solicits money on his behalf. It ends with a list of those who have agreed to collect donations, including Anna Richardson and Wilson Armistead. Asking rhetorically who he is, the article is expansive:

> He is one of those champions of freedom who has earned a name and a place in the annals of the struggle for Abolition in the United States, second to none, although his work has been prosecuted in a quiet way. He is one of those self-denying, self-helping men of action, as well as of thought, who, finding himself in the midst of a community, depraved and demoralized by Slavery, felt it to be his duty to combat the evil at its source, with such means he had at his disposal.[93]

On 2 December 1861 the *Anti-Slavery Monthly Reporter* published a letter Bailey had written to Louis Chamerovzow, the secretary of the British and Foreign Anti-Slavery Society. He tells Chamerovzow that he has just read two copies of the *Anti-Slavery Monthly Reporter* and has been "much obliged" to see a letter he wrote to Anna Richardson reproduced there.[94] As all of this suggests, there is a rich scribal, spoken, and textual backdrop to the tract that Anna added to the campaign of support she was engaged with from her Newcastle base.

Early in *Little Laura*, Richardson quotes from two letters from Bailey, the first telling her of Laura's death and the second following up with "a few more particulars respecting his precious child." After reading the second letter, "our thoughts turned to you, beloved young friends, and in a few hours' time we determined not only to tell you about Laura, but also to ask if YOU cannot assist her worthy family in their efforts to set the Negro free, in at least one of the Slave States."[95] This intimate direct address is emphasized by the repetition and capitalization of the word *you*. This form of direct address is echoed in the first-person commentary bookending the text. It opens with a short and accessible address noting that "Time was when the late Editors of the 'Olive Leaf' had the pleasure of talking from month to month to many of their dear young friends." Lamenting that "circumstances beyond their reach" (probably Henry's illness) had ended the possibility of engaging with those readers, she now aims for a new (and potentially greatly extended) audience. Indeed, she writes, her work is intended for "every little boy and girl whom we can reach throughout the British Islands who feels for the down-trodden American Slave, and wishes for him to be free."[96] Explicitly identifying her audience as juvenile readers already possessed of antislavery instincts (she addresses it "To the Young Friends of the Slave"), she intimates that they might develop a new purpose by reading her work and learning from the example of a juvenile activist she simply calls Laura B.

The tract describes the life of Laura Bailey, along with the description of an attack on the printing press and its financial and other consequences, as William Bailey describes them himself. Encouraging autonomy and reflection in her readers, Richardson makes a point of noting that Laura's antislavery sentiments were founded not just in what her parents espoused but also in her firsthand observation of enslaved people: "She had seen them in chains, and her heart ached very much over their wrongs and sorrows."[97] This is the rhetoric of white sympathy rather than Black emancipatory activism, and pushes for a sympathetic response from its juvenile readers by describing the enslaved as "poor blacks" and "poor creatures," but she also urges her readers to move beyond feeling for the enslaved by doing something about that feeling. She suggests that her young readers should follow Laura's example, and she draws on Stowe's depiction of the death of Little Eva to make this point. The day before her death, Laura sings the final verse of a well-known song whose lyrics of home and absence ideally suited the period's sentimental culture. Based on a poem Caroline Atherton Mason wrote while she was a young girl away at school and longing for her family, it was first published in the *Salem Register* in 1844. It became even more popular after it was set to music by S. M. Grannis in 1852. The lyrics of the final stanza ask,

Do they miss me at home? Do they miss me
At morning, at noon, or at night?
And lingers one gloomy shade round them
That only my presence can light?
Are joys less inviting and welcome,
And pleasures less hale than before,
Because one is missed from the circle,
Because I am with them no more?

Richardson signs off with a direct address, urging readers to "talk over this matter with your parents and teachers, and if they *quite* approve of your collecting small sums on the slaves' behalf, it would give us very great pleasure to forward those to Mr. B. as 'collected by the children of England, Scotland, and Ireland, in remembrance of his departed daughter.'" Each of the tracts was accompanied by a subscription form which could be returned "when more or less filled up." The following year she reported that £222 had been sent to Bailey, £62 of which was "chiefly collected by our dear *young* friends in England and Ireland, after reading the account of his little daughter 'Laura.'"[98] This campaigning was clearly effective.

Deborah De Rosa briefly discusses *Little Laura* as part of her larger analysis of antislavery juvenile texts produced in the period. A series of important juvenile texts were published in the United States, including Eliza Follen's collection *The Liberty Cap* (1846), Hannah Townsend's *The Anti-Slavery Alphabet* (1846 and 1847), and Jane Elizabeth Jones's *The Young Abolitionist* (1848).

By the late 1840s to 1850s the focus shifted to representations of what De Rosa calls "exemplary fictional, abolitionist children on which their young readers could model themselves and facilitate their quest 'to do something.'" These include *Uncle Tom's Cabin,* Aunt Mary's *The Edinburgh Doll* (1854), M. A. F.'s *Gertrude Lee; or, the Northern Cousin* (1856), and Maria Goodell Frost's *Gospel Fruits* (1856).[99] British juvenile antislavery tracts such as *Who Are the Slaveholders?* and *Little Laura* contributed to this shared culture. In addition, juvenile peace tracts such as Elihu Burritt's *Olive Leaflets,* collected from tracts published by Olive Leaf Circles in New York and Philadelphia, followed similar generic patterns.[100]

The importance of developing the sympathies and labor of juveniles was recognized on both sides of the Atlantic, though some figures (such as Lydia Maria Child) thought their activities should be subject to curbs. She particularly worried about the actions extending their involvement into areas she thought of as inappropriate. Writing in 1837 to express her reservations about children being encouraged to petition Congress, she argued that "it seems to be improper, because children are of necessity guided by others, and because this step is involved with questions evidently above juvenile capacities. Abolitionist parents ought thoroughly to prepare the hearts and minds of their children for the conscientious discharge of duties that will come with their riper years."[101]

Despite her reservations, many organizations, such as the Junior Anti-Slavery Society of Philadelphia, were set up specifically to engage and to educate the young. Many figures on both sides of the Atlantic worked hard to develop and expand the audience for short juvenile antislavery tracts. These were cheap to manufacture and easy to distribute, due to their length and portability. This was certainly the case for *Little Laura,* which was being circulated within Kentucky within a short period of its first appearance in Newcastle. Anna Richardson sent copies directly to Bailey, who may have subsequently reprinted it on his own printing press and then organized further distribution. In a letter dated 6 January 1860, he thanks her for a donation of fifty pounds and "another of the Little Laura books which, thank God, is doing some good in Newport and Covington, in the hands of two christian friends."[102]

The transatlantic journey of this short text is yet another example of the complex connectedness of activists who had developed sophisticated and rapid strategies for distributing and reproducing their work, building audiences and collecting funds. The story of Laura Bailey's short life shows the remarkable shift that had taken place within a few decades. While earlier antislavery girls sewed samplers, Laura's "nimble" fingers, along with those of her mother and sisters, set type.[103] The move into mechanical reproduction provided opportunities that activists were quick to take up and exploit. Anna Richardson moved with ease between handwritten letters to printed tracts, and William Shreve Bailey, like Elihu Burritt before him, laid down his anvil and took up the pen (and typeface).[104]

Meanwhile in West Yorkshire, antislavery activists were also working assiduously. The Leeds Anti-Slavery Association noted that its series of illustrated juvenile antislavery tracts "consists of 13 separate Tracts of 12, 24, and 36 pages each, at 9d., 1s. 2d., and 1s 6d. per dozen; or neatly bound in One Volume, with portrait of Ellen Craft, 1s. each," adding that Wilson Armistead will be happy to be sent "Orders for the above, or Donations toward their gratuitous circulation, or printing additional numbers."[105] The fact that the portrait was cited as a specific attraction speaks to the way the series sought to capitalize on Ellen Craft's celebrity status. Her remarkable escape from slavery, along with that of her husband, William, was well known in Britain. The drama of their escape made it appealing to a young audience, and the image of Ellen Craft in her celebrated disguise as "Mr. Johnson," a young white invalid, emphasized her courage and daring, characteristics being encouraged in young activists. Chapter 3 turns to one of the most significant members of the Leeds Anti-Slavery Association, who had a particular connection to Ellen and William Craft.

3

The Quiet Abolitionist

WILSON ARMISTEAD'S GUERRILLA INSCRIPTION

A striking entry from the U.K. census of 1851 transformed it from a routine piece of data collection into an abolitionist document. Together with the fugitives Ellen and William Craft and doubtless the support of his wife, Mary, and mother-in-law, Sarah Bragg, Wilson Armistead carried out a subversive activity. He added the words "fugitive slave" next to the names of Ellen and William Craft. The powerful authority of the unexpected presence of these words still compels attention, showing the subversive and resistant possibility of ink markings on pages. Feminist scholars have long argued that antislavery activism was an important precursor for women's activism, and this census entry anticipates the practices of suffrage activists in the early twentieth century. Indeed, it is quite possible that they were influenced by this event, which reverberated at the time but has subsequently fallen out of public knowledge.

My reading of this census entry assumes that archives themselves are multifaceted and disorderly sites—as Ann Laura Stoler puts it in her description of Dutch colonial archives, they are "active, generative substances with histories, as documents with itineraries of their own. What was written in prescribed form and in the archive's margins . . . oblique to official prescriptions and on the ragged edges of protocol produced the administrative apparatus as it opened to a space that extended beyond it."[1] The space beyond the administrative apparatus of local census data in the story recounted here is expansive, complex, and transatlantic. It shows that we must be attentive to reading and to seeking out multiple genealogies to produce the fullest picture of the past.

This census action attracted considerable contemporary media attention but appears to have been quickly forgotten. Understanding its significance requires locating it within a set of carefully calibrated contexts ranging from the local to the global. With this in mind, I consider what is at stake in bringing such a remarkable achievement back into the historical record as well as how it reveals the importance of microhistory. Telling this story allows for a reflection on how historical actors and acts often become hidden over time; it reminds us of how many remarkable stories of resistance and rebellion are still waiting to be uncovered. The account of how Armistead and others made a routine piece of U.K. data collection into an opportunity to protest U.S. slavery is at heart a tale of how activists and academics meet in the archive. But it is also a reflection on the complexity of official regimes of memory—in this case, census records and their relation to information-gathering processes involving speech, scribal writing, and their transformation into print.

One of the aims of this chapter is to understand why Armistead chose this mode of guerrilla inscription, and how he successfully carried it out. By "guerrilla inscription," I suggest markings ranging from illicit textual additions to emendations and marginalia that critique, subvert, or otherwise comment on the contents or significance of the documents on which they appear. These scribal interventions are carried out with a deliberate intent and are designed to be visible, create surprise, and provoke reaction and reflection. They are distinct from other kinds of markings, including the doodles that can be found in the personal collections of private readers. Guerrilla inscription demands to be read, to have its message heard, to make a lasting protest.

Armistead's inscription is both a visible protest and also, paradoxically, hidden and easy to miss. Together with his exhaustive body of written work—edited books, letters, and other works—it corresponds to what Simon Gikandi has called "the 'third text' of the archive . . . works written by people who were neither masters or slaves, observers whose relationship to the institution of slavery was tenuous, and whose intentions were driven by goals that were sometimes at odds with the systematizing function of the archive of enslavement."[2]

Energized by the prompt made (in a slightly different context) by Eric Gardner, who argues that "we must all rededicate ourselves to learning about and responsibly sharing the contexts surrounding the texts we study," I have scoured local records on both sides of the Atlantic to understand more about Armistead's activities.[3] Compared to the extraordinary and rowdy Quaker abolitionist Benjamin Ley's noisy performances of "guerrilla theater," which were staged on both sides of the Atlantic about one hundred years before Armistead's action,[4] Armistead's protest was less theatrical, though it was still dramatic. His quiet activism did not have the carnivalesque quality of Ley's stunts; it was pursued through writing rather than the live performativity Ley noisily favored.

By focusing on Armistead's 1851 intervention, it becomes possible to re-imagine the contours and climate of midcentury abolition and to reflect upon the kinds of work that can still take place by mining the archive. Relatively untapped British archives can help us rethink U.S. slavery and transatlantic abolition, revealing questions of visibility and invisibility and reminding us of how much can still be found. Telling the story draws attention to an underre-searched abolitionist and in the process involves what Lois Brown describes, in a discussion of writing about Black lives, as a reclamation of the ordinary.[5] Since Armistead's history also sheds new light on the lives of the Ellen and William Craft, Black and white historiography combine fruitfully, mirroring the ways in which Blacks and whites campaigned together against slavery, becoming allies and sometimes also friends along the way.

To contextualize this unorthodox moment, I will first give more details of Armistead's life and other work, turning to the traditional methods of biogra-phy and storytelling. I examine the editing and writing career that preceded it, situating his action in March 1851 within a long-standing set of abolitionist activities, yet doing this brings up a set of difficulties. Although Armistead was a noted editor, compiler, writer, and activist, his published work is now out of print, and his correspondence is dispersed across archives. His prolific output suggests that he must have possessed substantial personal records, notes, and manuscripts, yet none appear to have survived.

Personally unassuming, he was a dogged campaigner and regularly wrote to newspapers, especially about slavery. By the time of his premature death, he had developed a transatlantic reputation and had many well-known cor-respondents. He never sought to capitalize on this for personal gain and remained more interested in promoting the works of others than in having attention focused on himself and his achievements. He certainly understood that print was one of the crucial vehicles he could harness to effect political change. While other abolitionists gave speeches and lectures, he was happy to retreat to his study, to writing and behind-the-scenes activism, though he also undertook some public speaking, often introducing others or summarizing committee reports in public venues. Hence, he is one of nineteenth-century antislavery's introverted and relatively unsung protagonists, yet he was undoubtedly a figure of immense significance to the philanthropic endeavors of the midcentury period. Now, though, just over 150 years after his death, his contribution remains underestimated, his writing is neglected, and his name is unfamiliar except to a handful of scholars.

He only figures quite slightly in histories of abolition and antislavery, chiefly those focused on Britain, having largely, though not completely, passed from history. Richard Huzzey notes the importance of his leadership in Yorkshire, arguing that there "remains great scope for research on the local impact of anti-slavery societies in provincial towns and cities," but even this welcome and necessary recognition suggests a limited sphere of influence.[6] However, he had extensive transatlantic professional, social, and religious networks through business contacts as well as the often overlapping networks of the Society of Friends, through which he was able to achieve a far greater impact.

Restoring Armistead to the history of nonmetropolitan abolitionist activism in the United Kingdom and then to the transatlantic struggle and its legacy enables a recalibration of our view of his importance. It helps develop a richer understanding of the ways in which antislavery was pursued in the North of England, in turn adding to our understanding of the complexity of nonconformist and dissenting networks within histories of antislavery protest. George Shepperson argued nearly six decades ago that "Wilson Armistead's *A Tribute for the Negro* was one of the most outstanding—if not the most outstanding—ideological influences from the Abolitionist Epoch on African political thought."[7] In other words, it was an extremely significant influence on the political thinking of African intellectuals and nationalists in the period before the works of a new generation, notably W. E. B. Du Bois, were written. The African nationalist James Africanus Beale Horton quotes from it on several occasions in his *West African Countries and Peoples* (1868), and the Ghanaian nationalist S. R. B. Attoh Ahuma drew upon it over five decades after it was first published, in his *Memoirs of West African Celebrities, with Special Reference to the Gold Coast* (1905). Though it is outside of the scope of this chapter to test out Shepperson's claim, Armistead's commitment to contributing volumes to libraries helped the wide distribution of his writing, making it available to activists and intellectuals, including Frederick Douglass, who possessed a personal copy of the *Tribute*.

Armistead's antislavery work was pursued in conjunction with allies on both sides of the Atlantic. He was also a member of the Leeds Library—a meeting place, intellectual and social resource, and refuge, although members did not all share the same political affiliations. Men like Armistead were in a frustrating situation, thwarted in their commitment to conventional forms of public service due to their religious convictions. In a context in which public office was not something Friends could easily attain, library membership gave male Friends access to like-minded men, offering local connectedness, as well as to reading matter that connected them to broader culture. He championed libraries and frequently mentioned his admiration for them in his work. Writing of the Quaker merchant, politician, and bibliophile James Logan, who left his personal library to the Library Company of Philadelphia, he noted that Logan "was a great patron of learning, held an extensive correspondence with the literati of Europe, and, at his death, he bequeathed a library of 3000 volumes as a legacy to his countrymen, consisting of the best works in various languages, arts, and sciences; a splendid and durable monument of his munificence, and of his attachment to Pennsylvania."[8]

Meanwhile, Elihu Burritt argued that his own linguistic proficiency (he claimed to have a reading knowledge of fifty languages) was acquired by prolonged exposure to library books in the American Antiquarian Society in Worcester, Massachusetts. In *Sparks from the Anvil* (1846), he explained that he spent eight hours a day there, and a further eight hours working at his anvil.[9]

Library philanthropy was a quality Armistead especially admired, noting that upon his death Anthony Benezet bequeathed his books to the library of the Society of Friends in Philadelphia.[10] Benezet also left money to help enslaved individuals employ lawyers to assist them in their claims for freedom, and a bequest to continue his educational work with free Blacks and Indians, stipulating the importance of reading and writing, arithmetic, needlework, and account keeping. Doubtless influenced by what he knew of Benezet,

Logan, and like-minded figures, Armistead bequeathed his own membership of the Leeds Library to his sons. He also donated to the Leeds Library at least two foundational Quaker works from his own collection: the journal of George Fox (1694) and Robert Barclay's *An Apology for the True Christian Divinity* (1678).

In addition to the Leeds Library, Armistead would have had access to the resources of the library of the Society of Friends in Leeds. The Leeds collection was already substantial as early as 1794, and its catalog was more embellished than those of other towns and cities. The catalog opens with a valediction in praise of reading:

> The perusal of valuable Books, besides enlarging the Mind, and promoting our temporal Comfort and Advantage, may be the Means of spreading before us a pleasing View of the Beauty and Excellence of Religion; and may occasion some Desires for the Possession of the Happiness which it confers: But unless the *Divine Aid* be sought for and superadded, it will be defective in Principle, and will not be able to produce that Strength of Resolution, and steady Perseverance, which are necessary to crown our Labours with Success.[11]

Unsurprisingly, the library's holdings largely comprised religious books and works about and by Friends, encouraging participation in activities associated with Friends in good standing. These focused on active engagement with communities and with philanthropic and social justice work.

As I have already noted, unquiet libraries have often been critical to the activities of engaged citizens. They are spaces where the local encounters the global. They provide sanctuaries for those who face persecution and show how writing and print can be the foundation of alternative communities. This was exemplified by the significance of the People's Library of Occupy Wall Street, though many other examples might be cited.[12] For instance, in 1838 the Black abolitionist printer and journalist David Ruggles opened a reading room in his own home to counter the segregation of lyceums and other reading rooms. The cost of an annual subscription was $2.75, but visitors to the city were invited to use the room without a charge—something that fugitives, including Frederick Douglass, found invaluable.[13] Later, Ernestine

Rose's work in the Harlem branch of the New York Public Library in the 1920s actively aimed to champion integrated libraries.[14]

The novelist and activist Lydia Maria Child relied on the holdings of libraries to research and write her work, recognizing that her gender significantly restricted her access to print. As a child she was able to use the books in her brother's personal library, in the absence of a library of her own. Later in her life she was still able to avail herself of his ever-growing collection (numbering somewhere between seven thousand and eight thousand works at his death in 1863). She also was given free library privileges at the Boston Athenaeum by George Ticknor, a key figure behind the foundation of the Boston Public Library, even bequeathing it his collection of Spanish and Portuguese books in his will. These privileges had only ever been offered to one other woman.

But Child's good fortune did not last for long. Ticknor was outraged when she published *An Appeal in Favor of that Class of Americans Called Africans* (1833), demanding the immediate emancipation of the enslaved without compensation to slaveholders. Her uncompromising writing was without doubt unquiet, and the Athenaeum withdrew her access to its resources. Though Maria Weston Chapman rapidly led a campaign among her abolitionist supporters to purchase Child a membership, the Athenaeum nonetheless refused to allow Child access. Though deeply frustrated, Child thanked her supporters for their backing, exclaiming, "I have never in my whole life, met with anything that gratifies me more, or affected me so deeply."[15] She had grown up with her access to books always at one remove, and she appreciated their subversive power.

Exploring the histories and legacies of sites such as libraries reminds us of their valuable and unquiet contribution to freedom of thought and expression. Libraries are key resources for scholars as they pursue elusive leads and try to put together resistant stories, such as this one, which seeks to outline the activism of a quiet man. Discussions with archivists, scholars, and local historians who know the local terrain in unparalleled ways has allowed me to discover details that are the product of their intimate knowledge of collections and histories. In addition, this kind of research benefits from the joyful experience of what Jean Pfaelzer terms "hanging out—talking, sharing resources, telling and retelling this history."[16]

As I suggested earlier, human subjects are themselves living libraries, possessed of extraordinary and vital knowledge and memories waiting to be unleashed. Today's librarians often challenge their own profession's long-standing commitment to silence or quiet. For instance, many of us have memories of being told to be quiet in libraries, but the Newcastle Lit & Phil encourages noise. One of its bookmarks is decorated with an image of a stern-looking owl from a nineteenth-century chapbook stating firmly, "This is *not* a silent library, children can be seen and heard." In a similar fashion, the British Library currently has a podcast series titled *Anything but Silent.*

However, we should remember that subscription libraries were not open to all and that it was not until the development of a public library system that fuller possibilities of freely accessible libraries emerged. Further, though libraries have been important throughout history for dissidents and for radical and reforming movements, they also have been implicated in white supremacy and murky and exploitative business practices. More particularly for what is being discussed here, for some time, scholars have been exploring the foundational relationship between slavery and early American libraries, with disturbing conclusions. The Library Company of Philadelphia was located in a key center of book production and circulation and was a vital and progressive intellectual and social resource for many. Yet it was founded by a group of individuals who included both abolitionists and slaveholders. The library, like many other august institutions, was indebted to slavery. A key founder, Benjamin Franklin, was a slaveholder and dealer in enslaved people until the late 1750s, though Benezet was instrumental in turning him into an abolitionist. Indeed, Franklin's wealth was in part due to printing notices advertising runaway slaves in the *Pennsylvania Gazette,* and when he lived in London he circulated adverts seeking to find and return an enslaved man named King who had run away from his own household.[17]

Armistead made many and varied contributions to antislavery over a period of roughly two decades, between his first major antislavery publication in 1848 and his premature death at the age of just forty-eight, in 1868. His antislavery beliefs were formed by his deep personal commitment to the Society of Friends. He was particularly interested in the ways that Friends did not just espouse abstract principles but also acted upon them. He had broad interests that (characteristically) he wrote about with the kind of attention he brought to all areas of his life. Professionally speaking, he was a merchant, accustomed to ledgers, lists, order books, projections, and all the daily diffi- culties of trade. He was practical, disciplined, and ordered. Though he had an imaginative side, he was also morally earnest and retiring. He directed his energies to the kinds of philanthropic and benevolent activities deemed appropriate by the wider community.

Armistead's edited books can be divided into three main categories: miscellaneous writings, publications related to influential male Friends, and antislavery, united by a common methodology. He put together data about meteorological conditions on the one hand, and statistics on slavery on the other. He gathered snippets of folklore and fragments of local stories about the Lake District for his earliest book, and copied and pasted quotations from poets, politicians, religious authorities, and the enslaved and formerly enslaved, creating powerful polemics against slavery in the book that imme- diately followed. This discernible pattern, continuing across much of his writ- ing, corresponds to the popular nineteenth-century practice of scrapbook- ing.[18] Indeed, like scrapbooks, some of his edited volumes were composed of miscellaneous materials placed together for piecemeal reading.

All his activities were governed by his membership in the Society of Friends. Among his many letters was one he wrote to the *Friend* warning Quakers about Joseph Barker of Ohio, previously of Wortley in Leeds, who was publicly attacking his edition of the work of George Fox.[19] Armistead was well known for his letters to newspapers. In 1858 the *Leeds Intelligencer* published a notice announcing, "We must ask the indulgence of Mr. Wilson Armistead for a postponement of his fourth letter about the negroes, till our space is less demanded than to-day."[20] Posing as an apology, this sounds like chastisement. Still, the paper had covered local antislavery events for many years, such as a public meeting at which William Allen had delivered a lecture in 1853 (in which Armistead had also participated) and meetings of the Leeds Anti-Slavery Society, like the one that opens this book.[21]

His reading, like those of the Newcastle Friends discussed in chapter 2, was chiefly focused on religious texts, exemplary biographies, and nonfiction prose, especially newspapers and tracts. He also admired the work of the Ro- mantic poets Coleridge and Wordsworth, and loved the Lake District and the ways both poets wrote about the sublime and picturesque. Their writings accorded with his Quaker understanding that the divine could be discerned in the natural world. Like other committed Friends, he does not appear to have been a reader of novels, but he doubtless made an exception for *Uncle Tom's Cabin*. When Stowe and her entourage came to Leeds, he was a key member of the group honoring her, something covered in the antislavery press on both sides of the Atlantic.[22]

THE ATLANTIC WORLD OF WILSON ARMISTEAD

Wilson Armistead was born in Leeds on 30 August 1819. He spent his early life in Holbeck, South Leeds, where many Friends still lived. The city's first Quaker meetinghouse (built 1699) had been constructed nearby, in Water Lane. The local population was substantial: the 1851 census revealed that there were more Quakers in Yorkshire than in any other part of the United Kingdom.[23] His family's flax and mustard business was also based in Water Hall, Holbeck. He appears to have spent some time living in Cheshire in the late 1830s, and in 1844 he married Mary Bragg from Whitehaven in the Lake District, where there was also a significant community of Friends. The couple set up home together in Leeds, and at some point Mary's widowed mother, Sarah, moved to Leeds to live with the growing family. By the late 1840s Armistead was occupied by running the business, family life, and increasingly his extremely active involvement with abolition, alongside prolific and often overlapping writing projects.[24]

His first foray into print was made at the age of just twenty, when his detailed meteorological observations were included as a fifty-five-page appendix to T. B. Hall's *A Flora of Liverpool* (1839). Along with descriptions of the daily weather conditions in Woodside, Cheshire, he noted sun haloes and meteor showers, weather conditions across the globe, and early-flowering plants such as the primrose he spotted in full flower on 23 December 1838, several months early. His intellectual curiosity was combined with a notable attention to detail, encompassing readings of air pressure, rainfall, and temperature, all collated in careful charts that were the standard fare of meteorology. These were properly formulated scientific explorations, following established protocols. Rainfall was calculated using measurements from a simple water-collecting device he had constructed himself. The monthly charts he produced contained day-by-day recordings of the weather. His measurements of the temperature were divided into minimum, maximum, and mean readings, noting the direction and force of the wind. He also made barometric readings—divided up in the same manner as his readings of the temperature. He wrote a compressed description of each day's weather and summarized the overall readings in a column of results. After each of these charts is another full page of careful observations, in which he moves from numerical readings to a narrative account of the weather.

On 21 September, for instance, he observed rainfall in the morning and a rainbow in the afternoon; after a clear period, he watched the aurora over a period of several hours. In addition, he moved into experimental mode. Noting that the river was phosphorescent, he drew water from it and discovered that it "emits most light on being poured out of one vessel into another in a dark room. I found that by adding a few drops of the strongest solution of ammonia, the luminous property is at first much increased, but is soon entirely destroyed." On another occasion he noted that when an earthquake took place on Algiers, "similar shaking was also experienced in many places in Wales about the same time, though probably unconnected. It was very calm at the time, and a rumbling noise like distant thunder was heard."[25] This geologic connectedness may have returned to him when he reflected, years later, on Babbage's description of how sound travels, creating what he called a "vast library," and what we might think of as a vast *unquiet* library.

His interest in meteorology and plant species continued throughout his life, though as his involvement with antislavery took up more of his time, he had less opportunity to publish his findings. Meteorology, antislavery, and religion were all blended in this work, in a manner familiar to Friends and other dissenters. In the eighteenth and nineteenth centuries, several Quakers from Cumbria were quite committed to meteorology and botany, seeing their observations in relation to Friends' beliefs about ongoing divine revelation. Armistead may well have known John Fletcher Miller from Whitehaven, almost his exact contemporary, who was one of the many accomplished Quaker meteorologists and astronomers living and working in the Lake District. Miller became a member of the British Meteorological Society, traveled to Australia and Chile on the society's behalf, and gave scientific lectures in Whitehaven. Several other Friends became members of the Royal Astronomical Society as a result of their observations. Such figures were committed to their faith, its ethical provisions, and their scientific studies, regarding these as interdependent.

In 1845 Armistead published meteorological tables in the *British Friend,* revealing that the Yorkshire weather in December 1844 had been forbidding— none of them with experience of Yorkshire would have found this surprising. December opened with weather described as "Cloudy but fine," and within days, by 7 December, this developed into "Gloomy: continued hard frost." Though there were periods of better weather, December in Leeds was frequently "Dull and overcast," "Dull and gloomy," "Very slippy," "Much overcast," "Very dull and foggy," or "Very dull and gloomy," but New Year's Eve was "Fine and clear."[26]

While these descriptions are factual and can be found in similar records, adjectives like *gloomy* and *overcast* also have a poetic overtone that would find fuller expression in his subsequent works. The most significant of these was a substantial book in which he made a determined step into antislavery print. It was full of somber stories but also contained evidence that the inward light, as Quakers call it, was not just confined to one portion of humanity. Its title was *A Tribute for the Negro: Being a Vindication of the Moral, Intellectual, and Religious Capabilities of the Coloured Portion of Mankind; with Particular Reference to the African Race* (1848). In it, Armistead argued that people of African origin were equal to whites. In more than six hundred pages that would be unnecessary in a fairer world, he presented multiple pieces of evidence drawn from many diverse sources to demonstrate Black achievement. The book was undoubtedly paternalistic, especially by today's standards, but it is also a hugely significant piece.

The *Tribute* opens with a poem specially written by Benjamin Banner, the first stanza of which summarizes the project: "A TRIBUTE for the Negro Race! / With all whose minds and hearts / Have known the power of Gospel Grace, / The love which it imparts."[27] The book is divided into two empirically driven parts, the first titled "An Inquiry into the Claims of the Negro Race to Humanity, and a Vindication of Their Original Equality with the Other Portions of Mankind; with a Few Observations on the Inalienable Rights of Man, the Sin of Slavery, &c &c." The second comprises biographical descriptions of individuals (chiefly men), including Benjamin Banneker,

William Wells Brown, Alexander Crummell, Paul Cuffee, Ottobah Cugoano, Olaudah Equiano, Henry Highland Garnet, Toussaint L'Ouverture, J. W. C. Pennington, Phillis Wheatley Peters, Ignatius Sancho, and Francis Williams, to name just a few. The book also contained portraits of a series of men, ranging from Cinqué, who had led the *Amistad* revolt, to Douglass, Equiano, L'Ouverture, Pennington, and Jan Tzatzoe. Pennington's image was engraved from a photograph taken at Samuel Topham's gallery in Leeds, offering a vivid reminder of the relationships between visiting abolitionists and the local economies of the places they visited. It also suggests how much work remains to be done to trace the visual archives of Black accomplishment and to understand the interconnections between the sometimes conflicting demands of intimacy and publicity in the production and circulation of such images. As John Stauffer, Celeste-Marie Bernier, and Zoe Trodd have documented in *Picturing Frederick Douglass* (2015), Douglass took enormous care over his public image, captured in multiple photographs and daguerreotypes, astutely recognizing the importance of such self-fashioning.

In addition to the *Tribute*'s descriptions of familiar figures, there are details of many less familiar individuals, chiefly men but also women. These include enslaved Muslims such as Abon Becr Sadiki, sold into slavery and taken to Jamaica at the turn into the nineteenth century, who was fluent in spoken and written Arabic and a speaker of English, and Thomas Jenkins, originally from Guinea, who moved from being a farm laborer in rural Scotland to an autodidact who learned Latin and Greek, became probably the first Black schoolteacher in Scotland, and studied at the University of Edinburgh for a brief period. The women Armistead discusses include Eva Bartels of South Africa, who learned to read at the age of fifty and tried to convert those around her to Christianity, and Nancy Patchford of Hartford, Connecticut, who had been enslaved for forty years but through her labor amassed a significant amount that she bequeathed to charity on her death. Armistead's sources were varied and included descriptions drawn from the writings of Moravian missionaries, notably the German Moravian scholar and church historian Christian Georg Andreas Oldendorp, whom he calls the "excellent missionary Oldendorp."[28] This is the earliest indication that Armistead was familiar with the activities of Moravians, something I will discuss further in chapter 4.

Armistead made no claim to originality in this work; instead, he was keen to draw attention to the *Tribute*'s genesis in other texts, as well as the "kindness of many friends who have aided me during the progress of the work," listing several individuals on both sides of the Atlantic. He cites works including Abbé Henri Grégoire's *An Enquiry Concerning the Intellectual and Moral Faculties and Literature of Negroes: Followed with an Account of the Life and Work of Fifteen Negroes and Mulattoes, Distinguished in Science, Literature and the Arts,* first published in France in 1808 and then in translation in the United States two years later. Armistead recognized the importance of Grégoire's work and used it as a model. He writes,

I am indebted to Thomas Thompson, of Liverpool, for this scarce volume, who kindly presented me with a copy of it, which is rendered additionally valuable from its being one presented by the Abbé in his own hand-writing to the late William Phillips, of London. To Gerrit Smith of Peterboro', U.S., I am also indebted for an English translation of the same, by D. B. Warden, Secretary of the American Legation at Paris. This admirable work includes a mass of information, the accuracy of which may be thoroughly relied upon, being the production of a man of great erudition and rare virtues, well known in the learned societies of his day.[29]

He was keen to stress that his evidence corroborated the work of figures who were already well respected in "learned societies," since Nonconformists were barred from attending British universities until 1870. But as we have seen, his studies in meteorology and botany show his serious interests, as does the research behind the production of the *Tribute.*

Frederick Douglass, who had lectured in Leeds in late 1846 and early 1847 and is discussed in some detail in the book, reviewed it at length in the *North Star.* His review was republished in the *Liberator* on 20 April 1849, taking his comments to an even wider audience. Douglass's response was mixed. He writes that he was "deeply gratified that the work has been so ably and generously performed by Mr. Armistead, yet grieved and mortified that such a work seemed needful to be done." He also made a highly prescient statement: "The antiquarian of coming ages will search out this as one of the literary curiosities of the nineteenth century, and will produce it as evidence of the darkness of this age. What a commentary upon our enlightenment, that we must have books to prove what is palpable even to the brute creation—to wit: the negro is a man!" However, despite his profound reservations, he urged readers to buy the book, in a piece of stirring rhetoric:

> We recommend this work especially to the negro-haters of our own Christian land: we recommend it to our "negro pew" churches, and our negro-hating priesthood, and ask them to look at its facts, statements, reasoning, and lay its mighty truths to heart; remembering that the work is not that of a wild enthusiast, who bends facts, no matter how inconsistent and opposed to his theory, to suit his purpose; but that of a calm, disinterested Christian and scholar, with a heart alive to human woe, and whose only aim in these pages appears to be to befriend the helpless. We would also commend the work to our own beloved but heart-broken brethren, the victims of prejudice and slavery. The book should be in all your houses, and those who can ought to purchase one and possess it. We need and ought to possess it. We need it, as a means of refuting with their own weapons and on their own ground, the cruel calumniators of our race, as well as to inspire us with higher aspirations, and a nobler zeal and earnestness in the cause of our own elevation and improvement.[30]

Douglass's review was a crucially important mark of esteem, making U.S. abolitionists familiar with Armistead and his work. News of the book's impending publication had already been announced in transatlantic antislavery circles. A notice in the *Pennsylvania Freeman* on 11 May 1848 states that a previous notice publicizing the book should have advised readers that "subscriptions to the book will be received by George W. Taylor, North-west corner of Fifth and Cherry streets, and by Henry W. Longstreth, 347 Market street We presume that it will be a highly valuable and interesting work, and hope that it will be extensively circulated."[31] As I mentioned in chapter 2, Taylor was one of the editors of the American free produce periodical the *Non-Slaveholder*. Armistead's publishers used his authorship of the *Tribute* to draw attention to works he subsequently published, including *Calumny Refuted by Facts from Liberia* (1848), a work that included extracts from speeches of Henry Highland Garnet, Joseph Roberts, and Hilary Teague.

Four years later, in 1852, Armistead apparently published a collection

titled *Tales and Legends of the English Lakes and Mountains*, using the pseudonym Lorenzo Tuvar. While researching writing this book I was initially
unable to find much evidence to prove that Tuvar really was Armistead. Yet
there is a widespread assumption that the two are the same person that has
made its way into library catalogs as well as reprints of the book including
William Cushing, in his invaluable work *Initials and Pseudonyms: A Dictionary of Literary Disguises* (1885).[32] This claim is repeated in an 1891 edition of
Tales and Legends, which directly ascribes the work to Armistead, dropping
the pseudonym altogether. Subsequent editions follow this ascription, and a
1963 article by Wilfred Allot published in *The Journal of the Friends' Historical
Society* also repeats the claim. However, he adds the caveat that it is "curious"
that Armistead was able to produce this work, given his other commitments
in the period.[33]

I shared his sense of unlikeliness and kept pursuing the issue. Yet despite
all my reading, not only was I unable to find convincing evidence that Tuvar
and Armistead were the same person, but I found that at least one sketch in
Tales and Legends was written by someone else. Things did not add up. Given
the absence of archival evidence, the fact that Armistead did not seem to
have been the kind of writer who would have authored such a volume, and
the unlikeliness of him having the time to write it, I wondered why it was
routinely ascribed to him. The obvious inference is that he was not its author
but he was instead the compiler of a set of texts written by several anonymous
figures. This was the premise on which I proceeded and a brief comment,
attributed to Armistead in Joseph Smith's *A Descriptive Catalogue of Friends'
Books* (1867), confirms this. Armistead writes "This book was published under the assumed name of Lorenzo Tuvar, being got up chiefly to send to the
American Anti-Slavery Bazaars, or to aid the cause by its sale. –W.A."[34] This
bibliographical detail matters less for itself than for the way it exemplifies the
manner that assumptions can make their ways into scholarship, rapidly becoming certainties that can be difficult either to prove or challenge. Knowing
that Armistead "got up" the volume to raise funds adds to our understanding
of the development of transatlantic Quaker literary history as well as explaining the next book he would go on to publish, *A Garland of Freedom*.

At first glance, *Tales and Legends* could not be less like the *Tribute*, yet
once it is examined more deeply, continuities start to emerge. We know that

he had family connections to the Lake District and his interest in narrative, literary writing, and oral storytelling was already evident in the *Tribute*. *Tales and Legends* exhibits a clear, albeit conventional, nod to the Romantic poets and to Walter Scott—and even to the genre of the tale, associated with writers such as Washington Irving and Nathaniel Hawthorne. The volume quotes four lines of William Wordsworth's poem "The Somnambulist" before moving on to a discussion of the importance of the imagination, a key Romantic category. "Lorenzo Tuvar" writes,

> Imagination is a faculty in which we delight . . . leaving the practical speculations of the arts and sciences, we have chosen to select a field wherein imagination may fly her boldest flight, and we have allowed our fancy to rove amid scenes of fictitious bliss or woe, or amidst the real sorrows and joys of many an "owre true tale". . . should the pleasure of the tourist be enhanced by a perusal of any of the following tales connected with the Lake district, it will confer a still greater pleasure on the writer, even than that of culling them, from time to time, during his visits to those nooks hallowed by poetry, or consecrated by history, which a frequent residence in this locality has afforded him the opportunity of exploring. They are offered to the lover of nature, and to the admirer of the picturesque, with the hope that, whilst delighting in nature's sublimities, which are self-evident, proclaiming, at every step, their Divine original, he may not pass by unheeded some of the remarkable spots of history or romance without feeling interested in their associations.[35]

The author is positioned as a Romantic tourist, collecting and displaying a miscellaneous array of conversations, incidents, legends, personal experience, ballads, and other poetry derived from "frequent residence" in the Lake District. Overall, it is a fascinating mélange suggesting a talent for imaginative writing, including verse. Drawing attention to "poetry," "history," "nature," the "picturesque," and finally the sublime and the divine, are all familiar as part of the repertoire of Romantic responses to the Lakes.

A few pieces stand out. In "The Inscribed Rocks of Windermere" the narrator describes being taken by a local man to see the work of John Longmire, a stonemason from Troutbeck. Longmire had suffered from mental illness and had spent about six years carving words, with great skill and expertise, into the flat rocks on the shore of Windermere. Like the girls and women who sewed antislavery samplers around the same period, Longmire used the skills available to him to express his views in the manner with which he was comfortable. Combining materiality and abstract thought, he created a lasting natural physical monument to progressivism and human achievement. The words he carved were all capitalized, and the height of the letters ranged from about six to twenty-four inches.

Longmire's beautiful carvings are not well known today, though some of them can still be found on a tranquil spot on the edge of the lake, something I discovered when researching this book. Coming across them was both thrilling and poignant, and I stayed with them for a long time, the silence of their surroundings only punctuated by birdsong. Though the acts of creating the carving would have been noisy, once he had completed his work Longmire may have sat, as I did, contemplating their meaning.

In performing his solitary labor, Longmire participated in an ancient tradition of leaving markings on the landscape. So did more famous figures such as Dorothy, John, and William Wordsworth, Samuel Taylor Coleridge, and Mary and Sarah Hutchinson, who in 1802 inscribed their initials into a rock by the turnpike road between their respective homes in Grasmere and Keswick, a few miles north of Longmire's rocks. Unlike them, however, Longmire's focus was on recording people, events, and concepts beyond himself, in the public realm. On one large rock he carved the names of poets, including Burns, Dryden, Gray, Milton, and Scott, and dramatists and public figures, including Edward Jenner, who created the smallpox vaccine. In addition, Longmire carved short and suggestive phrases, including "The Liberty of the Press," "Magna Charta," "Money is the sinew of war," and on another rock the single word "STEAM" in large letters.

Particular attention is drawn to two stones, both of which were related to antislavery: "On one large red stone of at least ten feet square, was engraved '1833. MONEY. LIBERTY. WEALTH. PEACE';—a catalogue of blessings very much to be desired . . . on another, in larger characters, 'A SLAVE LANDING ON THE BRITISH STRAND, BECOMES FREE.'"[36] While the words *liberty* and *peace* are self-explanatory, it is less clear why *money* and *wealth* are part of this list. Perhaps Longmire was referring to the compensation paid to British planters in 1833, an injustice that continues to resonate today. The longer sentence "A slave landing on the British strand, becomes free" references the 1772 Somerset case, one of the early legal milestones in abolition. Here, it simply seems to stand alone in a declarative manner, while also implying further narratives about freedom and possibility, such as those engendered by the Slavery Abolition Act. Yet, imagined differently, it is also more literally illustrative. The word *strand* refers to the shore of a sea, lake, or river, and the rock on which the sentence is carved is itself on a strand on the edge of a lake. Thus, in the very act of reading, an individual might pause and allow themselves a particularly vivid sense of its implications. Situated within the natural world, carved into rock, using unadorned language not dissimilar to what Wordsworth called the "real language of men," Longmire's inscriptions responded to current events and human achievement and aimed for longevity. Indeed, Longmire's carvings echo Wordsworth's insistence in the preface to *Lyrical Ballads* of the importance of a language that communicates precisely because of the powerful connection between human emotion and the permanence of the natural world. The liminal site is both "hallowed by poetry" and "consecrated by history," but it was also the product of human skill and the anguish of mental illness.

Longmire's engravings were produced in a period in which there was a particular attention on rock formations. The word *paleontology* was first used in France in 1822 to describe the way the study of fossils allowed humans to develop an understanding of ancient organisms. Longmire's work was created between that moment and the publication of Charles Darwin's *On the Origin of Species* (1859), which drew attention to the long history of evolution and the uses of fossils as evidence of the explosive theory that would challenge the faith of many Christians. One such figure was Joseph John Gurney, who published an essay titled "Conversation on Geology" in the Newcastle-produced *Aurora Borealis*, in which he tried to reconcile science and creation.[37]

A professional stonemason such as Longmire would doubtless have had personal experience of the ways that rocks can contain and embody evidence about the historical past. Likely he had come across fossils, faults, mineral deposits, and so on in the stones on which he worked. Armistead certainly understood the connectivity of land masses, for as we have seen he had personal evidence that an earthquake in North Africa could be felt in the United Kingdom. But it is possible that neither man knew that though the landscape

of the Lake District might seem timeless, its mountains and lakes have themselves migrated across the earth's surface over many years. They are, as Doreen
Massey memorably wrote, "*Immigrant rocks* . . . just passing through here . . .
and changing all the while."[38] Longmire's inscriptions speak to a history that
we are continuing to explore and explain, one which needs reimagining as
more evidence is unearthed. As we add new contexts and explore unfamiliar
sources, we demonstrate that history, like historiography, is never set in stone
but is always subject to change and movement. This can sometimes be rapid,
but at other times it is slow and inexorable.

With this in mind, I return to the question of authorship I raised earlier
by reflecting upon a piece in *Tales and Legends* titled "The Quakeress Bride.
A Tale of the Mountains." The tale is a love story, depicting the fortunes of
a young merchant, born in the Lakes and visiting from London, where he
now lives. Lonely and disenchanted with his work, he falls in love with a
young Quaker girl he had known in his Lakeland childhood and finds solace
in his burgeoning love and in his connection to her welcoming family. The
story ends with the couple's marriage and a conventional though keenly felt
discussion of domestic happiness:

> No longer neglectful, or indifferent to the result of his mercantile engage-
> ments, he entered upon them with increased ardour, not with the base and
> grovelling view of amassing unprofitable wealth, but as an honourable em-
> ployment, affording him the means of supporting those who are dependent
> upon him, and of relieving the distresses of his fellow-creatures . . . No longer
> ill at ease with himself or the world, he became a useful member of the great
> human family, desirous of fulfilling his allotted part, by engaging actively
> in schemes of philanthropy, and in the exercise of a pure, unostentatious
> benevolence.[39]

He credits this new focus to the joy and sense of responsibility accompanying
marriage and fatherhood, as well as to the positive the influence of his wife.
The end of the story is followed by seventeen lines from Cowper's *The Task*
in praise of "domestic happiness," described as "thou only bliss / Of Paradise
that has survived the fall!" Since the lines are unattributed, the author must
have thought that readers would be familiar with them—or that, even if they

were not, the sentiment itself was significant enough simply to quote them without attribution. Armistead quoted passages from Cowper throughout his works, harnessing his interest in poetry for his antislavery writing. But as we have seen, so did other Quakers, including the Newcastle group that contributed to the *Aurora Borealis*.

The annual is prefaced with an image of a young woman wearing a Quaker bonnet, simply titled "The Bride." This was engraved from an original drawing produced by George Richardson, the father of Henry. She stands in front of a table on which a basket lies, as if she has just come inside or is about to leave. Further suggesting the connection between interior and exterior, in the background a drape is pulled halfway across a window to reveal a large tree. She looks directly toward the viewer with a steady and intelligent gaze, appearing simultaneously capable and modest. Opening with this visual image of a young bride, the annual closes with a written piece titled "The Bride: A Sketch," which apart from a few minor changes, is essentially the same as "The Quakeress Bride."

The table of contents names the author as J. W., or Joseph Watson, a Newcastle-based solicitor who was one of the editors of the annual. He was the northern secretary of the Anti–Corn Law League, founded by John Bright, a Quaker MP. Bright had been educated for a period at Ackworth and was a strong supporter of abolition, not least because his father had been the owner of a Manchester cotton mill. In 1839 Bright married Elizabeth Priestman, the daughter of two Newcastle Friends, Jonathan Priestman and Rachel Bragg. One other piece, a poem called "The Angel of Pestilence," is signed with the same initials.

One additional detail, taken from John Steel's *A Historical Sketch of the Society of Friends*, decisively confirms Joseph Watson's authorship. Steel describes Watson as having "considerable literary powers," noting his contributions to a number of publications, including this *Aurora Borealis* sketch (though he does not name it specifically), calling it "one of the few quaker stories which have been written by a Friend and full of the right quaker atmosphere."[40] While all of this confirms that Armistead was the compiler of *Tales and Legends*, rather than its author, I turn now to a book that can also be securely attributed to Armistead in his role as compiler.

The collection of antislavery poems titled *The Garland of Freedom* (1853) contained the work of British and U.S. writers, including William Cowper, Eliza Lee Follen, Henry Wadsworth Longfellow, James Russell Lowell, James Montgomery, Hannah More, Harriet Beecher Stowe, and John Greenleaf Whittier. In addition to poems by well-known writers, others were from antislavery figures known to Armistead, such as the Quaker Jane Bragg. Her poem "The Day of Freedom" notes "'Tis not sympathy alone / Nor is it joy that can atone / For the poor Negro's wrongs," lines combining an element of paternalism with an implied reminder that action is needed to effect change. Bragg had earlier translated a hymn by the Xhosa poet Ntsikana (or Sicana as he was often known), which Armistead included in the *Tribute*. Sicana had converted to Christianity and became well known for his hymns.[41]

Bragg also wrote a seven-stanza valedictory poem for a series of Leeds antislavery tracts Armistead collected and issued as *Five Hundred Thousand Strokes for Freedom* (1853). In his preface, Armistead justifies placing the tracts into a single volume by arguing that it was something he had been considering for some time. He believed it could serve a useful purpose, not least because it had established precedents, like the other works he had published. There are an "abundance of Tracts on Peace and on Temperance, &c., in extensive circulation—*Olive Leaves* are scattered the wide world over. Why should we not have something equally available for diffusing information on the question of Slavery."[42] He was inspired by Elihu Burritt's *Olive Leaf* series, again suggesting the interconnections among the reform activities and activists associated with peace, temperance, abolition, and free produce. Going on to describe the new antislavery series, he writes that there currently were eighty-two tracts of a variety of lengths. Some were original and specifically produced for the volume, while others "consist chiefly of reprints from American, or other publications adapted to the present purpose." Overall, he anticipates that they will help develop "an Anti-slavery feeling—deep, strong and practical," revealing the importance that he and other Friends ascribed to the quality of practicality.[43] In the spirit of such practicality, he suggests ways the tracts might be distributed to maximize circulation and impact. Here, as in other areas of his antislavery work, he harnessed and adapted his business knowledge. He used his mercantile experience to engage "actively in schemes of philanthropy, and in the exercise of a pure, unostentatious benevolence," like the protagonist of "The Quakeress Bride."

The titles of the tracts suggest their variety: "Slavery Described. By a Member of Congress," "The Farewell of a Slave Mother to her Daughter (a Poem)," "Auctioneering Advertisements," "Slaveholding Piety," "Abstinence from Slave Produce," "Intellect and Capability of the Negro." In addition to statistical and factual details, corresponding to the way he put together meteorological data, poetry recurs throughout, adding a literary quality to the more dominant polemical narrative tone. Tract 6, titled "Workings of American Slavery as Regards Caste and Prejudice," ends with lines from the abolitionist Thomas Pringle, secretary to the Anti-Slavery Society. Pringle was also known for his work helping to bring Mary Prince's narrative into the public domain, as I discuss in chapter 4. Armistead had previously used the poem on the frontispiece of *A Tribute for the Negro* and would go on to use it elsewhere:

—"The long scorned African,—
His Maker's image radiant in his face,—
Among earth's noblest sons shall find his place."

The use of familiar quotations created a shared set of reference points for readers, cutting across their varied geographic locations and personal situations and creating a kind of familiarity, akin to the creation of an imagined community. Armistead relied on this practice extensively in a further collection titled *A "Cloud of Witnesses" against Slavery and Oppression: Containing the Acts, Opinions, and Sentiments of Individuals and Societies in all Ages* (1853). He drew from a wide variety of well-known sources, chiefly British and American. These included the Bible and extracts from the writings of Anna Laetitia Barbauld, Anthony Benezet, Henry "Box" Brown, William Wells Brown, Edmund Burke, Elihu Burritt, Lydia Maria Child, Alexander Crummell, Frederick Douglass, Olaudah Equiano, Benjamin Franklin, Margaret Fuller, Henry Highland Garnet, William Lloyd Garrison, Henry Wadsworth Longfellow, Harriet Martineau, James Montgomery, Hannah More, Amelia Opie, Phillis Wheatley Peters, Alexander Pope, Samuel Rhoads, Benjamin Rush, James Thomson, John Wesley, Ignatius Sancho, and Henry Greenleaf Whittier.

He had already used a similar practice in *Select Miscellanies: Chiefly Illus-*

trative of the History, Christian Principles, and Sufferings of the Society of Friends (1851), a book focusing, as its title suggests, on Quakers and Quakerism. After the success of the first series (two volumes), he extended them with a second series comprising a further four volumes. On the title page of the sixth volume was a view of Ackworth School, and the focus on the school was developed with fifteen pages of anonymous reminiscences by a former boy scholar from Ackworth, along with a short poem by another boy scholar. In addition to this substantial series, Armistead updated existing works about or by eminent Quaker men, adding new material when he could locate it. In this vein he published a further series of books: *Memoir of Paul Cuffe a Man of Colour* (1840), *Memoirs of James Logan* (1851), *Journal of George Fox* (1852), and finally *Anthony Benezet* (1859).[44]

Armistead also contributed to the work of others, invited not just because his words carried some weight but also because of his generosity and commitment. He wrote an introduction to *Incidents in the Life of the Rev. J. Asher* (1850), by the Black Baptist minister who was visiting England to raise money for the Shiloh Baptist church of Philadelphia. After he returned home, Asher became a chaplain in the Sixth U.S. Colored Infantry, and died of typhoid fever in July 1865. A note at the front of the memoir informed readers that it was being published to enable Asher to purchase books to assist his ministry. Armistead's introduction opens with a quote from *Othello* (who had also featured in the *Tribute*): "Mislike me not for my complexion, / The shadowed livery of the burnished sun." He continues by describing his personal relationship to Asher, who "has been a frequent visitor at my house for the last few weeks."[45]

Armistead's introduction is dated 10 March 1850, showing that he was working on it shortly before he left for his only visit to the United States. On 29 June he embarked from Liverpool on a journey he would later document in the *British Friend*. During his visit he met with several abolitionists and political activists, as well as Friends and business contacts. Frustratingly, the fact that the location of any substantial quantity of surviving personal papers is unknown means that only an abridged account of his travelogue exists. In consequence, meetings he may have had with American abolitionists may never be known, though reference to his presence can be traced in some of their writings. Indeed, the only evidence for the fact that he traveled to Philadelphia comes not from his "Reminiscences" but from a letter published in the *British Friend* on 21 June 1865. He writes, "For the past sixty years a statue to William Penn has stood in front of the south entrance to the Pennsylvania Hospital. This being one of the objects of interest I remember to have seen when in Philadelphia some years ago, I observed with regret it has fallen from its pedestal, where, however, it will probably soon be replaced."[46] He also visited Baltimore, something revealed by his son Joseph years later: "We may get an idea of the state of society in some of the States in those days from the fact that on one occasion, after he had been addressing some Christians on their duties to others whilst on his way to Baltimore, one of them coolly said, 'Wal, if you go to Baltimore, I guess you'll swing.'"[47] Characteristically, in addition to collecting antislavery material throughout his visit, he also continued his study of the natural world and his religious observances, even combining the two. While he was in Lynn, he visited a Quaker meeting and encountered a knowledgeable female Friend who gave him a sample of moss.

Having established his international reputation, Armistead was also building locally, using his U.S. connections. His leadership in Leeds would continue until the end of his life. A pattern of his ongoing investigations about all of the subjects that interested him is exemplified by an italicized note at the end of his 1851 book on Logan, which simply states, "Parties possessing publications, MS. letters, or any information respecting James Logan, not contained in the foregoing pages, will oblige by communicating particulars of the same to the Compiler, addressed, WILSON ARMISTEAD, Water Hall, Leeds."[48] The spirit of openness and quest for knowledge is striking. He would make this kind of invitation repeatedly in his publications, envisaging his work as neither complete nor definitive but instead subject to change, development, and improvement.

In particular, the public appeal demonstrates his ongoing commitment to collectivity over individuality—even in writing. He was keen to encourage the written contribution of others. In 1854 the Leeds Anti-Slavery Society announced that it was launching a fund to raise money for an essay writing prize to encourage work "on the sinfulness of slavery, the best mode of terminating it; and the benefits that would result therefrom." The model of the essay competition was familiar to Quakers. Individuals who wished to contribute to the fund were instructed to send money to Armistead in

Leeds, George Taylor in Philadelphia, James McCune Smith in New York, Samuel J. May in Boston, or Frederick Douglass in Rochester.[49] In October 1855 he hosted May in his own home at a combined meeting of the Leeds Anti-Slavery Society and the Leeds Young Men's Anti-Slavery Society. In December he delivered an address in Leeds at a meeting that included Parker Pillsbury.[50] He continued campaigning after the end of the Civil War. By 1866, he was raising money for emancipated slaves, writing to the *Leeds Intelligencer* to ask for contributions.[51] He became the treasurer of the Leeds Freedmen's Aid Association, lobbying for contributions for funds to support freedmen. When William Lloyd Garrison spoke in Leeds on 21 October 1867, Armistead gave an address to honor him.[52]

GUERRILLA INSCRIPTION: TRANSATLANTIC ABOLITION AND THE 1851 CENSUS

As I have suggested, Armistead's 1850 visit to the United States fortified his abolitionist principles and gave him a new confidence, firsthand experience, and a renewed sense of purpose. It was his single most significant life experience after marriage and children. He wrote about his experiences in "Reminiscences of a Visit to the United States, in the Summer of 1850," an incomplete series in the *British Friend,* published from November 1850 to December 1852.

Among the contexts for Armistead's action was the series of fairs and peace congresses in the period around 1851, attended by abolitionists and peace activists, many of whom were Quakers. These highly organized transnational events were premised upon the belief that participants could create societal change through individual and collective acts. David Nicholls argues that they were "dominated by the British radical bourgeoisie," a group to which Armistead, like the Richardsons, undoubtedly belonged.[53]

Armistead's unauthorized intervention in the census should be seen as emerging within this climate of optimism and vision. It is an early example of other important acts of peaceful protest, including the suffragette activism centering on the 1911 U.K. census. Many women were unwilling to participate in the census until they were accorded full rights as citizens. While so-called census evaders tried to avoid representation altogether by various strategies, including staying away from their homes on census night, "census resisters" subverted the official document by adding written comments such as "VOTES FOR WOMEN" on the household schedules. These protests were inspired both by strong feeling of antipathy toward a document collecting their data while they were denied the vote and by the traditions of peaceful practices such as tax resistance.[54] The idea of resisting unjust laws had been given new impetus by the political philosophy of Mahatma Gandhi, who met with Charlotte Despard of the Women's Freedom League in 1909. Nonstate actors understood that they could make a profound intervention in the activities of the state, even when it did not fully recognize them.

Armistead's intervention was specifically intended to draw attention to the way the politics of abolition had been geographically reshaped by the passing of the Fugitive Slave Law. An important consequence of the law was that the Mason–Dixon line was effectively no longer a boundary separating free from slave states. Thus, the Atlantic became the new frontier for fugitives like the Crafts. Armistead understood that his addition to the census yoked the United States to the United Kingdom in the pages of a piece of state bureaucracy with no obvious or official link to the politics of abolition. He used the U.K. census to raise issues of personhood and liberty across national boundaries and to create a subversive form of textual witnessing. He had responded to a particular crisis in the history of abolition, the passing of the Fugitive Slave Law by the U.S. Congress on 18 September 1850. Days later, forty fugitives fled from Boston to Canada, while several self-emancipated figures, including the Crafts, made their way across the Atlantic.[55]

On the night of the census, with the Crafts staying in the family home as honored guests, Armistead was faced with a particular set of obligations. As nominal head of the family, it was his responsibility to complete the household schedule (a slip of paper) with a list of all those currently residing with him. The following day, this was to be collected by the local enumerator, who would transfer the data to the headed columns of the census book. Specific information had to be recorded. First were details of the residence and occupants: names, relation to the "head of family," marital status, age, "rank, profession, or occupation," place of birth, and "whether blind, or deaf-and-dumb." As a law-abiding man, Armistead was committed to upholding his civic duty by completing the schedule. Yet he was also actively involved in protests against the Fugitive Slave Law and seized the opportunity the census provided to take his protest into a state document.

The evidence for this can be found in the census book itself, since the household schedules from that year have not survived. From it we learn that Wilson Armistead, age thirty-one, is the head of the household. In the column headed "Rank, Profession, or Occupation" he is described as a "seed crusher and oil merchant." The next entry records the presence of his thirty-two-year-old wife, Mary. After this, the couple's three children, Joseph, Sarah, and Arthur, are recorded. Ending the list of family members is Sarah Bragg, the sixty-year-old widowed mother of Mary. Between the list of family members and the list of domestic workers—Mary Ann Elland, Jane Elland, and Caroline Barraclough—are the names William and Ellen Craft. They are described as a visiting married couple, both born in the United States and ages, respectively, twenty-four and twenty-six years. In the column for "Rank, Profession, or Occupation," William is described as a cabinetmaker, while Ellen is simply designated the "Wife of Wm. Craft." But in an extraordinary, unasked-for additional detail—unique to the entire census—each is also described as a "fugitive slave." The two powerful words are underlined and stand out clearly from the routine information surrounding them.

How did these two words get there? The obvious inference is that either they were initially written on the schedule and subsequently copied by the enumerator, or that the enumerator added them to the census book independently at a later point. Since the schedule no longer exists, we need to rely on evidence. From this evidence, I have established that Armistead took personal responsibility for adapting the schedule.

The 1851 census entry is remarkable in more than one way, as a few key details will demonstrate. First is the fact that two fugitives from Georgia came to be staying in Leeds. Second is Armistead's recognition that the census could be used for a political protest. Third is the fact that this extraneous—even incendiary—information made its way from the household schedule, via the enumerator, into the census record. This required it to take a journey through the hands of a series of individuals tasked with checking and confirming each entry to ensure accuracy and uniformity. Since this involved the process of copying words from the schedule to the census book, this leads to other questions: Why would the enumerator transcribe information with

Census entry from 1851 for Wilson Armistead, with permission
of the National Archives, Kew, Surry, United Kingdom.

no connection to the official data being collected? Was he also an abolitionist? Were he and Armistead working together? In the preliminary stages of
research, I suspected that this was the case. However, as I will outline, the
situation was far more complex. Producing an answer has required detailed
local research and the help of local librarians with specialist knowledge.

The entry for the Armistead household is a striking anomaly in the U.K.
records; though other fugitive slaves were also recorded in the 1851 census,
none of them are described using the language of fugitivity. For instance,
William Wells Brown, who was lodging at a boardinghouse in the center of
Leeds, is described simply as a "lodger."[56] Henry "Box" Brown was staying on
the other side of the Pennines, in Burnley, Lancashire, along with James C. A.
Smith, the free Black man who had helped him escape. By the time of the
census, Brown and Smith had successfully exhibited the panorama show
Henry Box Brown's Mirror of Slavery on both sides of the Atlantic. Audience
members watched as a series of moving canvas images, mounted on verti-
cal spools, passed in a sequential manner. Brown, like Smith, is listed in the
census as a "lodger," but the occupation of each is described as "anti-slavery

advocate." Though this is itself noteworthy, it is not comparable with the ways the Crafts were described.

Sympathetic abolitionists often invited lecturers to stay with them in their own homes, and it is likely that Armistead offered the Crafts hospitality in this spirit, building on an acquaintance made when he visited Boston the previous year. Understanding how the three encountered each other in Boston, however, requires a brief account of their respective histories. The Crafts have been better served by scholars than Armistead, and key details of their lives were also revealed by the couple themselves, in William Craft's *Running a Thousand Miles for Freedom: The Escape of William and Ellen Craft from Slavery* (1860).[57]

Ellen Craft was the enslaved half sister of Eliza Smith by the pair's father, Major James Smith, and Maria, a woman he held in slavery. When Eliza Smith married Robert Collins of Georgia in 1837, her mother "gave" her daughter the eleven-year-old Ellen as a wedding "present." She was, as William Craft put it, angered "at finding her [Ellen] frequently mistaken for a child of the family" and saw an opportunity to remove the reminder of her husband's infidelity from her sight.[58] The sisters both moved to Macon, where Ellen met William Craft. He had also been born into slavery in Georgia and his family had been separated early in his life. His enslaver had sold his parents to different slaveholders and had continued to split up the family little by little. He sold William's brother and then mortgaged both William and his sister to obtain money for cotton speculation. When he could not repay the bank, he sold them both.

The shared histories of being subjected to the whims of white slaveholders had a lasting impact on the Crafts. Fearing that they might be separated at any moment, they decided upon an audacious and risky and plan for self-emancipation involving a justly celebrated strategy of disguise, partly relying on Ellen's sewing skills, but also on her ability to pass as a young white man. After successfully escaping from Georgia in December 1848, they were initially sheltered by a Quaker family near Philadelphia, where they met William Wells Brown. Three weeks after arriving in Philadelphia, they traveled to Boston, where they stayed in the house of Lewis Hayden, a formerly enslaved man and by this time a prominent Bostonian and key figure in the Underground Railroad. Both Crafts, like Brown, who was also based in Boston, were actively involved with abolition, just as they would be when they moved to England.

The drama of the Crafts' escape made for a narrative that translated well onto the lecture circuit, and they and Brown formed a highly effective team. In January 1849, all three, along with Box Brown, addressed the Massachusetts Anti-Slavery Society to tell their stories. Meanwhile, British abolitionists were making sure that news of their remarkable escape was being circulated in the press. On 10 March 1849, for instance, the *Newcastle Guardian* published a letter from Wells Brown, who was himself described by the paper as "a fugitive slave." It called the Crafts' escape "one of the most wonderful accounts of the escape of fugitives from American slavery, which has ever come under our notice."[59] By the time Wilson Armistead arrived in Boston in the summer of 1850, the Crafts were well known as part of Boston's abolitionist community. Since Armistead was eager to be introduced to American abolitionists, a meeting between the three was assured.

Armistead's background could hardly have been less like that of the two fugitives, and his journey to Boston was certainly unlike theirs. By the time he left Liverpool for the United States on 29 June 1850, he had established a reputation on both sides of the Atlantic as a thoughtful and sympathetic ally. Sailing on the *Hibernia,* Armistead described his trip in some detail in a series of well-written and unsigned articles. He opened his account in a conventional epistolary manner:

> Dear Friends,—
> When you kindly forwarded me a letter of introduction to William Lloyd Garrison, previous to my departure to the United States of America, you expressed a wish to have an occasional line from me during my absence in the far West . . . I fear, however, from a lack of descriptive powers, that my narrative will neither be very instructive, nor comprise much that will prove new or interesting.[60]

His narrative was one of the many travelogues circulating in the period, including Harriet Martineau's *Society in America* (1837) and Charles Dickens's *American Notes for General Circulation* (1842).[61] He specifically mentions

Joseph Sturge's pithily titled *A Visit to the United States in 1841*, held in the library at Ackworth School by 1850.

While in the United States, Armistead certainly met a few key abolitionists, including William Lloyd Garrison. News of his visit circulated within Quaker abolitionist circles. William Cooper Nell informed Amy Post that after dining with Lewis Hayden on 14 July 1850 he went to visit Robert Morris. Here he heard of Armistead's visit, since he immediately adds that he hopes to meet the Yorkshireman.[62] Through these networks of conviviality and activism, the Crafts and Armistead encountered each other in a city far away from their usual places of residence, shortly before the political storm caused by the Fugitive Slave Law

A different kind of writer might have capitalized more on the fame of the Crafts, who were rapidly gaining celebrity status, to boost his own profile. But Armistead only revealed his meeting with them in an extract published in the *British Friend* in March 1852, giving additional details the following month. Readers would, as he reminded them, have known the story of the Crafts from earlier issues of the journal. He writes,

> During my stay in Boston, I called several times on the notoriously interesting fugitives from slavery, William and Ellen Craft, who were then located there for safety . . . Little did we then think how soon the city of the Pilgrim fathers would yield them no longer security that they would be compelled to flee from the land of their nativity to escape the grasp of the manstealer, and to seek protection in the dominions of Queen Victoria.[63]

At the time of the appearance of this installment the "notoriously interesting" Crafts had been in England for some time and were well known in the British press. The phrase "land of their nativity" was used in the British press in April 1851 to describe Armistead's census activism, suggesting that he was aware of the stir this had caused. But his focus is chiefly on his favorable impression of the city, his choice of a hotel in a "retired and quiet location," and his contact with William Lloyd Garrison, John Tilson, and Robert Morris.[64]

Armistead called first on Garrison, who was away. Tilson was busy, though he agreed to meet the following day, and so Armistead went to meet with Morris. For this serious British Quaker, this encounter with Morris was particularly memorable. The Black lawyer represented exactly those qualities that Armistead admired; he was intellectually able and politically committed. He had been born in Salem, Massachusetts, and went to work for the abolitionist lawyer Ellis Gray Loring, who had given him legal tuition. Professionally successful despite discrimination, he was called to the Massachusetts Bar in 1847. For Armistead, Morris's achievements were unmistakable evidence of the equality of the races.

Armistead was always looking out for arguments by which he could make the case for equal treatment of Blacks and whites, and he would go on to mention these Black professionals in his contribution to H. G. Adams's *God's Image in Ebony* (1854).[65] He admiringly mentions meeting with other Black professionals, including three pioneering lawyers, all of whom had overcome significant obstacles. Macon Bolling Allen had studied law in Maine with Samuel Fessenden, an abolitionist and lawyer, and was awarded a license to practice law in 1844. He was the first Black lawyer in the United States, and the following year, now living in Boston, he was admitted to the bar and became the first Black lawyer to argue a case before a judge in a jury trial. George Boyer Vashon was the first practicing Black lawyer in the state of New York, though he was twice denied the right to practice in Pennsylvania. He had attended Oberlin Collegiate Institute and was its first Black graduate in 1844 as well as the class valedictorian. Samuel Ringgold Ward was a newspaper editor, orator, and Congregational minister. He was born into enslavement in Maryland but escaped with his parents to New Jersey and was educated at the African Free School in New York. Ward's participation in the Jerry Rescue in October 1851 led him to flee to Canada with his family in November. He was already a newspaper editor, and in Canada he cofounded the *Provincial Freeman* in 1853 with Mary Ann Shadd Cary. Cary was its chief editor, though she hid her true involvement, fearing the paper would not be taken seriously if it were known that it was operated by a Black woman.

Morris was involved in campaigning for social justice and racial equality, work which would have a profound legacy. Early in his career, he and Charles Sumner were appointed by an African American man, Benjamin Roberts, in an important legal case, *Roberts v. The City of Boston*, brought after Roberts's five-year-old daughter, Sarah, was refused entry to a whites-only school that was close to her home. The suit was unsuccessful, but five years later a state law requiring integration was passed. *Roberts v. The City of Boston* would later be cited in two groundbreaking cases that resulted in the integration of schools: *Plessy v. Ferguson* (1896) and *Brown v. Board of Education* (1954).

Morris showed Armistead around Boston, introducing him to Allen, whom they met by chance while walking. The fact that Morris and Allen knew each other has not been established until now. It is a delightful fact that the three men encountered each other this way, since, as Davis and Bilder, speculating about a meeting, write, "It seems likely that the two men would have crossed paths, but we found no direct evidence that they knew each other."[66] The fact that their paths quite literally crossed is another of the intriguing revelations to be found in Armistead's "Reminiscences."

These meetings were clearly significant to Armistead; until this point his personal acquaintance with Black Americans was still limited. The men are specifically mentioned in the *Tribute*:

> George B. Vashon, a talented young Coloured gentleman was recently admitted, after due examination, as Attorney, Solicitor, and Counsellor of the Supreme Court of the State of New York. On his examination, he evinced a perfect knowledge of the rudiments of law, and a familiar acquaintance with Coke, Littleton, Blackstone, and Kent . . . Robert Morris, jun., in addition to the excellence of his character, has acquired correct business habits . . . Macon B. Allen, who successfully passed the ordeal of a rigid examination, now holds the office of Justice of the Peace for Middlesex county, United States.[67]

Armistead argues that in New England, Blacks "have more privileges or rather *just rights* extended to them; and, as a natural consequence, they advance in proportion" and that racial prejudice is diminishing in New England. "As a proof . . . I may mention, that in the city *Directory* it has been invariably the custom to class the names of the coloured residents (numbering above 1700), together, at the end of the book, instead of including them in proper rotation. Last year, or the previous one, they were for the first time printed indiscriminately amongst the names of the other residents."[68]

What Armistead specifically notes is the way in which formal documents signal broader social attitudes, draw attention to social justice and injustice, and can be used as evidence to develop political agendas. He remarked upon other examples of the importance of accurate recordkeeping too. For instance, when John Tilson took him to the Merchants' Exchange, Armistead paid special attention to the way in which information was recorded in the reading room: "My friend pointed out to me the exact method adopted here of recording, in books kept for the purpose, the entries of ships' cargoes, &c."[69] Twice, within a few paragraphs, he describes the importance of precise documentation for households and their inhabitants, and for ships' cargoes. The Quaker merchant, accustomed to the importance of accurate recordkeeping, was probably writing this installment in the period of the 1851 census date. This focus on disciplined administrative practices is particularly apposite.

Official records also play a vital role in trying to trace the lives of the Crafts prior to their escape to England. The U.S. census of 1 June 1850 documents the presence, in Macon, of Robert Collins; Ellen's half sister, Eliza Collins; their four children, Juliett (age 10), Thomas (9), Mary (6), and Robert (3); and several others, all of whom are white. Robert Collins is described as a speculator, with real estate valued at $60,000. Up until 1850, the enslaved were not recorded as part of the census. But an innovation of that year was the publication of separate slave schedules.[70] These were organized according to the names of white slaveholders, meaning that enslaved people simply appear as the property of whites, while their own names are not given. Instead, columns are provided for age, sex, color (B and M indicated whether those recorded were Black or mulatto), whether they were "fugitives from the state," the numbers of those manumitted, and finally whether they were "deaf and dumb, blind, insane, or idiotic."

The list of individuals held in slavery by Robert Collins was recorded slightly after the census date, on 9 August 1850. Listed among the forty-one people held by him are two fugitives, each denoted by a diagonal mark in the appropriate column. One is described as a mulatta born in 1835 and the other as a Black male born in 1830. Could this female fugitive be Ellen Craft? It is probably impossible to know for certain, yet the date of birth is not that of Ellen. She was born in 1826, and the family must surely have known this, given her relationship to Eliza Collins. If this female fugitive is not Ellen, then the schedule suggests that more than one enslaved woman may have escaped from the Collins household. This would also mean that Ellen is absent from the slave schedule. Given the concerted and highly publicized efforts Collins would make to bring her back to Georgia in 1851, including petitioning President Millard Fillmore, this seems like a surprising omission.

A slave schedule provides considerable evidence of ownership and could undoubtedly be used as evidence in support of other kinds of claim. More work needs to be done before it is possible to be certain about the identities of these fugitives, meaning it is another story yet to be told. Yet, before moving on, we should pause to look at the way in which this official document, filled out by hand, records the history of human lives while rendering it as anonymous data. What thoughts might have passed through the head of the figure who recorded these anonymous lives? Did he ever pause to reflect upon the gravity of the task he was undertaking? Was it just another bureaucratic task or was he disturbed by its implications? Or did he find beauty in the order he was creating, ignoring or being uninterested in the processes that led to the creation of the document? Most importantly, how do we honor the dignity of lives reduced to ink strokes on the pages of an administrative system denying them humanity?

Reflecting on the power by which these schedules define people as property, I am reminded of Hazel Carby's discussion of the relationship of cursive script and the making of imperial ledgers in *Imperial Intimacies* (2019). Her demonstration of the systemic way that such systems hide the violence of enslavement is particularly apposite:

Empire is accounting: continuous and rigorous accounting. The technologies and techniques of imperial governance were wielded by its bureaucrats in myriad colonial offices and in the metropole. Scriveners created order from disorder with pen and ink, purging the subterfuge and insurgency of the enslaved from their account books. Clerks concealed horror within the gracious lettering of English calligraphy. Bookkeepers invented and maintained an imperial fiction of order when they rendered the turmoil and violence of plantation existence into regimented rows and columns with headings and subheadings. Accountants transposed people into profits and losses in their ledgers as they whipped them into shape as numbers. Colonial officers erased black life from their correspondence.[71]

The violence the U.S. slave schedules seek to hide, and the textual violence they enact upon the lives of the enslaved, are both closely related, formally and in terms of intention, to the slave registers Carby discusses. These registers were used to account for the enslaved in the West Indies after 1807, since the ban on the Africa trade meant that new bodies could not simply be stolen and transported as they had been previously. Looking at them together reveals the ways that bureaucratic systems by which enslavement was regulated were truly international.

Whether or not the fugitive on the Macon slave schedule was Ellen Craft, both she and William were certainly explicitly mentioned elsewhere in the 1850 U.S. census. Both are listed as staying in the Boston household of Harriet and Lewis Hayden, along with several others.[72] These others included two children, Joseph (age 14) and Elizabeth (5). Four of the occupants, most likely formerly enslaved or even fugitives, were born in South Carolina, one was born in Virginia, one in Pennsylvania, and two (the Crafts) in Georgia. Three occupants (Harriet, Joseph, and Lewis) were born in New York, and one (Elizabeth) in Massachusetts. All are described as Black, with the sole exception of a twenty-six-year-old English-born woman, "Bridget E*ly."

Within the space of two years, then, the Crafts figure in two different census records, on the opposite sides of the Atlantic. In both cases they were staying in what was a racially mixed household. In direct contrast to the way they are listed in the 1851 census in the United Kingdom, neither of the Crafts is recorded as a fugitive in its U.S. counterpart. Yet within weeks of their appearance in the U.S. census, the new law made their positions insecure, and their presence in the census made their geographic location extremely clear and their situation especially precarious. Thus, the census both attested to their status by naming them and affording them humanity but also rendered them vulnerable.

When Armistead met the Crafts in Boston, their situation had seemed stable, but the passing of the Fugitive Slave Law radically changed their lives and the lives of many others, creating social and political upheaval.[73] The atmosphere of anxiety and expectation would have been all around Armistead during his time in the United States and clearly had an extremely significant impact on him. Despite the existence of an active vigilance committee (whose most committed members included Hayden and Morris), the Crafts were

SCHEDULE I.—Free Inhabitants in _____ in the County of _____ of _____ enumerated by me, on the _____ day of _____ 1850.

Robert Collins, line 32, Bibb, Georgia; Bibb County;
United States Census, 1850 (NARA Microfilm Publication M432, roll 88).

Washington D.C.: National Archives and Records Administration.

SCHEDULE 2.—Slave Inhabitants in _____ in the County of _____ of _____ , enumerated by me, on the _____ day of _____, 1850.

Robert Collins, line 36, Bibb, Georgia; Bibb County; United States Census
(Slave Schedule), 1850 (NARA Microfilm Publication M432).

Washington D.C.: National Archives and Records Administration.

too well known to be safe. Capturing and returning them would be a major strike against abolitionists.

Indeed, two slave catchers, Willis H. Hughes and John Knight, arrived from Georgia in October, openly looking for the Crafts, and Ellen went into hiding in the houses of long-standing abolitionists. First, she stayed in the home of Henry Bowditch and then she moved to the home of Theodore Parker, who would subsequently officiate at the Crafts' wedding on 7 November 1850. William initially remained in his workplace, arming himself against attack and helped by a supportive community of watchful abolitionists, especially Blacks. He then moved back to Hayden's house, which had been reinforced by the addition of gunpowder in the basement in case of an attack.

After a series of dramatic but failed attempts to capture the couple, Hughes and Knight were forced to leave Boston, but it was clear that the Crafts were no longer safe. They also left Boston, traveling to England via New Brunswick and arriving in Liverpool in December 1850. Ellen was initially unwell, and though no details are known about her state of health, it is reasonable to speculate that she may have had a miscarriage during or after the ocean crossing. She certainly had a period of convalescence out of public view once they arrived in England. By this time their escape story was already well known to newspaper readers, and their arrival was noted in the press.[74] A decade later, their memoir would further cement public interest and add details of their lives in England.

Disturbing accounts of the treatment of other fugitives were also being circulated. Armistead would undoubtedly have been updated by U.S. abolitionists about the involvement of men he had met in Boston, including Lewis Hayden, Samuel Gridley Howe, and Robert Morris, in the celebrated case of the fugitive Shadrach Minkins. After escaping from Virginia and seeking refuge in Boston, Minkins was arrested there by U.S. marshals in February 1851. Sensationally taken from court by force, by a group of activists led by Hayden, Minkins was first hidden in Boston and then supported in his escape to Montreal, where he remained for the rest of his life. Hayden and Morris were tried and acquitted for their roles in his escape.[75] All three men actively defended Anthony Burns, who was captured in consequence of the 1850 law.[76]

In the period immediately before the 1851 U.K. census, Wells Brown and the Crafts appeared together in several British cities and towns, often on consecutive days. They first visited Scotland and addressed groups in Edinburgh on 2–6 January, Glasgow on 8–9 January, Dundee on 22 January, and Aberdeen on 10–13 February. They then traveled back to England, touring Yorkshire and the North East. They lectured in Newcastle on 13 March, Sunderland on 17 March, York on 24 March, Bradford on 28 March, and Leeds on 29 March—the day before the census. There was extensive newspaper coverage of their activities. An advertisement in the *Aberdeen Journal* on 12 February gives a sense of the ways in which their self-presentation combined elements of politics and entertainment. The event is clearly envisaged as multidimensional. It takes place over two days and incorporates a lecture, a panorama, singing, and the presence of the fugitives themselves. The event was advertised as follows:

WILLIAM WELLS BROWN, (assisted by WILLIAM CRAFT—whose Wife, ELLEN CRAFT, the "White Slave." Will also be present—) will deliver, in the MECHANICS' HALL, his THIRD LECTURE ON SLAVERY, illustrated by his SPLENDID PANORAMIC VIEWS,

(Painted on 2000 feet of canvas.)

The Lecture will be enlivened by the Recital of

ANTI-SLAVERY MELODIES;

and Wm. Craft will relate some of the most interesting circumstances connected with the Escape of himself and his Wife from Slavery.

The Lecture to commence at half-past 7 o'clock.

Tickets, 3d. each; Reserved Seats, 6d,;—to be had at the Booksellers, and at the Door of the Hall.

To-morrow Evening (THURSDAY), at half-past 7 o'clock, A PUBLIC MEETING

Will be held in BLACKFRIARS STREET CHAPEL, when WILLIAM WELLS BROWN will give an enlarged detail of the Horrors of American Slavery, and will explain the Nature and Operations of

The Fugitive Slave Bill.

Admission by Tickets, 3d. each—to be had at the Booksellers, and at the Door of the Chapel.[77]

The title of the panorama was *Views of American Slavery*, though that is not specified in the advert. Attendees would have understood that the title suggests a visual perspective (literal views or scenes), while the Crafts and Brown would (by their very presence as well as by what the men say—and sing) give further perspectives on American slavery and would themselves be on view. At least some of the potential members of the audience would have read accounts of the trio's recent engagements in other Scottish venues and would have had some prior expectations for the event.

Importantly, there was no promise that Ellen Craft would speak. Following the conventions of the period, she remained silent even when on stage. The advertisement draws attention to her fair complexion, encouraging potential attendees to see her themselves and judge whether she corresponds to their preconceived ideas of what an enslaved woman looked like.[78] Her fair skin is something newspapers repeatedly commented on, for it was a talking point for white British audiences unfamiliar with people of African origin and curious to get a firsthand look at people who had been held in slavery and then escaped so dramatically.

Undoubtedly, then, the event relies on an audience's curiosity, even prurience, and their desire to be entertained and diverted, as well as on a more elevated political and moral commitment to abolition and to building opposition to the new law. The adjectives used to describe the two evenings cover all parts of this spectrum and contain a strong promise of entertainment. Words such as *splendid, enlivened,* and *interesting* all suggest diversion—albeit of a potentially enlightening variety. The fact that tickets were to be purchased both at bookshops and outside a chapel also indicates the significant moral and educational elements the event promised to deliver.

Equally, the description of Ellen Craft as a "white slave" is reminiscent of the way circus or stage monikers were used for celebrity figures in the public sphere. Wells Brown, like Henry "Box" Brown, recognized the sensational possibilities of activism—as the name Box Brown shows quite clearly. At the same time that the Crafts and Wells Brown were touring in Britain, the Swedish singing sensation Jenny Lind (popularly known as the Swedish Nightingale) was on a wildly successful tour of the United States, organized by the showman P. T. Barnum. He recognized the commercial possibilities created by the combination of her stupendous voice and well-known commitment to charitable work. A little later, Charles Beecher compared the reception experienced by Harriet Beecher Stowe on her celebrity tour of the United Kingdom in 1853 with the "Lind mania" in the United States.[79] Meanwhile, Elizabeth Greenfield, known as the Black Swan, had embarked on her singing career. She performed in the United States but also in England in 1854 and was celebrated by abolitionists, including Harriet Beecher Stowe and the Duchess of Sutherland.

The Crafts and Wells Brown were conscious of the political and moral urgency of abolitionism but could also see the importance of cultivating celebrity identities through their performativity.[80] Using a register that encompassed a set of separate (even opposing) possibilities helped to build an audience and raise the public profile of abolition within and beyond its active and loyal radical and dissenting base. After the build-up of the first evening, the second evening's events turned to the more somber matter in hand.

The language of fugitivity was being widely used in the U.K. press, with the Crafts repeatedly represented in contemporary newspaper accounts as fugitive slaves. This shows the effective way their self-presentation drew attention to their personal predicament. An important way of creating sympathy was to combine their gripping escape story with their physical presence. Care was taken to build a sense of outrage that even after their escape they could be subjected to recapture and return at any time. The drama of their escape, therefore, was tempered by the fact that they were still unable to live in the so-called free states of the North with any safety.

An article titled "Anti-slavery Meeting in Newcastle," published in the *Newcastle Guardian* on 15 March 1851, gives a detailed account of events, including audience reaction.[81] Reports like this help us recreate not just what was said on such occasions but also how the meetings sounded. They give a sense of interactivity, bringing the voices of people long lost to the archive back into the record once more—if only as part of a community of vocal responses rather than as individual interlocutors. This noisy vocality is the counterpart to Armistead's quiet activism, situating his guerrilla inscription in a broader context of vocal responses to fugitivity and activism.

First, Ellen (described once more as a white slave) was asked to join the men. Sitting next to her husband, she remained silent but was "loudly cheered" by the audience. After a brief introduction by the local chair, William Craft gave an account of their escape from slavery, including their arrival in Philadelphia (at which the audience enthusiastically cheered once more) and their meeting with Brown. The audience's excitement at being told of how they gained their freedom was then challenged by his revelation that after almost two years of living "quietly" in Boston, the passing of the new law led to them being pursued by enslavers and having to leave for England. This last announcement also met with applause, heralding their escape. He then preempted what must have been anticipated criticism about any "deception" they had entered into "even to obtain their liberties," arguing that they were obliged to act as they did because of the "cursed institution" of slavery.

Brown was then asked to speak. He had already given lectures in the city in December 1849 and November 1850, and so "as on former occasions, [was] most enthusiastically applauded." He described his meeting with the Crafts, and their experiences as fugitives. He told the audience, "They were the first to have been driven from their country by the fugitive slave bill" and stated that the sympathy they experienced in New England was largely because Ellen "was so much fairer than most slaves who escaped." He went on to seek financial help for the founding of a school for fugitives in Canada and to build support for abolition by making sure that fugitives were visible at the Great Exhibition, opening in in London on 1 May. The meeting closed with pledges of assistance and with the two men "singing a negro melody."

This model was regularly repeated in the venues where the three appeared. For instance, on 24 March 1851 they addressed a "very large public meeting" in York.[82] The meeting ended with the signing of resolutions, including a statement of "a deep abhorrence of the unrighteous provisions of the 'Fugitive Slave Law.'" By the time the census was taken, then, the three fugitive activists had established themselves as regulars on the lecture circuit and had set up a pattern for their self-representation. They would reiterate this in Leeds on the eve of the 1851 census.

Several key circumstances and events played a part in Armistead's action on census night: the passing of the Fugitive Slave Law, the escape of the Crafts to England, the wide publicizing of cases of fugitives such as Shadrach Minkins, and the opportunity offered by the upcoming Great Exhibition to draw attention to U.S. slavery. A mixed tonal register characterized the way the *British Friend* covered the story. Crediting the "Leeds papers" as its source, it combines bare facts with a degree of embellishment. Italics make the moments of particular emphasis stand out, recreating a sense of the drama that the Crafts invoked in their public performances.

> William and Ellen Craft, who gave last week, at Woodhouse Mechanics' Institute, so touching an account of their escape from Slavery, were the guests of our esteemed fellow-townsman, Mr. Wilson Armistead. Being that gentleman's lodgers on the 30th March, it was requisite that their names and places of nativity, as well as their rank and profession, should be inserted by him in the Government Census paper to be filled up and returned on the 31st.
>
> These two individuals were accordingly entered by Mr. Armistead under their real designation, *"Fugitives from Slavery in America, the land of their nativity."*
>
> What a disgrace to a professedly free and Christian country as America, that such an acknowledgment should have to be made—that it should be published to all the world that *America's own born citizens are driven to seek refuge in a foreign clime from the man-stealer, and from the horrors of Slavery.*[83]

The article assumes that its self-selecting audience of Quaker readers would already know the contexts of contemporary antislavery.

The huge public interest in the Crafts, combined with Armistead's existing reputation as a principled abolitionist, made great newspaper copy. The compositional methods of newspapers, which often simply repeated stories from one another, also meant that his intervention was to become highly visible. For instance, the *Hereford Journal* and the *Cheltenham Chronicle* both repeated the article word for word, while paratexts on the same pages noted the opening of the Great Exhibition. This pattern was widely repeated. In nearby Bristol, an article about the Crafts was published on a page drawing attention to an abolitionist meeting.[84] Since this was exactly the outcome Armistead wanted, I now turn to the opening move in the process that achieved it.

By this point in the history of the U.K. census, an administratively standard and specific pattern had been established. It had been developed and refined in consequence of previous censuses, and there was, it seemed, little opportunity for deviating from these established protocols. Enumerators, until 1891 always men, were appointed by local registrars for each of the enumeration districts. The enumerators had to meet requirements of literacy, numeracy, health, and good behavior, both to carry out the necessary tasks and to command the respect of the households they visited. In 1851, 38,740 enumerators and 3,220 registrars were responsible for the census. In urban areas enumerators were often teachers and other men of good standing.[85]

The process enumerators followed was governed by specific protocols. They were issued household schedules to be distributed to the houses for which they were responsible, and filled in by the householder on census night. In addition, enumerators were given books of instructions. The enumerator was required to visit the households for which he was responsible on the morning after the night of the census. He had to collect the schedules and check they were properly completed. Where necessary, he had to ask for additional details, or if the householder was illiterate, he would fill out the schedule on their behalf. Guidelines for dealing with those who refused to give information, or who gave false answers, were clearly outlined in a lengthy clause. Fines of between forty shillings and five pounds could be issued, after due process. Once the schedules were collected, the enumerator transferred the details into the enumerator's book. He was allowed one week to complete transferring the details and compiling other information required of him.[86]

At this point his responsibilities were complete. The book was then checked by the registrar and the superintendent registrar before being dispatched, with the household schedules, to the census office in London. Once there, it would be checked through once more "to sort out any problems or ambiguities in the data, reference no doubt being made to household schedules."[87] Finally, the enumerators' books were gone through to access detail about births, ages, and so on for the published table. It is by chance that household schedules were still being used for the collection of data in 1851. Thomas Henry Lister, the first registrar general, was unconvinced by their usefulness, and it was only the passing of a Census Act, two months before the 1841 census, that kept them part of the process taking place a decade later.

When Armistead completed the household schedule, he prompted a lengthy procedure in which a series of individuals, starting with the enumerator, read, checked, and approved the record. Once the schedule was completed it was returned to the local enumerator, William Fryer Beckwith. At this point Beckwith might have ignored Armistead's comment and simply transferred the expected information into his book. As we have seen, enumerators were supposed to make sure records were accurate and complete. Five decades later, in 1911, this even led to some enumerators intervening to challenge and correct census entries. For instance, though the Reverend Cummin of Sussex returned a census entry listing himself as the sole occupant of his residence, the enumerator altered this to include four daughters, two of whom were described in the census as "suffragettes wandering about all night."[88] While Cummin was obviously supportive of his daughters' protest, which was why he claimed to live alone, the enumerator was not. So the fact that Fryer Beckwith did not challenge Wilson's inscription implies either sympathy for abolition or, alternatively, a sense that not copying the entry as it stood would create additional problems. It is important to try to establish what happened after he collected the schedules, and what any relevant "problems or ambiguities" might be.

Here, things become still more complex. The final part of the story of Armistead's intervention shows the unlikelihood of its eventual success. Little is known of Beckwith, though he is listed in the 1851 Leeds trade directory as a painter and in the census of that year as a painter and paper hanger. At face value, this is surprising, since enumerators in larger urban areas were more likely to be professional men. However, he was related to two powerful brothers, George Beckwith, a printer and the registrar of marriages for Leeds, and John Beckwith, a journalist on the Conservative-leaning *Leeds Intelligencer* and the superintendent registrar of births, deaths, and marriages for Leeds. It was this family connection, rather than his personal standing, that led to William Beckwith's appointment.

Edward Autey, an ally of the Beckwiths, was registrar of births and deaths for Leeds West and superintendent registrar of the census. Autey and the Beckwiths were all Conservatives, whose politics opposed those of Armistead in every obvious way. None of their names appear in the membership list for the Leeds Anti-Slavery Association, and the voting patterns of the men are instructive. When Joseph Sturge stood as a Radical in Leeds in 1847, the Beckwiths and Autey did not vote for him. Instead, they cast the two votes they each had for the Whig candidate James Garth Marshall and the Conservative candidate William Beckett. Armistead, like other abolitionists such as Edward Baines, each cast a single vote for Sturge, wasting their second vote rather than casting it for the other candidates. This pattern repeats the way the men voted in the 1841 elections.[89] Sturge was routed, in an episode that characterized the toxic conflicts dominating local politics, which had an impact on the events of 1851.[90]

Of all the Beckwith men, most is known about John Beckwith. He was held in extremely low esteem by his political opponents. After his sudden death in 1856, the *Leeds Mercury* published an openly hostile obituary. While he was admired as an able journalist and a Poor Law administrator, he was attacked as an unfair promoter of biased Poor Law guardians and "a person of notoriety as a local politician . . . [whose] conduct as a partisan was, however, such that perhaps few men have had less confidence reposed in them by political opponents."[91] Further accusations about his behavior appeared in the paper a few days later, making it clear that dissenters in Leeds had not had faith in Beckwith's impartiality as a local official. Indeed, in an extraordinary episode, their ministers collectively sent a petition to be read to the Leeds guardians when they met to appoint a successor. This explicitly stated their desire to make sure that the new superintendent registrar "discharged his duties courteously and respectfully towards the memorialists and the congregations of which they are ministers."[92] In other words, they did not want another figure like John Beckwith to be appointed.

William Fryer Beckwith, appointed as an enumerator due to his connection to a group of partisan Conservatives, would not have been sympathetic to a Quaker abolitionist or to the two fugitives who were his guests. However, as a painter rather than a professional man, he did not have the social standing of Armistead, a member of the merchant class. He was therefore unlikely to have the personal confidence to openly challenge Armistead's guerrilla inscription.

A critical further consideration is more significant. William Beckwith would undoubtedly have known of the hostility (including accusations of impartiality and partisanship) directed toward John Beckwith. Doubts had already been raised about how John's activities were managed. Refusing to incorporate Armistead's inscription in the census would have created a situation that abolitionists could have exploited even more substantially. Indeed, it might have led to unwelcome attention, exposing how John Beckwith operated at a local level.

Though it may be impossible to prove this beyond doubt, it seems that William Beckwith was effectively pushed into allowing Armistead's illicit addition to be entered into the census book due to a brilliant piece of political strategizing by the quiet Quaker. Against the odds, and despite hostile officials, Armistead's guerrilla inscription remains in the census, testifying to his activism and a courageous vision of social justice, which was shared by individuals on both sides of the Atlantic. It was an act of principled opportunism in a local climate in which more unprincipled self-interest and biased behavior was commonplace. Furthermore, it is part of a compelling hidden story.

What initially is a curious anomaly in census records has significant ramifications. Armistead's imaginative protest remains an example of the many small acts of courage out of which larger campaigns are built and sustained. It reveals patterns of activism that extend well beyond their immediate environments, participants and temporalities linking like-minded individuals across space and time. As an example of the way protesters question and challenge official regimes of memory, it is important both for what it tells us about the past and because it points to the possibility of future stories to be told. Armistead's canny guerrilla inscription invites us to reexamine the archive for other neglected texts, figures, and modalities, giving us an opportunity to revisit the larger archive of transatlantic antislavery and trace previously unknown connections between the local and global.

Seemingly exhausted after a life spent writing and campaigning, Armistead died on 18 February 1868, three years after the Thirteenth Amendment formally abolished slavery in the United States. In the last few years of his life he lived with his family in a house that had been built by a local tobacco manufacturer, who named it Virginia Cottage to acknowledge the source of his wealth which was dependent on slave-produced tobacco. Though the Armisteads did not change the name of the house, they did transform it into a site of abolitionism. It became a collection point for goods being donated to support newly-emancipated individuals after the abolition of slavery. Right up until his death he remained deeply committed to the situation of people of African origin in and beyond the United States. A fulsome obituary in the *Leeds Mercury* draws attention not just to his constant work but also to the fact that he was content to remain in the background, working for change:

> We greatly regret to have to announce the unexpected death of our estimable townsman, Mr. Wilson Armistead, which took place on Tuesday. In the deceased gentleman the African race have lost an earnest friend, the best energies of whose life may be said to have been spent in the endeavour to secure their liberties and rights, and to promote their welfare. From an early period of his life he devoted himself to the cause of the oppressed slave and the scarcely less oppressed free coloured man . . . Mr. Armistead was an indefatigable correspondent on behalf of the oppressed with friends of the anti-slavery cause throughout Great Britain and North America; and he was as liberal with his pecuniary means as his pen. He was a man of a singularly amiable disposition and retiring habits. From his marked preference for undemonstrative means, such as quiet correspondence and private influence, for effecting his cherished objects, it happened that he was earlier and better-known as a philanthropist in America, Scotland, and elsewhere at a distance, than here in his own town, where, however, he was much and deservedly esteemed . . . During his last illness his mind was occupied with the cherished objects of his life. He sent messages and suggestions to his friends on behalf of the freedmen of the United States; and one of his latest efforts was to send some volumes as a contribution to a library for the negroes at a Moravian mission station in Jamaica.[93]

In addition to its reflections on a set of activities this chapter has traced, the obituary includes an intriguing phrase, "one of his latest efforts." Its semantic uncertainty provides an opportunity for further reflection. Does "latest" mean his final work or his most recent activity or both? More importantly, it suggests a further area for investigation, namely how much Armistead knew about Moravians and to what extent were they a part of the transatlantic antislavery networks I have been tracing. Moravians are a kind of absent presence in the story this book has told up until this point, something I will remedy in my closing chapter. I now turn explicitly to an examination of the significance and impact of the Renewed Unitas Fratrum or Moravian Church, which had an established presence in the Atlantic world by the middle of the eighteenth century.

4

Mobile Moravians and British Antislavery

A recent exhibition in the Moravian Historical Society's Whitefield House in Nazareth, Pennsylvania, contained three extraordinary items made by the talented luthier John Antes, who was born in Pennsylvania in 1740. One was a violin, constructed from maple, walnut, and ebony and completed in 1759; another was a viola made from maple, spruce, and ebony in 1764. The final instrument, also completed in 1764, was a cello made from maple, ebony, and pine. These are among the earliest surviving string instruments constructed in colonial North America, though Antes also made several other instruments in a workshop in the Moravian settlement in Bethlehem, where he lived for several years before he departed Pennsylvania permanently in 1764. He subsequently traveled first to Germany, where he trained as a missionary, and then to Egypt, where he lived before settling in Fulneck in Yorkshire, dying in the Moravian settlement in Bristol in 1811. In addition to making musical instruments, he was probably the earliest composer of chamber music to be born in the colonies, and his compositions include three string trios he wrote in Cairo, signing himself "Dilettante Americano."[1] His mobility, like his musicality, was far from unusual among Moravians.

The Renewed Unitas Fratrum had a significant impact in the Atlantic world, despite its small membership. It was a notably mobile and polyglot organization, though many of the detailed records of its activities across its settlements are in German. Its extensive communications network enabled church members to know what was taking place throughout the diaspora— the word used for its scattered community—well before it entered the critical lexicon of cultural scholars. Though the *Oxford English Dictionary* associates the primary meaning of *diaspora* with the dispersal of the Jews after the destruction of the First Temple, a second and extended definition links it to any dispersed group of people living "beyond their traditional homeland or point of origin," noting its relationship to the Renewed Unitas Fratrum. Due to the evangelizing reach of its missions and its organization structures, the church has been called a "transatlantic religious community."[2] To maintain a sense of identity, its leadership established sophisticated methods, especially regarding recordkeeping and communications. By carefully managing the processes of recording and circulating information, they also maintained control of the church's wider reputation.

Scholars have written groundbreaking works on the Moravians' history and impact, based on its rich, underexplored archives.[3] For instance, Katherine Faull has assembled valuable information about women's lives by using the Lebenslauf (or memoir) produced by Moravians before their death and subsequently read aloud by the minister at their funeral, prior to wider circulation among congregations. These include Black Moravians who held respected positions, such as Magdalena Beulah Brockden. Born in Guinea, she was captured as a child, enslaved, and then spent years living in Bethlehem, where she had been sent by her enslaver, Charles Brockden. Manumitted in 1758, she remained in Bethlehem, where she died in 1820. She married Ofodobendo Wooma, of Igbo origin, who had also been enslaved in West Africa as a child and was known as Andrew. Her Lebenslauf fills in a gap in an incomplete archive, challenging Saidiya Hartman's claim that "there is not one extant autobiographical narrative of a female captive who survived the Middle Passage."[4] It should be noted that it does this in a manner governed by the specific form of the genre. Neither Brockden's gravestone (which notes that she was the wife of "Andrew a Negro" and was born "in Africa in 1731") nor her Lebenslauf reveal detail about the harrowing journey from freedom to enslavement. Still, the prospect of what can be learned from Black Moravian autobiography is exciting, enabling new knowledge about Black agency.

But what of the impact of Moravians who lived in Britain? Their contributions to traditions of working-class dissent were raised, albeit fleetingly, by E. P. Thompson in his seminal *The Making of the English Working Class* (1963), written in Yorkshire while he was an extramural lecturer at the University of Leeds. However, work remains to be done on the place of British Moravians in antislavery, especially on the way their missionary labor helped shape debates about West Indian slavery despite the church's ownership of enslaved people. By reevaluating the archives of enslavement, we can gain new perspectives on the relationship of more familiar and well-researched antislavery networks (such as that of the Quakers) to less well-studied groups. This matters, because it enables a more complex understanding of transatlantic antislavery, adding to our knowledge of the paradoxes and contestations ongoing in a period of often hostile debate. Indeed, the past looks different if we pay more attention to divergences and discrepancies from the neat categories that are often used explain and simplify positions or groups that frequently are untidy and do not seem to fit. In turn, this shows the need for fluid and capacious ways of interpreting and telling historical narratives.

In this chapter I tell a messy and even open-ended story, and in consequence both the chapter and the book conclude with an acknowledgment of how much work remains to be done. The first part of my discussion is concerned with a constellation of connected Anglophone texts whose shared origins lie in a German-language work written in Egypt by John Antes. He later translated this into English when he was living in Fulneck, publishing *Observations of the Manners and Customs of the Egyptians* in 1800. His work capitalized on both a wider public interest in Egypt, prompted by Napoleon's 1798–1801 campaign, and an interest in the invaluable information missionary texts provided about natural history and geography.

After his death, his Lebenslauf was published in German before appearing in English as *Extract of the Narrative of the Life of our Late, Dear and Venerable Brother, John Antes, Written by Himself* (1811). It repeated some of the material from his earlier book, while also including an account of his final years and death. The English-language publications were key sources for two tracts published by the Religious Tract Society (RTS), *Confidence in God, Illustrated in the Life of John Antes* (1819) and *Anecdotes in the Life of John Antes, Giving an Account of His Residence in Egypt, and His Sufferings from the Inhumanity of Osman Bey* (n.d.). The RTS tracts also contained material in common with each other, though there were key differences between them.

What is immediately evident from the varied titles of all these works from 1800 onward is the indication of a repeated reshaping of material. For instance, in *Observations,* Antes focused in detail on a variety of his experiences in Egypt, but understanding that his audience was niche, only a limited amount of this material made its way into the 1811 text. This was further distilled in both the RTS tracts, which also included Antes's account of being kidnapped and tortured in Cairo by men working for a figure called Osman Bey. Both tracts contained a new element, namely a vivid woodcut illustration depicting the moment Antes was subjected to the bastinado, being beaten on the bare feet by a hard whip made of hippopotamus hide.

What this reveals is that as his story made its way through a series of distinct though related publications over several decades, it took on a new form. It started to accrue varied meanings by proximity to a set of contemporary contexts ranging from Barbary captivity to racial slavery.

Situating my discussion within the history of the Renewed Unitas Fratrum and the impact of Moravians in Yorkshire, I explore the extent to which the antislavery networks I describe in this book were influenced and shaped by their local knowledge of Moravian customs and publications. To do this, I trace the under-acknowledged impact of Moravians on the British culture of the late eighteenth and early nineteenth centuries. I conclude the chapter with a discussion of two key texts bookending the key abolitionist milestones of 1807 and 1833: John Gabriel Stedman's *Narrative of a Five Years' Expedition, against the Revolted Negroes of Surinam* (1796) and Mary Prince's autobiographical *The History of Mary Prince, a West Indian Slave* (1831). While both of these works have been given significant attention, by emphasizing their connections to the development of Moravians in Britain, I add complexity to our understanding of the contexts within which they were published.

JOHN ANTES AND THE RELIGIOUS TRACT SOCIETY

The RTS was established in 1799 as a U.K.-based evangelical Christian organization, with its origins in the London Missionary Society. It was always connected to interdenominational missionary work, and in a nonsectarian spirit, it embraced a wide range of Protestant groups, including Moravians. In its early years it was solely devoted to publishing religious tracts, though it later expanded into books, broadsheets, handbills, sermons, and almanacs. Its first series of tracts, which eventually ran to 514 separate titles, opened with a tract simply titled *Address on Distributing Religious Tracts*. Following this, its general committee agreed a series of additional texts—thirty-four in the first year and twenty-seven in the second, after which the rate of publication slowed.[5]

The second series of tracts were also known as Hawker's tracts and were designed to be more sensational than their earlier counterparts to appeal to an existing market of readers, namely purchasers of popular tracts that the RTS held in low regard.[6] Since only a small number of carefully chosen items were reprinted from the first series, new tracts were specifically written for the second series and appeared in multiple languages, positioning the RTS within an increasingly commercial and global market. There were tracts in Chinese as well as Gaelic, Irish, Welsh, and a variety of other European languages. The work of Moravian missionaries was part of the RTS series from its earliest days. It published the sermons of John Cennick, who had become a Moravian in 1745, and a tract titled *Mission in Greenland*.[7] In addition, it printed two tracts on John Antes, *Confidence in God* in the first series, which described him simply as a missionary in Egypt, and *Anecdotes* in the second series, which named him as a Moravian missionary. This seems to indicate that by the time *Anecdotes* appeared, its readers would have had growing public knowledge of Moravians.

Regardless of how familiar readers would have been with Moravians, the story of Antes's encounter with Osman Bey was certainly compelling. On the afternoon of 15 November 1779, Antes and his friend, an unnamed secretary to the Venetian consul, were walking together in fields just outside of the city limits of Cairo, which was part of the Ottoman Empire. The city was protected from attack by several provincial rulers known as beys, who could be hostile to foreigners. Antes was familiar with local customs and was possibly wearing the Turkish clothing often favored by the small group of Moravian missionaries in Egypt. This style of clothing was appropriate for the climate and meant that the missionaries were less visibly different from many of those around them. He regularly left the city to sit in the shade of trees during the summer or to shoot fowl in the winter, even though he knew that outside the city's perimeter, dangers included kidnap and ransom. He was willing to risk this possibility for the sake of the exercise and the air, since he lived close to a polluted and unsanitary canal.

Just before sunset the pair turned to head back toward the city gates, but before they could reach them they were accosted and robbed by a group of Mamluks, or enslaved soldiers, who answered to Osman Bey. Antes's companion could not speak Arabic, so Antes, a proficient linguist, offered to remain as a hostage while the Consul returned to the city. He was then taken to their powerful leader.[8]

The bey was suspicious about why Antes was outside of the city gates at that time, accusing Antes of being a thief. After their initial encounter, Antes was immediately taken to a castle used by the beys who guarded the city. He was placed in a dungeon and chained by the neck to a heavy piece of wood to prevent escape. About half an hour later, he was taken up to speak once more to the bey. What followed is recounted in considerable detail:

> On entering, I found a small Persian carpet spread for me. This was a marker of civility due only to a gentleman, for the common people, when about to receive the bastinado, are thrown upon the bare ground. The Bey again asked me who I was? *A.* "An Englishman." *Q.* "What is your business?" *A.* "I live by what God sends" (a customary Arabic phrase). He exclaimed, "Throw him down." I asked what I had done. "How, you dog," answered he, "dare you ask what you have done? Throw him down." The servants then threw me flat upon my face, and with a strong staff, about six feet long, having a piece of iron chain fixed to each end, confined my feet above the ancles [*sic*]; when two men, twisting staff and chain together, turned up the soles of the feet, and being provided with what they called a corbage, (which consists of a strap of the skin of the hippopotamus, about a yard in length, rather thicker than a man's finger, half cured, and very tough and hard) waited for their master's orders. When they had placed at me in this position, an officer came, and whispered into my ear;—"Do not suffer yourself to be beaten; give him a thousand dollars, and he will let you go." I reflected that, should I now offer any thing, he would probably send one of his men with me to receive it, and that I should then be obliged to open my strong chest, in which I kept not only my own money, but considerable sums belonging to others, left with me in trust; and that the whole of this would, in all probability, be carried away at the same time. Being, therefore, determined not to involve others in my misfortunes, I answered;—"I have no money to give," upon which he

immediately ordered them to begin. This they did, at first moderately, but I immediately gave myself up for lost, well knowing that my life depended entirely upon the caprice of an unfeeling tyrant; and not expecting to fare better than others who had been the victims of this barbarity, I had no other refuge but the mercy of my God, and commended my soul to him. I also experienced his support on this trying occasion so powerfully, that all fear of death was taken from me, and I could cheerfully resign my life into his hands. After they had continued beating me for some time, the officer again whispered into my ear, the word, *money*; but now the sum was doubled. I again answered, "I have none here." They then laid on more roughly, and every stroke felt like the application of a red hot poker . . . When, at length, the Bey saw that no money could be extorted from me, he probably thought, that after all, I might in reality, be a poor man; and as I had done nothing to deserve such punishment, he ordered them to let me go.[9]

Antes's description of his experience shows clearly that the motive for beating him was extortion, something he explicitly avows. However, the moment in which his faith sustained him would have been of particular interest to the RTS. His submission to and faith in God were tropes that would have been appealing to its readers. Shortly after the beating, Antes was released, and his ordeal, lasting less than twenty-four hours, was over. But the story of his experience, reproduced in the early decades of the nineteenth century, circulated within a print environment where overlapping depictions of Barbary captivity, West Indian slavery, and slavery in the U.S. South came up against one another, creating a print environment in which readers were introduced to scenes of violence and brutality. Though accounts of Barbary captivity had a long publishing history, they became particularly popular in the first decades of the nineteenth century. They complicated existing representations of Black and white bodies in a period of rapidly expanding slavery in the United States.[10]

Both tracts included a vivid image of the most sensational moment in Antes's text, when he was whipped by men working for Osman Bey. It uses iconography drawn from separate, though connected, traditions. First, it drew from the kinds of orientalist depictions widely circulating in the West for centuries, while second was a newer iconography of the violence of racial slavery increasingly circulating in antislavery print. As we know, images cross from one field of representation to another, maintaining elements of earlier meanings while also being resituated in a new frame of reference.[11] When seeking to interpret the overall image, we should remember that though the scene it depicts took place in November 1779, the image was produced several decades later. Thus, while it draws from the written text and several representational modalities, it also needs to be situated within other frames of reference.

On the left of the image is a group of four men, all of whom are sitting in a cross-legged position. While three are obscured within the dark background, the fourth (Osman Bey) dominates both the group and the entire left side of the image. He sits in front of the other men, his authority made highly visible by his positioning, demeanor, and light clothing. His left arm is raised horizontally across the front of the scene, emphasizing his role in the punishment being meted out. This shows that he is the overall director of the scene.

Meanwhile, Antes lies facedown in the center of the image with his arms and legs spread-eagle and his torso bare. His trousers are so dark that his legs are scarcely visible on the carpet, but his ankles are clearly weighed down by a heavy wooden pole that lies over them, keeping them in the required position. In the foreground and middle of the image, the bare soles of his feet stand out of their surroundings because they are lighter than either the carpet or his trousers. Two men tower over his prone body, as if captured midstrike in the process of beating him. One of their whips is S-shaped to show its movement backwards before it is brought down upon him once more. A turbaned man stands behind these two active figures, his hands on his hips, supervising their work.

Hierarchies of skin tone and rank abound in the image. While Osman Bey and Antes are both fair-skinned, the other six men are all darker and appear to be of African origin. This reverses the many antislavery images that depict violence being meted out to Black bodies. Ironically, the men who were beating Antes may well have themselves been enslaved. Nonetheless, the imagery positions him as the sole victim of the situation.

Though Antes specifically explains that he was subjected to the bastinado, the men in the image appear to be whipping him on his naked back, not his feet. The image thus speaks less to Antes's own experience than to the kind repeatedly depicted in accounts of the tortures of the enslaved, including in the work of Stedman, Prince and the antislavery tracts being circulated by Wilson Armistead in Leeds. An 1853 illustrated advertisement drew attention to the publication of half a million antislavery tracts in Leeds. It notes, to pique further interest, that they were illustrated with woodcuts.[12] One of these depicte a prostrate Black figure tied to the ground and beaten in a manner that certainly resembles the RTS image of Antes. Yet the figure is naked, and the torture takes place in the open air, further stripping away the humanity of an enslaved Black figure even as it purports to create sympathy. On the other hand, the RTS illustration reverses the hierarchies of race as we have seen, but it retains the disturbing violence, suggesting a factitious kind of equivalence between Antes and an enslaved Black man.

Confidence in God was less sensational than *Anecdotes,* which was eight pages long and priced at one penny, making it both cheap and portable. Its format corresponds to a standard pattern in which the title, text, and illustration all work together. As its title suggests, it emphasized the more sensational elements of Antes's experience, offering a shorthand of what readers will encounter. Readers might expect it to be broadly biographical, to include details of living in an unfamiliar land, and to contain elements that connect it to the kinds of sensation or adventure narratives that had long been a staple of popular writing.

Anecdotes is clearly located in the contemporary commercial climate, even more than *Confidence in God.* It sought to emphasize the more dramatic elements of Antes's life experiences, as its title suggests. No longer contextualized by and subsumed within all the elements of a lengthier publication or damped down by a less sensational title, *Anecdotes* had a new set of inflections. While the use of the word *sufferings* in the title might imply the kinds of anguish which come from a crisis of faith, its Egyptian setting, along with the words "inhumanity of Osman Bey," invokes an almost novelistic tale of orientalist cruelty and tyranny.

The tract thus explicitly speaks to popular accounts of Barbary captivity circulating in the period, some based on reality and some imagined, such as the fictitious *An Affecting Narrative of the Captivity and Sufferings of Thomas Nicholson* (1816). Like the RTS tract, it uses the word *sufferings* in its title.

But there are more sinister similarities too. For instance, it also contains a bastinado scene. Its protagonist, Thomas Nicholson, along with two fellow Americans who have been taken into slavery, are subjected to ruthless punishments. Nicholson is given the bastinado, something not described in any detail, while his companions are brutally executed by being first impaled upon a spike and then beheaded.[13] But John Antes was a real man, albeit one with a life more eventful than many, and I now turn to this life.

"THIS MAN AM I"

Antes was born to the large family of Christina DeWees, who was from Germantown, just outside of Philadelphia, and Johann Heinrich Antes, who was German born. Antes described his father as a Calvinist and "very upright follower of Jesus" who argued with the minister of his church and became a Moravian after a meeting with August Gottlieb Spangenberg, leader of the church after the death of the Pietist nobleman Count Nikolaus Ludwig von Zinzendorf.[14] This conversion would lead to a series of events that resulted in some of the family members becoming highly active in the church, including Antes's sister Anna Catherine, who was integral to the establishment of congregations in North Carolina.[15]

Antes and another sister, Anna Margaretta, left the colonies permanently to work for the church, both living for periods in Fulneck. Anna Margaretta was the first to go, moving to London as part of the entourage of Zinzendorf, who had arrived in New York in December 1741 for the start of a two-year missionary visit to the colonies. Zinzendorf's connection to the Antes family had a considerable impact on them all. Antes's description of Zinzendorf does not mention his sister, perhaps because he was young when she left. Instead he notes, "On taking leave of my father, the Count desired to see all his children, and on that occasion, placing his hand upon my head, in a very solemn manner, commended me to the grace of God our Saviour, praying him to preserve and guide me, throughout my whole life. This circumstance made an indelible impression on my mind."[16] Since Antes was not even three years old when this took place, his description may well have come less from his personal recollection than from the way this parting was recounted to him by others.

After their father's conversion, most of the family moved to Bethlehem. Their house in Nazareth became a school for boys and Antes remained there, receiving a Moravian education. In 1750, when the school moved to a different location, the family returned and was reunited. But just two years later Antes moved to Bethlehem to be trained for service in the church. In this capacity he would be the fortunate recipient of an excellent and well-rounded education in Pennsylvania and Germany, an education in which both intellectual and technical skills were highly valued. Before he left Pennsylvania he had, as we have seen, made several string instruments. His four years' training as a watchmaker in Neuwied gave him sufficient skill to adapt this, and when he moved to Fulneck he invented a mechanical page-turner for music stands. Benjamin Latrobe had made a flax spinning wheel, and an ingenious door latch for which he was awarded a silver medal from the Royal Society, when he was at Fulneck

Before Johann Antes's early death in 1755, he advised his son to follow the advice of Spangenberg, whom he had asked to take on a paternal role. Torn between his father's express wishes and his own sense of doubt, reinforced by ongoing family opposition to the church, Antes experienced a crisis of faith. But on 19 December 1756 he found that his faith was restored.[17] Despite continued opposition from some family members, he determined to remain in the church and eventually left for Europe in 1764, after accompanying Indian converts part of the way from Philadelphia to New York during an infamous period of backcountry violence.[18] That year, he attended the synod at Marienborn, and after a year in Hernnhut he moved to Neuwied, where he was asked to join a mission to the Coptic Church. Leaving Germany, he first traveled to London in the autumn of 1769, reacquainting himself with his sister, who was living in Fetter Lane. He set off in October on a vessel heading to Larnica, and after an extremely difficult journey he arrived in Egypt.[19]

While working in Cairo from 1770 to 1781, he produced a series of German-language notes, letters, and diary entries. Not all his papers have survived; some were lost during a sea journey, an ongoing hazard for all those who took such voyages and a frustration for those who must speculate about what was contained in these lost archives.[20] We can see from the evidence of his *Observations* that he kept a detailed record of many aspects of his daily life, travel, and experiences. He combined these with additional details about natural history and botany. He speculated about the source of the plague; wrote detailed information about the Nile, its flooding, and its water quality; described the climate and related details; and discussed the commercial prospects offered by Egypt's geographic location. It is fascinating to speculate about whether John Marshall of Leeds read the book during the period in which he was planning the construction of his Temple Works factory in Leeds.

In addition, Antes wrote letters to a few well-known figures. Just a few months before his fateful encounter with Osman Bey, he wrote an important letter that reveals a great deal about the construction of white masculinity in the post-Revolutionary period. On 10 July 1779 he wrote to Benjamin Franklin, the United States' minister to France, informing him that he wished to send a musical gift of six "Quarttetto's wich I have lately composed in my leassure hours for my Frind the Marquis de Hauteford, to make use of at the Harmonical Society of Bengal." Reminding the older man that they had met once before, sixteen years earlier on the other side of the Atlantic, he wrote, "You may perhaps still remember a young Man wich in the Year 1763 amussed himself with making Musicall Instruments such as Harpsichords Violins etc. whome Curiosity and Desire of Learning once led to your House at Philadelphia, without anything to introduce him but a little American Cordiality. This Man am I."[21]

The halting hesitancy of the opening words of the first long sentence is offset by the confident four-word pronouncement of the sentence that immediately follows. Just three years later, the French-born J. Hector St. John de Crèvecoeur would famously pose the enduring question "What then is the American, this new man?," which Antes's four words, "This Man am I," seem to anticipate and answer. Antes, of European ancestry, conformed to the willed act of imagining that would envisage white men as the epitome of American masculinity.

There is no evidence that Franklin remembered the "young Man" specifically, but he was certainly familiar with Pennsylvanian Moravians. He had printed a number of their early publications, including work by Zinzendorf himself. He also admired their musicality. In 1756 he had visited the Moravian settlement in Bethlehem (where Antes was then living) and wrote to his wife Deborah Read Franklin expressing his admiration for the "very fine music" he had heard there.

In his letter, Antes goes on to update Franklin on his progress since they met in Philadelphia, telling him, "Since I left America, wich has been in the Year 64, I employed all my Talents to Mechanic, and chiefly to the Watch-making Branch, in wich I have been pretty lucky, so that I did something above the comon Way . . . If I could here be of any Service to my Mother Country or to you in Particular I should allways embrace every Oppertunity with the greatest Plassure."[22]

Overall, the letter is highly revealing. For starters, it suggests a long-standing admiration for Franklin. Antes had tried to see the older man in the autumn of 1769, when he spent two months in London just before leaving for Egypt. But it also tells us something about Antes's understanding of his situation as a Moravian missionary. By the time of his letter, he had lived on three continents and had become increasingly aware that what we now call identity is a complex affair. In his day-to-day life he chiefly communicated using German, the language in which he was most comfortable. But growing up as a Moravian in Pennsylvania and then moving to Germany gave him an early exposure to several different languages, not all of them European. He lived in Bethlehem during the same period that Magdalene Beulah Brock-den and Ofodobendo Wooma were living there, and though we know that Wooma could speak English, it seems probable that he also spoke German and presumably Igbo, the language he would have spoken until he was taken into slavery as a child.[23]

Thus, Antes was an accomplished linguist, and it is likely that he also spoke at least some Italian and had a smattering of other European lan-guages.[24] Once he moved to Cairo he certainly learned to speak and read Arabic. Yet he repeatedly expressed his anxiety about his competence in En-glish, concluding his letter to Franklin, "Pray excuse the Trouble I give you with my long Letter and bad Language. Be assured that it comes from a cordial and sincere American Heart."[25] His use of the word *cordial* echoes, consciously or not, the quality of "American Cordiality" that he associated with Franklin himself, boosting his own claim to being in possession of an "American Heart." Even so, he was troubled by his lack of fluency in English, or his "bad language" as he called it. He may have been aware of the hostile comments Franklin made in 1751 about the use of the German language among Pennsylvania Germans, which meant that it is "almost impossible to remove any prejudices they once entertain," showing his belief that they were not assimilating into Anglo-American culture in the manner of English-speaking immigrants.[26] In contrast, Crèvecoeur later approvingly noted that because Moravians lived communally rather than as individuals, they did not degenerate in the backcountry as did European settlers.

Antes retained a sense of the way in which debates about white settlers were shaping ideas about belonging, understanding that as a German-speaking Moravian he had a particular status. The spelling in his letter is certainly idiosyncratic, though eighteenth-century spelling was frequently eccentric by contemporary standards. But the manuscript text contains orthographic unorthodoxy, which points to the fact that he was not a native speaker of English. For instance, in places he incorrectly uses a German scharfes S when standard English requires a single letter S. From the evidence of this letter, then, one might surmise that Antes thought of himself as a German-speaking American. If so, he would have been in good company: by 1790, Germans represented about 8.6 percent of the total population of the United States, and about one-third of the population in Pennsylvania was German. Since he refers to the United States both here and elsewhere as his "Mother Country," the case seems closed. And there we would leave it, were it not for a series of other occasions (and their interesting afterlives) in which he described himself somewhat differently.

As we have seen, he called himself a "Dilettante Americano" when he completed his musical compositions in Cairo, and in November 1779 in his letter to Franklin. On the other hand, eight months after he wrote to Franklin, he described himself as an Englishman when he was challenged by Osman Bey.[27] His performative Englishness on this occasion gives pause for thought. That conversation took place within the polyglot and cosmopolitan world of Cairo, in which he seemed to have moved with relative ease. In the original German-language account of this interaction, he describes himself as saying "Ich bin ein Engländer," which became "I am an Englishman" in his book on Egypt and all subsequent English-language versions. However, since he was speaking Arabic to the bey, both statements are already translations. This draws attention to complex kinds of identification determined by politics of the situation in which he found himself.

Antes was a stranger, a Christian in a predominantly Muslim country that was part of the Ottoman Empire, who was not speaking in his own language. He was also a missionary, who had become accustomed to meeting with hostility in the face of his attempts to evangelize. Since his captors were Mamluks, they came from many different ethnic backgrounds and spoke many languages among them. Given his Moravian background, the experience of being in an environment where many languages were spoken would have been entirely familiar to him. Describing himself as an Englishman, useful shorthand within the specific context of capture, had inflections that are quite distinct from those of a monolingual Englishman born and brought up in, say, London or as a subject of the Crown in pre-Revolutionary Philadelphia. It was certainly highly pragmatic, for in the context of Egypt in that period, identifying as English was recognizable in a way that being American would not have been; the Moravian missionaries in Egypt called themselves English on more than one occasion.

Nine years later, on 30 April 1788, he wrote to the English naturalist Daines Barrington, sending a copy of *Observations*. Its title page describes the author as "John Antes, Esq. of Fulnec, [*sic*] in Yorkshire," suggesting that he was now an English gentleman. Either styling himself or allowing himself to be styled in this manner reveals that he was positioning himself as a highly respectable minister. It is not clear whether he had chosen to use an honorific that Crèvecoeur had specifically celebrated as being redundant in the more egalitarian New World or this was a publishing decision and not within his immediate control. However, he soon builds a more complex picture.

The book opens with an address titled "To the Public," which reads in part,

The following sheets were never written with a view to publication; but as they had passed through the hands of several respectable men, who gave it as their opinion, that they contained some useful information, which should not be withheld from the Public, as they might throw additional light upon that dreadful disorder, the Plague: this argument had some weight with the Author, as even the probability of doing the least good would encourage him to publish his observations, which otherwise were noted down merely in order to gratify his own curiosity.[28]

Once again he intimates, as he had in his earlier letter to Franklin, that he had a certain amount of leisure time, suggesting that he considered himself to bear a relationship to a better-off class of "respectable men" and had cultivated habits of reflection and "curiosity." Encouraged by them he considered writing "a history of the country, its customs, inhabitants, trade, &c.," but the appearance of Claude Étienne Savary's *Letters on Egypt* (1787), and *Travels through Syria and Egypt* (1787) by Constantin-François de Chasseboeuf, comte de Volney, made him "abandon that scheme entirely." Such a work, he reasoned, would have to "contradict not only one, but both of them, and thus confound the Public" and this was not his intention.[29] He added that his manuscript notes predate their books but that he had only read two other celebrated books after writing his own work, namely James Bruce's *Travels to Discover the Source of the Nile* (1790) and Alexander Russell's *The Natural History of Aleppo* (1756). By including such specific references and detailed maps of Egypt, he clearly situates his book within the genre of the Egyptological work he outlines.

Following this is a letter addressed to "the Honourable Daines Barrington," opening,

> Some time ago the Rev. Mr. Latrobe informed me, that it would be agreeable to you to see some of those remarks, which I had made on different subjects in Egypt. In consideration of the friendship and esteem which my late worthy brother-in-law had for you, I would have immediately complied with this request, had I made them in the English language; but having noted them down in German, it required some time to translate them, which on account of my other employments, I could not finish till lately. I now take the liberty to send them.
>
> But I beg leave to observe that, although I have always considered myself as an Englishman, my father having been naturalized and intrusted with offices in the King's service, in America, yet having been educated, and having spent most of my time among foreigners, I am far from being able to express

myself in the English language with any degree of accuracy; and you will, therefore, excuse my presenting you with such an imperfect account.[30]

Barrington would doubtless have known that at the time of writing, Benjamin Latrobe was helping his own lifelong friend David Bruce prepare the manuscript of *Travels to Discover the Source of the Nile*. He may not have known that Latrobe heartily regretted his involvement with the project, finding Bruce rude, egotistical, and stingy.[31] Antes had met Bruce in Cairo in 1773 and had what he diplomatically termed "the pleasure of his company for three months almost every day."[32] Given his own experiences in Cairo, where he routinely spoke to merchants and traders and witnessed the operations of the Ottomans, Antes understood himself to be writing within a Western marketplace that reflected a growing commercial and imperial interest in Egypt and Africa.

In his letter he spends some time challenging claims made by other writers and even ridiculing their methods of collecting information, arguing that the fact that travelers and writers could not speak Arabic limited their access to reliable sources.[33] He also discusses his own contributions to the store of knowledge of European travelers. Finally, in the last section of the prefatory matter, the book includes a letter to Captain John Blankett, responding to his letter requesting details about caravans leaving Egypt "to the interior parts of Africa."[34] Blankett would subsequently become an admiral in the British navy, fighting with the Ottomans against the French forces in Egypt.

How was it possible for Antes to reconcile his two distinct claims? Could he believe himself to be possessed of an "American Heart" but also have always thought of himself as English? Further, how and to what extent does his obvious anxiety about his grasp of the English language at that point impact either of these assertions? What of his German tongue? Understanding Antes's position involves questioning the familiar evaluative frameworks on which scholarship often relies, challenging existing models of inter- and transcultural exchange. He certainly seemed to believe that it was possible to be simultaneously a German-speaking American and a German-speaking "Englishman," the description he used for himself on at least one other occasion.

It might seem that he was pragmatically presenting himself in a manner he thought might be more highly regarded by his two correspondents, and this certainly is the case. Three years before he wrote to Franklin, the American Revolution caused a political schism between Great Britain and its former colony, and a personal one (that would never heal) between the Founding Father and his Loyalist son, William. Antes may have realized it would have been politic, at the very least, to emphasize his "American Heart" as he wrote his letter to the older man.

There was one other pressing, though delicate, reason for him to stress his loyalty to the new nation. American heart or not, he used his letter to petition on behalf of American Moravians. Like other pacifists, Moravians had been exempted from bearing arms in the English colonies, something protected by the 1749 Moravian Act.[35] Moravians had to register their places of worship, but they repeatedly denied that they were dissenters, instead emphasizing their status as members of a Protestant episcopal church. They were subsequently expected to make a financial contribution in lieu of taking up arms during the War of Independence, while they were also permitted to make affirmations rather than taking oaths, something resented by some other dissenters. At the same time, some outsiders thought that Moravians were themselves dissenters.

In his 1779 letter Antes told Franklin that while he was "fully convinced that nothing can be more just" than making an appropriate payment, the amount currently demanded was too high: "I need not to inform you what Utility this Society might be to the Colonies, and that the[y] will be as faithful Subjects to the Congress as ever the[y] have been to the King of England, and that out of a religious Principel." Such "faithful subjects" should not be penalized for their religious beliefs. In fact, he suggests, their loyalty was the very consequence of the religious principles that resulted in their pacifism. Ironically, that was what led some to question their loyalty to the new nation.

Yet in his letter to the aristocratic Barrington he returns, differently, to the issue of loyalty, stating explicitly that his father was a loyal subject of the Crown, "intrusted with offices in the King's service." His German-born father's naturalization was made possible by the 1740 act allowing for Protestant aliens who fulfilled certain criteria to become subjects of the king.[36] Given this, he could also tell Barrington quite legitimately, "I have always considered myself as an Englishman." He had indeed grown up as an English subject in the colonies, though the outcome of the Revolutionary War would turn him into an American citizen, something he appears to have embraced when he wrote to Franklin. Furthermore, living in England might subsequently have deepened a sense of Englishness.

However, his repeated claim to faithfulness or loyalty to both Crown and Republic was also a familiar rhetorical mode. Individuals who understood themselves to require additional evidence of fidelity because their faces, hearts, or tongues did not obviously conform to the norms of an increasingly rigid and dominant Anglo Atlantic worldview also used the mode. This is evident in a moment in 1780, for instance, when the Fulneck-based George Traneker wrote to defend Moravian loyalty. First noting that Moravian practices were not like those of Catholics, he then turned to the issue of loyalty, explicitly linking it to the question of national identity, that is, Englishness:

> As to the members of the Brethren's congregation in Fulneck, they are, like all the rest of the Brethren in the British dominions, his Britannic Majesty's very loyal and faithful Protestant subjects; and but very few of them are foreigners, and not one of these carries on, or even serves as a journeyman in any of the staple-manufactures of this country; and these few persons are Lutherans, so denominated from Dr. Martin Luther, the first venerable reformer in Germany, whose confession of faith is the well-known Protestant Augsburg Confession, which is fully received by the Church of the Brethren, and is one and the same thing in substance with the Thirty-nine Articles of the Church of England.[37]

Linking the Moravian Church to the Church of England was an important move in emphasizing that it was part of the familiar Protestant fold rather than a cult or a dissenting group. Emphasizing the fact that Fulneck Moravians were largely not "foreigners" suggests the extent to which its Germanic origins and the wide use of the German language made Moravians appear alien and suspect in Britain. Antes's embrace of respectability a few years later was part of a defensive strategy. The Moravians of Fulneck had made loyalty to the Crown a key part of their *Brotherly Agreement,* printed in 1777 and regularly reviewed by the community. It announces that "we will approve ourselves, in all things, as loyal subjects, sacredly and religiously submitting ourselves to the laws and constitution of the realm; and whoever shall act knowingly contrary thereto, shall forfeit his or her place among us."[38]

While John Antes possessed the shield of whiteness, nonwhites also had to demonstrate loyalty during the same period—and for them it was even more of an imperative. Vincent Carretta notes that Olaudah Equiano, James Albert Ukawsaw Gronniosaw, Briton Hammond, John Marrant, Phillis Wheatley Peters, Ignatius Sancho, and Francis Williams all made written claims of loyalty.[39] His letters to Franklin and Barrington indicate that Antes understood the strategic significance of also making such a claim, though he was able to claim privileges unavailable to those of African origin. He was an elite figure from a wealthy background, belonging to a church whose most revered leader was an aristocrat, but he also recognized that he belonged to a religious group often regarded with suspicion. His claim to be an Englishman and an American (albeit one for whom the English language was a source of anxiety) is thus both extremely simple and profoundly complex. It was useful and appropriate shorthand in the various contexts—revolutionary, religious, evangelizing—in which he found himself. In other words, it was expedient. But it was also a social and political claim that does not correspond to the familiar and available categories of modernity, notably national identity, by which scholars often evaluate the past.[40]

THE RENEWED UNITAS FRATRUM

The fifteenth-century origins of the church were in a Protestant group known as the Unitas Fratrum, formed after the 1415 execution for heresy of the Czech religious leader Jan Hus. Hus's religious views were shaped by the ideas of the Yorkshire-born Protestant reformer John Wycliffe. Hus and his followers challenged papal authority and corruption and wished to have the Bible translated into vernacular languages to allow direct personal access to the word of God. This continued focus on the vernacular was a crucial element of the distinctive identity of the Moravians. For a start, those intended for the ministry received an excellent education, which included language instruction. Part of the consideration behind this was practical; though the proselytizing church's official language was German, many members of its congregation spoke other languages.

Another element of this rationale was theological. Alexander Regier has argued that while in eighteenth-century Protestantism, broadly, the "multiplicity of languages is understood as a reflection of our Babelian condition and therefore an expression of loss," Moravians instead understood "the variety of languages as a sign of generosity rather than of limitation."[41] We can see an example of how radically polyglot Moravians were by noting a description of the *Singstunden*, or "singing hours," of the early American Moravians, in which hymns were sung using the vernacular of individual church members: "The Singstunden were embellished by polyglot singing that is, by the congregation singing the hymn simultaneously in their respective vernacular tongues. The macaronic carol, 'In dulce jubilo,' was sung in eleven languages! English, German, Swedish, Bohemian, Dutch, French, Greek, Irish, Latin, Welsh, and Wendish, as well as in two Indian dialects, Mohawk and Mohican."[42]

The start of the eighteenth-century revival is attributed to the moment in 1722 when Zinzendorf offered Moravians sanctuary and land on his estate in Saxony. Five years later, with Zinzendorf established as a charismatic leader, the Renewed Unitas Fratrum was established in Herrnhut, Saxony, a name meaning "The Lord's Care," marking the start of a rapid renewal and expansion. Moravian missionaries traveled to England, Ireland, and other parts of Europe, as well as the North American colonies, South America, Greenland, Africa, and the Caribbean. While not all its missions were successful, the church made many converts of both enslaved and free individuals, leading to a strikingly diverse membership and becoming what Colin Podmore has called "the first international Protestant Church."[43] Currently, most of its members live in Africa, particularly in Tanzania.

Since Moravians had an ecumenical vision, they worked closely with members of other evangelizing Protestant groups. Famously, John Wesley was profoundly influenced by his conversations with Moravians, after encountering them in 1736 on board a ship bound for the American colonies. He subsequently visited Herrnhut in 1738, and the same year, along with London-based German Moravians, established the Fetter Lane Society in

London. However, he quickly fell out with the Moravians over theological and doctrinal differences, and in 1740 he formed the Foundery.[44] Forty years later, and now somewhat reconciled with the Moravians, he visited Fulneck. James Montgomery, who was a pupil there at the time, later recounted that "the name of Mr. Wesley was an unwelcome one among the boys, on account of what he said about the Moravians in his writings."[45] Wesley was not the only figure to express his differences with the Moravians, to question their distinctive way of living, or to articulate puzzlement about what they believed.

The social and communal practices of early Moravians were profoundly influenced by Zinzendorf. Historical accounts of the church invariable make a distinction between the years of his leadership and the changes that took place after his death in 1760. At that point its new leader, August Spangenberg, sought to distance the church from elements of its early history that had resulted in a degree of notoriety. These included the period from 1743 to 1750, known as the "Sifting Time," during which devotional attention was paid to the blood and the side wound of Christ, using highly eroticized imagery and language, as well as the impact of a monetary crisis in 1753.[46] Spangenberg wrote a key text that helped in the repositioning of the Moravian church, which was translated into English by Benjamin Latrobe as *An Exposition of Christian Doctrine as Taught in the Protestant Church of the United Brethren, or, Unitas Fratrum* (1796). Ackworth library held a copy of this by 1850.

In addition to the early focus on the physical and bodily, the aesthetic orientation of the group's devotional practice also caused a mixed response. Religious services included music, for which the church is still renowned. Trombone choirs announced deaths and accompanied religious services, which included a rich repertoire of hymns. Rituals such as "love feasts" combined prayer with music and eating in surroundings decorated with elaborate paintings. Many Protestants were more accustomed to plainness and austerity, while some also found the Moravian pattern of communal living odd, even threatening.

Community organization replaced the family unit, instead emphasizing the union of the wider group of believers. A careful system enabled this to operate with characteristic efficiency. Young children were separated from their parents and placed in gendered groups known as choirs. The consequence of a formal and segregated choir structure across all ages, groups, and stations in life was to encourage female as well as male leadership. In addition, each choir had considerable autonomy within the congregation. Choirs all kept meticulous records; indeed, the practice of recordkeeping and circulation enabled sharing of information about what was going on in its various parts. Even church members who were not themselves especially mobile would have regular access to missionary reports, enabling Moravians to understand themselves as part of the diaspora.

Missionaries wrote formal "Diaspora Accounts" and sent them to Herrnhut to be hand-copied and redistributed in scribal form throughout the church community. These were then read aloud in services, so all members knew what was happening throughout the whole church.[47] This was an extraordinary and carefully managed form of information sharing and community organization, yet at the same time it seems perverse in an age of print. Nonetheless, the church's administrative hub in Germany saw advantages in maintaining control of the dissemination of this kind of official material, including by avoiding print, even though it authorized other print publications. Thus, handwritten "Gemein Nachrichten," or "Common News," were passed from one community to another to be read aloud communally rather than privately, sustaining group identity through the process of collective listening rather than individual and private reading.[48]

This was especially important as the church expanded across the globe and encompassed converts from an ever wider set of backgrounds, languages, and print competencies. This system continued until 1818, when the church elders finally sanctioned print. But some two decades before this, British Moravians were already agitating for print, with some early success. From the 1790s onward, Moravian missionary activity was gaining increasing attention. The Brethren's Society for the Furtherance of the Gospel Among the Heathen issued its first publication, the *Periodical Accounts Relating to the Missions of the Church of the United Brethren, Established Among the Heathen,* in 1790. Through this act of stepping into print, British Moravians continued what would become the highly effective and systematic method of public rehabilitation and profile building that would result in Armistead and others applauding their missionary work while largely overlooking their slaveholding.

As the church elders embarked on a process of reimagining the church and actively reshaping its image and reputation after Zinzendorf's death, a good deal of archival material was destroyed. Materials were carefully selected either for destruction or preservation, to control the way the church was represented. Moravians issued a series of printed publications about missionary work, recentering the church in the Protestant mainstream during a period of evangelical enthusiasm.[49]

Moravian missionaries had started their labors in the Caribbean in the first decades of the eighteenth century, establishing a mission to the Danish colony of St. Thomas in 1733. This took place after a meeting in Denmark between a formerly enslaved Black man named Anthony (Anton Ulrich) and a David Nitschmann, a Moravian carpenter. Ulrich gave firsthand testimony about his experiences as well as describing the continued conditions of his sister and other enslaved people in St. Thomas. Nitschmann and another Moravian, Leonard Dober, seized upon Ulrich's request for a mission to be sent to the enslaved and volunteered, even naively stating that they would allow themselves to be enslaved to make themselves more accessible to the population they hoped to convert. While this shows that at that point they had a limited understanding of the racial nature of slavery, it also, as Katharine Gerbner argues, shows the "general disregard for earthly standing" that characterized Moravian theology.[50] This was one reason why, when Moravian missionaries preached to the enslaved, they included the strong injunction that the enslaved ought to obey their enslavers and be satisfied with their temporary (because earthly) condition. The missionaries did not endorse the violent excesses of some enslavers, but they also took care not to encourage insurrection.

Missionaries wanted the enslaved to develop a set of behaviors and beliefs modeled on European ideas, moving away from practices such as polygamy. They also hoped their presence and influence would help to mitigate the worst excesses of slaveholders' behavior, though they also endorsed the curse of Ham and insisted on the validity of the biblical injunction that the enslaved should serve their masters. At the same time, since they taught reading and encouraged Bible study, they found that literate enslaved people used their own knowledge of the Bible to challenge missionary teachings, questioning textual interpretations and injunctions. Newly literate enslaved people were effectively creating a Black liberation theology. When the enslaved seized upon tools such as literacy to lay siege to the system that kept them enslaved, they were actively repudiating the teaching of the very missionaries who gave them biblical instruction and promoted reading and writing. In contrast, Moravian missionaries were actuating the evolution of Christian slavery.

An increasing number of scholars are revealing the extent to which the Moravian church not only included but also relied upon the ownership of enslaved people. Yet the church also taught believers that there was a spiritual equality between all Moravians and encouraged Blacks and whites to work alongside each other. Summing up the paradoxical position of (on the one hand) the repeated endorsement of slaveholding by the church and (on the other) the inspiration provided by Afro-Christianity, Jon Sensbach concludes that "black Christianity—the spiritual freedom that the enslaved claimed for themselves—was fundamental to the antislavery politics of the late eighteenth century."[51]

The situation was indeed complicated. The eighteenth-century Renewed Unitas Fratrum, Sensbach argues, had a "deeply ambivalent relationship to the key indexes by which many Europeans measured their ideas of progress, and . . . national identities." While Moravians understood themselves to be "reacting against modernity," they also "embraced and promoted it." Thus:

> In an age of reason, their worldview was militantly antirationalist. In their home communities, their diaspora settlements, and their missions around the world, they wanted only to live by their understanding of God's word, shunning worldliness and the things they associated with it—acquisitiveness, politics, militarism, the intellect, immodesty. Yet with no sense of irony and no moral qualms, they participated in the quintessential invention of the modern world, the American plantation system and all it entailed: the African slave trade, international capital, management of an enslaved agricultural and industrial labor force.[52]

Nonetheless, Moravians developed a reputation for antislavery among British abolitionists and were frequently praised for their missionary work. This was due to the church's highly effective propagandistic rewriting of its history in the last decades of the eighteenth century and its careful cultivation of a reputation as an evangelizing Protestant church rather than an eccentric cult or group of dangerous dissenters. The writings of the missionary Christian Oldendorp were important to this reputation building.

Oldendorp's *Geschicte der Mission der evangelischen Brüder auf den Caribischen Inseln S. Thomas, S. Croix und S. Jan* was published in 1777. Christian Ignatius Latrobe (a nephew of John Antes and leading figure in the British Moravian congregation) translated extracts into English following requests by abolitionists such as William Wilberforce and James Ramsey, the Anglican minister who published his well-known *Essay on the Treatment and Conversion of African Slaves in the British Sugar Colonies* in 1784. *Geschicte der Mission* was rapidly translated into Swedish but was not available in its entirety in English until as recently as the 1980s. Armistead only had a limited knowledge of the work, stating in the *Tribute*, "Would our limits allow, numerous evidences might be adduced of the operation of divine grace on the hearts of the Negroes in the Danish West Indies. Oldendorp's account of the Moravian Missions in those Islands abounds with evidences of this kind. To that work I must refer the reader, after giving a few translations from it, kindly made for me by my friend Martha Shipley, of Headingley."[53] His comments suggest that his lack of familiarity with German meant that he had not read the entire work. Had he subjected it to detailed attention, he would have been wary of unqualified allusions, since it was by no means advocating abolition. However, by including it in the *Tribute* in this manner, he was contributing to a reshaping of the reputation of the church.

By the time the church elders chose Oldendorp to visit the Danish West Indies and report back, the mission there was well established. Leaving Germany in 1767, he stayed in the West Indies for eighteen months, returning via colonial North America. He spent four months in Bethlehem, also visiting nearby Nazareth. In Bethlehem he would have met the recently manumitted Magdalene Beulah Brockden and might also have encountered some of the enslaved women and men purchased by the Bethlehem congregation. He certainly would have already encountered individuals owned by the church in the Danish West Indies. Visitors to the Moravian archives in Bethlehem can still examine the catalog listing individuals purchased by the church.[54] Oldendorp moved from the violence of the Danish West Indies to what has been described as "an eccentric type of slavery" in Bethlehem, in which the enslaved lived and worked alongside white Moravians but were nonetheless unfree.[55]

Leaving the colonies, he returned to Germany, spending the next five years turning his notes into a three thousand–page manuscript. Meanwhile, the church had appointed Johann Jakob Bossart, the head of the church archives, as the text's editor. Bossart made wholesale changes to the manuscript, leaving Oldendorp dismayed and furious when he discovered the extent and consequences of Bossart's work. Oldendorp wrote a letter of protest, arguing that he felt disgraced by the inclusion of his name. Bossart, who had never been to the West Indies, made editorial decisions that entirely removed or toned down what has been called "a scathing critique of the West Indian slave society and a passionate appeal for the human dignity of its African and African Caribbean victims."[56]

Oldendorp's unrevised work showed "eighteenth-century readers a group of enslaved people who were not barbarians or nameless drudges but mighty strivers fortified by God's word against terrible odds," Jon Sensbach argues, though he also notes that because it was "intended partly as a promotional tract to entice planters to engage the Brethren's services, [Oldendorp] put his own proslavery opinions in full view."[57] He echoed the teachings of the church itself, emphasizing the God-given nature of human hierarchies, in which slavery was an accepted part.

This was a position very clearly articulated by Zinzendorf, who, during a period of crisis between the slaveholders and Moravian missionaries to the Danish West Indies in 1739, unexpectedly arrived on the islands. He intervened between the missionaries, Black converts, and white planters and attempted to convince the planters that Moravian missionaries were not encouraging slave rebellions. In the face of ongoing white planter resistance, Zinzendorf took a decisive step in the direction of defending racial slavery. He preached to Black converts in St. Croix, instructing them to accept their position in life and to understand that whites were guiding them away from Satan. As Gerbner states,

Zinzendorf reiterated that Christian baptism was in no way connected to manumission. "A heathen must have no other reason for conversion than to believe in Jesus . . . The Lord has made everything Himself—kings, masters, servants, and slaves. And as long we live in this world, everyone must gladly endure the state into which God has placed him and be content with God's wise counsel." Not only had God ordained earthly stations, but he had also created race-based slavery."[58]

This position would be repeated in 1769 in the general synod and endorsed in 1782 by Spangenberg.[59] Yet years later Oldendorp's descriptions of St. Thomas would be cited positively by Armistead and other British antislavery activists, many of whom did not read German and encountered extracts that were circulating in translation. What they gleaned from it (and subsequently championed) was a positive message of uplift, improvement, spiritual equality, and fellowship brought by conversion. It is this, rather than the justification for racial slavery, that antislavery activists were focusing on when they quoted from works written by Moravians.

Armistead's scrapbook-like clipping-and-assembling methodology resembles a mode also widely used within the period's newspaper industry. The volume of the material he collected and the speed at which he worked meant that he did not always subject his materials to challenge or deep scrutiny. He was reliant on unchecked sources and on information circulating in the burgeoning world of print, from texts either in his own library or libraries to which he had access via his friends or in collections. In consequence, he repeated statements about Moravian attitudes to slavery and antislavery that were simply untrue. A striking example is the mistaken claim in A "Cloud of Witnesses" that "the Moravians, although they abstained from verbally urging on masters the duty of liberating their slaves, bore their silent but convincing testimony by invariably liberating all who came into their possession.— About 1780."[60] Armistead gives no source for this quote, though fourteen years earlier the religious tractarian Esther Copley used precisely the same words in A History of Slavery and its Abolition (1839).[61] Perhaps he and Copley relied on the same sources or he simply reproduced what she claimed and added a date, since both also mention a meeting in Bristol between Thomas Clarkson and Henry Sulgar, a member of what she called "the Moravian society."[62] Elsewhere, Copley inaccurately refers to Zinzendorf as a Danish nobleman, compounding a general sense of confusion.

Apparently slight and unimportant details like these suggest the problems caused when inaccurate claims are repeatedly cited as if they are true, accruing unwarranted status and authority through repetition. We have already seen this at work in chapter 3. Since some of these religious writers were connected, the probability of this circulation of inaccurate information is further amplified. For example, Copley edited a periodical titled *The Domestic Visitor*, helped by George Stokes, who himself prepared several tracts (including that of Antes) for the Religious Tract Society.[63] The false claim about manumission implies that Moravians had a principled passivity that enabled them to resist enslavers and act by persuasion and example. Even if it were true, the numbers manumitted would be relatively small. More pertinently, whatever its original source, it was certainly not true. Yet because Armistead accepted and repeated the claim, it no doubt gained credence among his readers who amplified them further.

YORKSHIRE MORAVIANS

Living in Leeds meant that Armistead and his antislavery coworkers were close to Fulneck Moravian Settlement as well as to Moravians in Baildon, Gomersal, Horton, Lower Wyke, and Wellhouse, all in West Yorkshire. These areas had been highly receptive to the preaching of dissenting evangelists. The population was largely composed of working-class communities of weavers and other textile workers. Moravians had an impact on the areas surrounding their churches and settlements. Fulneck was well known for its architecture and the beauty of its carefully chosen situation. The musical education and practices of Moravians were also famous, as we have seen. Trumpets were blown from the roof of the church on occasions, and crowds of thousands would come to listen to the musicians because their accomplished performances were a rare interlude in lives that were often hard.

The impact can be imagined by reading this description of an open-air Easter service held in Fulneck in the early nineteenth century. The settlement is in a beautiful location with a fine view over the surrounding valleys. The service included a hymn "sung by the vast assembly, led by horns, trombones, and other wind instruments, and echoed along that beautiful valley, and mingled with the hum of bees, the ripple of the waters, the wild music of the birds."[64] There is evidence that the Brontës, living close to several Moravian settlements, had connections to the church. British Moravians carefully nurtured their relationship to the Church of England and Patrick Brontë, an Anglican curate, was certainly familiar with his Protestant neighbors. Charlotte Brontë's closest friend, Ellen Nussey, was educated for a period at Gomersal Moravian Ladies' Academy, while another friend, Mary Taylor, attended Moravian church services in Gomersal with her family. Intriguingly, when Anne Brontë was dangerously ill, she asked to be attended by a Moravian minister, something fictionalized in Charlotte's novel *Shirley* (1849).

This was not the only occasion when Moravians were represented in literary texts around this period. The American novelist C. B. Mortimer wrote two novels centering on Pennsylvania Moravians. After the first of these, *Bethlehem and Bethlehem School* (1858), was strongly criticized by church members, Mortimer defended herself in the preface to her subsequent novel, *Marrying by Lot: A Tale of the Primitive Moravians* (1868). She had been raised as a Moravian and described the church as "a denomination of Christians whom, taught from my cradle to reverence, I have ever regarded with unqualified respectful admiration."[65] Her second novel sought to explain the principle of the lot, a decision-making process favored by Moravians in the earlier period.

Other well-known local figures also had Moravian connections. The Leeds-based factory reformer Richard Oastler, a Tory, had spent eight years being educated at Fulneck, later arguing that the Moravian emphasis on the fact that only sin was to be feared had made him willing to take risks throughout his life. Though he was an abolitionist, he famously argued in 1830 that Yorkshire antislavery activists should look closer to home and alleviate the conditions of children working unregulated hours and under terrible conditions in what he famously called Yorkshire slavery.

More particularly known, as we have seen, was James Montgomery, the abolitionist, newspaper editor, and poet. He was born in Scotland to Irish Moravians and spent his early years in the Moravian settlement in Grace Hill, Ireland. In 1777 his father traveled with him to England to have him educated at Fulneck with a view to having his young son trained as a minister. In 1783 he was joined there by his two younger brothers. Meanwhile, his parents embarked on missionary work, first in Barbados and subsequently Tobago, as "messengers of the Gospel from a land of religious freedom to a community of slave-owners, slave-drivers, and slaves!"[66] The couple both died there after less than a decade, having had little success in their missionary efforts. Montgomery later memorialized this in verse:

My parents dwelt a little while
Upon a small Atlantic isle,
Where the poor Pagan Negro broke
His heart beneath the Christian's yoke.
Him to new life in vain they called,
By Satan more than man enthralled,
Deaf to the voice that said, "Be free!"
Blind to the light of Truth was he.[67]

His younger brother, Ignatius, became a Moravian minister, but Montgomery left Fulneck at sixteen, with the support of the church, when it became clear that he was not flourishing. He was sent into business in nearby Mirfield, working with a member of the church, but quickly ran away with the intention of going to London. Yet the church continued to show extraordinary forbearance and loving support, as it had done when the future architect Benjamin Henry Latrobe abandoned his studies in Germany and turned his back on the church about a decade earlier. Montgomery's employer sought him out and after a tearful reunion (on both sides) agreed that he should be supported in his wish to go to the capital.

The impact of Montgomery's Moravian upbringing remained profound, however. He authored a poem in 1827 to commemorate the centenary of the event marking the church's spiritual "birthday" (as it is often known) in Herrnhut. At public meetings he was known to proclaim, "'I *am the* SON *of a* MISSIONARY!"[68] His abolitionist poem "The West Indies" (1809) was written in response to the 1807 abolition of the slave trade but has additional significance if read with knowledge of his parents' missionary work.

Thereafter, he continued to use the church as an inspiration for his writing. In 1819 he published his unfinished epic poem *Greenland*, which drew upon the history of the Moravian church missions. In a preface he lamented that it was incomplete, writing, "The original plan was intended to embrace the most prominent events in the annals of ancient and modern Greenland;—incidental descriptions of whatever is sublime or picturesque in the seasons and scenery, or peculiar in the superstitions, manners, and character of the natives,—with a rapid retrospect of that moral revolution which the Gospel has wrought among these people by reclaiming them, almost universally, from dark idolatry and savage ignorance."[69]

What might seem an unusual choice of subject for early nineteenth-century poetry becomes much easier to understand once Montgomery's religious background is taken into account. *Greenland* is divided into five cantos, the first three of which draw heavily in content and structure from the two-volume *Historie von Grönland* (1763) by the Moravian missionary David Crantz (translated into English in 1767), and writings by fellow Moravian Jeremias Risler. Their work was familiar to Moravians and contributed to the rich textual resources through which church members understood and shared their history. In addition to this poetry, Montgomery wrote approximately four hundred hymns, many of which are still sung today.

His wide social and political network encompassed members of the Society of Friends and fellow abolitionists and radicals. In 1795, after publishing an antiwar ballad in the Sheffield *Iris,* he was convicted of sedition. He was imprisoned in York Castle, and then sent there again the following year when he spoke out against treatment of political protesters. While confined, he deepened his connections to abolitionists and Friends. During his first period of imprisonment, for instance, he spent considerable time with Henry Redhead Yorke, an Antigua-born mixed-race man charged with treason after speaking at an antislavery rally in Sheffield. During the second period, Montgomery met several Friends from Lothersdale (North Yorkshire) who had been imprisoned for refusing to pay their tithes, keeping up a warm correspondence with one of the men, Henry Wormall, after he was released.[70] He may have met George Richardson, the father of Henry, who came to visit the imprisoned Friends. His firm also printed the book catalog for the Sheffield Society of Friends, suggesting ongoing friendly relations. Wilson Armistead admired this work and quoted from it repeatedly, while the Ackworth library held a copy of Montgomery's poem "The West Indies."

Indeed, pausing at Ackworth for a moment allows us to trace further connections between Friends and Moravians, groups that had long maintained good local relations. The school's records show that Fulneck Moravians visited the school in 1797. Around this time, during his three-year long visit to

Europe, the eminent Philadelphia Quaker William Savery also visited Ackworth. He had just spent two periods as part of the Quaker group involved in negotiations between Indigenous leaders of the Western Confederacy and the U.S. government. Writing to "our Brethren The Moravian Indians settled on the River La French" on 26 June 1793, he called his group "your wellwishing Friends of the People called Quakers."[71]

He also was familiar with the two important Pennsylvania Moravian settlements of Bethlehem and Nazareth, and with Moravians such as John Heckewelder, the English-born Moravian missionary to the Indians. In 1833, Adolph Rosmer from Fairfield settlement in Manchester visited Ackworth to mark the passing of the Slavery Abolition Act. Among the many other connections between Friends and Moravians, one deserves special mention here. Anthony Benezet's father and three of his sisters became Moravians after moving to Philadelphia, developing deep connections to Bethlehem and Nazareth. Armistead did not mention this in his memoir of Benezet (possibly not knowing of it), but he did know of a recently discovered letter mentioning Benezet's discussions with Moravian Indian converts, linking him to the contexts of frontier settlement.[72]

WILSON ARMISTEAD AND THE MORAVIANS

Armistead's published work indicates that he had been familiar with the writings of missionaries since at least the 1840s, as we have seen. References to Moravians thread their way throughout his publications, first appearing the preface to *A Tribute for the Negro* in a passage describing the principles governing his selection of extracts. He is keen to emphasize a wide set of choices:

It may be observed, that in making the Biographical selection for this work, the author has been governed by no sectarian prejudice. With due regard to the primary object in view, he has embraced, in support of the proposition maintained, all classes, irrespective of their particular religious tenets. The Episcopalian, the Presbyterian, the Quaker, and the Moravian, are all alike included, not even excepting the half-civilized barbarian, on whom the light has but dimly shone. Whatever our own particular views may be, charity compels us to believe that the virtuous and the good are acceptable to the

Universal Parent. A good life is the soundest orthodoxy, and the most benevolent man is the best Christian.[73]

Starting with a claim to the equality of all, Armistead nevertheless suggests an uncomfortable hierarchy whose chief and unacknowledged taxonomy is race. As we saw in chapter 3, Frederick Douglass praised the contribution made by the *Tribute* but expressed strong objections that it was necessary to explain that people of African origin had the same abilities as whites. He probably also smarted at the paternalism exemplified by some of the comments in this passage, including the expression of an egregious commonplace, the characterization of the "half-civilized barbarian, on whom the light has but dimly shone." But Douglass knew firsthand that mass-produced printed texts could be extremely effective tools for changing public perception and that works like the *Tribute* had a significant role to play in abolition.

At this point, early in his antislavery writing career, Armistead had a more abstract knowledge of people of African origin than he would develop later, especially after his inspirational face-to-face meetings with free and formerly enslaved Blacks in the United States. Before he compiled the *Tribute* he would not have had the opportunity to meet many nonwhite people, something that undoubtedly had an impact of the way he thought about slavery and antislavery. This was one of the significant differences between British and U.S. antislavery activists. Most white British participants in antislavery had limited (if any) contact with Blacks, something that changed when Black abolitionists crossed the Atlantic for their lecture tours and developed personal relationships with British activists.

Many elements of the kinds of work carried out by Moravian missionaries would have accorded with his beliefs. A man who held Anthony Benezet's educational work with Black students in Philadelphia in the highest regard also applauded the Moravians' strong focus on teaching the enslaved to read and write. In contrast, this was often regarded with suspicion or outright hostility by slaveholders, who disrupted lessons and destroyed books to stop this literacy work, fearing it would lead to rebellion. By the time the *Tribute* appeared, Moravian missionary work was well known in Britain. Moravians had contributed to the 1788 inquiry into the slave trade and had taken a bold step into print, spearheaded by British Moravians who capitalized on the way involvement with the inquiry had given the church a new status. Over-all, the church had come a long way since its deliberate and highly effective campaign to take control of its public reputation.

Armistead cites two Moravian writers in particular. One is John Holmes, who in 1818 published *Historical Sketches of the Missions of the United Brethren for Propagating the Gospel among the Heathen, from their Commencement to the Year 1817* to raise the profile of missionary activity. He issued an extended edition in 1826, by which time he was living in Fulneck. Holmes acted as compiler and editor, including the work of others in his book. His own work included details of many successful missions as well as a brief account of missions that failed, such as the mission to Tobago that had claimed the lives of both of James Montgomery's parents. Holmes's work was part of the growing body of material drawing attention to missionary evangelizing in a period characterized by a transatlantic evangelical awakening, and Fulneck's geographic proximity to Leeds may have been a factor in Armistead's familiarity with a book that was passed around locally. Several of Holmes's sources were originally written in German and would have been unfamiliar to an English-speaking audience prior to his own translations in the first two decades of the nineteenth century. Holmes also reproduced brief memoirs of several Black Moravians, giving access to personal histories in a manner anticipating the slave narratives that would proliferate in the next decades.

WILLIAM BLAKE, JOHN GABRIEL STEDMAN, AND THE MORAVIANS

Having established the existence of local connections between Yorkshire Moravians and Quakers, I now turn to the works of John Gabriel Stedman and William Blake, which each, in diverse ways, had a considerable impact on contemporary discussions of slavery and abolition. Stedman moved to Suriname to join the forces putting down a rebellion of Maroons who had fled enslavement in the coastal plantations of the Dutch colony and estab-lished themselves in the rainforests of the interior. By this time, Moravian missionaries were an established presence in the region, and though Stedman doubtless knew this, his work does not focus on them. William Blake, whose mother, Catherine Blake, and first husband, Thomas Armitage, were active

Moravians, made many of the book's most famous engravings. The shadow presence of this Moravian background is an underappreciated element of the context within which it was produced and read.

Meanwhile, Moravians also had a considerable impact on Mary Prince's life on both sides of the Atlantic, something I discuss in the final section of this chapter. A crucial element of her 1831 autobiographical text is the description of her conversion in Antigua and her marriage to Daniel James, a free Black man, in a ceremony presided over by a Moravian missionary. Her Moravian connections subsequently enabled her to situate herself within a transatlantic network of believers and to establish an independent life for herself in London, away from her abusive enslaver. Reflecting on the significance of Moravians in relation to the work of Stedman and Prince gives a more nuanced framework for both, as well as for the period. It also allows for discussions of other texts, including that of Antes, which take on new meanings within this reframed context.

A key figure in London circles in the 1790s was Joseph Johnson, the publisher of Stedman's *Narrative of a Five Years' Expedition, against the Revolted Negroes of Surinam* (1796). Johnson added Stedman's work to a distinguished publishing list that included many dissenters and others with an overt commitment to abolition. These included the poets Anna Laetitia Barbauld and William Cowper; political thinkers Benjamin Franklin and Thomas Paine; the Yorkshire-born natural scientist Joseph Priestley, who was minister of Mill Hill Chapel in Leeds from 1767 to 1773; and figures associated with the dissenting Warrington Academy, where Priestley taught modern languages and rhetoric.

Johnson's London home was a meeting place for a variety of individuals whose ideas had a significant impact in shaping the ethical, intellectual, and political currents of the Atlantic world. Guests at his celebrated weekly dinners included Priestley, the Swiss painter Henry Fuseli, and Anna Laetitia Barbauld, while later visitors included William Godwin, Thomas Paine, and Mary Wollstonecraft. Blake, who produced the most graphic and well-known engravings, attended one of Johnson's events.[74] Guests discussed revolution, abolition, scientific development, and the rights of women.

Stedman's work had a significant impact on transatlantic abolition and provides unmistakable evidence of the way abolitionist campaigns strategically capitalized on what could be gleaned from the evidence available in materials circulating in the growing realm of print. In addition, its publishing history links a set of late eighteenth-century British dissenters with overt commitments to antislavery to Moravians whose position was less clear-cut. Stedman's book involved an unlikely triangulation of author, publisher, and engraver. He carefully edited his written journal, including hiding salacious details about interracial sex with enslaved women. His manuscript would be further reworked by William Thompson, whom Johnson employed as an editor—much to Stedman's fury.[75]

Stedman, though detailing systematic abuses and atrocities routinely taking place in Suriname, believed that slavery should be reformed rather than abolished. Johnson's beliefs are harder to gauge, though. While his publishing list included Barbauld's "Epistle to William Wilberforce Esq. on the Rejection of the Bill for Abolishing the Slave Trade" (1791) and Alexander Geddes's satirical abolitionist work *An Apology for Slavery* (1792), he also published works supporting slavery. Indeed, during the very same period he published John Collins's *Case of the Sugar Colonies* (1792). After considering the evidence for his sympathies, Daisy Hay concludes that the "idea that Johnson was personally ambivalent about the slave trade is at odds with many of the decisions he took and the company he kept," suggesting that though he agreed to publish Collins's work, he did so to allow the rhetoric itself to show the inadequacies of Collins's argument. And in the context of Johnson's overall list, Collins's "voice was overwhelmed by those of writers who took up their pens to condemn everything for which he stood."[76] However, a principled refusal to publish a proslavery work would surely have made his commitment to antislavery clearer.

Blake was certainly an abolitionist and had established his credentials in his poem "The Little Black Boy," one of the best-known poems in his collection *Songs of Innocence* (1789). The engravings he produced to accompany Stedman's words remain among the most powerful, graphic, and disturbing images of the violence of transatlantic enslavement. They were widely circulated as part of the visual iconography of the growing antislavery and abolitionist campaigns, often separated from the text they originally accompanied.

Descriptions of Stedman's relationship with an enslaved woman named Joanna, with whom he had a son, made their way into later work by other authors, including Lydia Maria Child's antislavery collection *The Oasis* (1834). This collection was read within women's antislavery sewing groups as they sewed the objects to be sold in antislavery bazaars. The story of Joanna continued to resonate within the antislavery world, amplified through these readings and echoing in the minds of these antislavery women as they pieced together and stitched their work. Four years later, Child produced an extended version, complete with new illustrations. While in the earlier text she had acknowledged the inconsistency of Stedman's attitudes and his selfish preoccupation with his personal (that is, sexual) fulfillment, in the second text she created a more wholesale critique of slavery and of what Martha Cutter calls Stedman's "failed masculinity."[77] Child once more acknowledged Stedman as a source but now moved away from his authority, seeking to afford Joanna separate agency and imagine her in fuller ways.

The reception and circulation of Stedman's work exemplifies the way in which antislavery activists seized on evidence of Black humanity and virtue, understood as fundamental qualities for future citizenship. Advocates of slavery repeatedly challenged the idea that these characteristics existed among people of African origin, and as arguments were made on both sides, they were also played out, sometimes in hidden ways, in the emerging form of the novel. The experiences of white female protagonists in fiction of the period have sometimes been read as coded analogs for those of enslaved Black women, even in texts that do not directly address slavery. In addition, anxieties about contamination and miscegenation, familiar from slave societies, are easily transposed to the incest plots that frequently recurred in novels of the period. The American novelist William Hill Brown's *The Power of Sympathy: Or, The Triumph of Nature* (1789), for instance, reveals that the relationship between Thomas Harrington and Harriot Fawcet is doomed when it becomes apparent that they are siblings, due to their father's adultery. The text assumes that readers will be sympathetically inclined toward the pair. Sentimental culture would play a significant role in shaping nineteenth-century antislavery rhetoric, in ways that are now well known, and this in turn developed into tropes used by Black writers themselves within antebellum slave narratives.[78]

Likewise, Stedman used a rhetorical register that relied upon sympathetic tropes. This is unsurprising, since he was an admirer of sentimental novels, notably the work of Henry Fielding, Tobias Smollet, and Laurence Sterne.

While his own persona was modeled on the protagonists of such writers, he depicts Joanna responding to forms of adversity in the manner of the virtuous female protagonists of sentimental novels. This cynically suggested that the position of a fifteen-year-old enslaved Black girl and an imaginary white heroine were somehow equivalent. His borrowed and adapted representational mode enables him to intimate the connection between Joanna's personal beauty and her virtue, a structural position familiar from depictions of many eighteenth-century fictional heroines.

Drawing from the circulation of fictional narratives about forbidden and disastrous relationships, Stedman also sought to elevate himself through a depiction of Joanna's natural gentility. He represents his relationship with her not as one of radically uneven power, which it clearly was, but as forgivable, even inevitable. In his account, Joanna possesses virtues to which any heterosexual man would understandably respond. Tellingly, his published work avoids repeating the sexual crudity of his notebooks, in which he recounts his encounters with enslaved women. The women themselves scarcely warrant a mention and are silenced and rendered anonymous while Joanna is allowed a voice, albeit one controlled and shaped by Stedman.

In earlier scholarship, Blake's abolitionism was credited to his early exposure to dissenters, namely Baptists, Muggletonians, Quakers, and Swedenborgians.[79] The more recent focus on the impact of the Moravian beliefs and practices he was exposed to as a child suggests a newer line of inquiry. In her detailed summary of evidence for Catherine Blake's close involvement with the community of Moravians centered in London's Fetter Lane, Keri Davies writes that "Moravianism . . . *marked* Blake."[80] This research, derived from the archives of the British Province of the Moravian Church in London, gives access to a Blake whose mystical images have a relationship to Moravian theology. Blake's connections to Johnson, Stedman, and Fuseli provide evidence for connections between familiar antislavery networks and lesser-known narratives linking British Moravians to antislavery. This is an exciting new Blake, who warrants further research.

Blake's abolitionist position, as we have seen, was not the official position of the church itself, though at least one prominent British Moravian, Francis Okely, explicitly supported abolition. Christian Ignatius Latrobe appears to have been personally sympathetic to abolition, though publicly he espoused the official Moravian position.[81] When William Wilberforce contacted him about abolition in 1786, Latrobe was careful not to involve the church in any way that would compromise that position or threaten its missions in the West Indies.

Fuseli was certainly a Moravian, and it is probable that Blake and Fuseli discussed religion—certainly they shared a mystical iconography with links to Moravian theology. Fuseli was also connected to prominent abolitionists. He knew and produced work for the Liverpool-based abolitionist and Unitarian William Roscoe. He also taught the painter Benjamin Haydon, best known for his 1841 painting of the British and Foreign Anti-Slavery Society's celebrated meeting, *The Anti-Slavery Society Convention, 1840.*

Blake also had connections to other British Moravians, which stretched back to the 1780s and 1790s. He certainly would have been familiar with the work of the satirist James Gilray, whose father was a Moravian. Gilray's images critique both slavery and abolition: while his 1791 *Barbarities in the West Indias [Indies]* depicts an atrocity documented by William Wilberforce, in which an enslaved man was thrown into a boiling vat of sugar, *Philanthropic Consolations after the Loss of the Slave Bill,* from four years later, depicts William Wilberforce and his fellow abolitionist Bishop Samuel Horseley in unsparing and grotesque detail. The caricature depicts the men as hypocrites and immoral lechers, smoking and drinking with two unnamed and highly sexualized Black women, one of whom has bare breasts. These two works show that his skills could be deployed on both sides of a bitterly divisive argument.

Blake certainly knew the artist Jonathan Spilsbury and poet James Montgomery, both of whom had attended worship at the center of British Moravian operations in Fetter Lane. Spilsbury produced portraits of leading British Moravians, including Benjamin Latrobe (the father of Christian Ignatius and brother-in-law of John Antes), who was the highly respected and successful leader of the church's British Province from 1768 to 1786, though he had spent many years in Fulneck before 1768. Spilsbury's ministry was sufficiently regarded for him to be invited to deliver a sermon in the Chapel of the African and Asiatic Society, in Peter Street, Soho, as well as in Fetter Lane. He also appears to have been familiar with missionary activity. When turning down the invitation to preach in Peter Street, he wrote,

Next Sunday it has been expected that I should preach to the Africans who assemble in Peter Street but this my present indisposition obliges me to decline. If You should on that day be at liberty to supply my place in inviting, at least, I suppose forty or fifty Africans & other persons who attend at the same time, to partake of redeeming love I should be extremely gratified, & I am persuaded You would enjoy a blessing in the opportunity if You can embrace it.—

As we have Missionaries in Africa and You are well acquainted with the success attending their labors in that part of the World, You would have it in your power to communicate many things, which would afford pleasure & encouragement to the members of the African Society in London; If You cannot preach to them, perhaps some one of our other Labourers, now in London, may be disposed to embrace this opportunity of publishing the Glad Tidings of the Gospel.[82]

Spilsbury therefore had ongoing and close connections with the British Moravian Church, Moravian missionaries, and churchgoing Black Londoners. He would have known about the success of the Moravian mission to Suriname, where missionaries first traveled in the 1730s at the invitation of the Dutch authorities. Following a rocky start, they had become a well-established presence by the time Stedman lived there. Though initially instructed to maintain "strict neutrality in all worldly colonial affairs . . . [they] had placed themselves in a complicated network of dependencies, commitments and expectations," as Jessica Cronshagen has written. When the missionaries started their labor, they adhered to the church's instruction to maintain political neutrality and abstain from interference, but gradually the missionaries began using the idea of European civilization, long a crucial colonial tool, to suggest a model that converts should emulate.

Moravians had always observed highly systematized ways of being in the world, and the idea of order underwrote the colonial system. Cronshagen writes, "Christianity thus became a lifestyle. It was performed by a daily life that could be named as 'order' by the European inhabitants of the colony," whose missionaries took snuff on balconies, hair powdered as it might have been in Europe, while the enslaved worked on plantations. Some of those enslaved people were owned by the Moravian Church, and this Moravian slaveholding "made them—whether they liked it or not—representatives of colonial power."[83] Taking this all together, the ongoing uncertainty about the impact of Blake's mother's Moravian beliefs on him is apposite, particularly given this chapter's engagement with the ambivalent status of the Moravians in any discussion of transatlantic antislavery.

As several scholars have suggested, Blake's images both interpret and challenge Stedman's text. Ralph Hoermann argues that in his well-known image *A Negro Hung Alive by the Ribs to a Gallows,* Blake moves beyond a critique of slavery in situ, and by including a slave ship in the background of the image, he "implicates the European viewer on the other side of the Atlantic in these atrocities," extending the sense of participation in violence beyond that suggested by Stedman's text.[84] This kind of tactic was widely used by abolitionists—as, for instance, in the sugar boycott of the 1790s. But one of the most infamous and brutal depictions of torture is Stedman's discussion of the execution of a man named Neptune, who was pinned down and broken on the rack. In the face of an agonizing death, as they slowly subjected him to astonishing brutality, Neptune consistently mocked his torturers. Marcus Wood argues that Blake's image offers a critique of Stedman's representational mode and restores to Neptune an agency and humanity denied to him by Stedman.[85] Blake's shocking illustration contained elements that would circulate within the visual culture of abolition, including in one of the many scenes of violence being meted out to Mary Prince in the West Indies.

THE MORAVIAN MARY PRINCE

By the end of the eighteenth century, several key texts about or by Black British figures were in circulation, influencing antislavery arguments. These included *The Letters of the Late Ignatius Sancho, an African* (1792), Ottobah Cugoano's *Thoughts and Sentiments on the Evil and Wicked Traffic of the Slavery and Commerce of the Human Species* (1787), and the best known of this trio, *The Interesting Narrative of the Life of Olaudah Equiano* (1789). Importantly, too, Phillis Wheatley Peters's *Poems on Various Subjects, Religious and Moral* (1773) was circulating to wide acclaim. In 1831 a text by another Black woman was added to this list: *The History of Mary Prince, a West Indian Slave. Related by*

Herself. With a Supplement by the Editor. To which is added, The Narrative of Asa-Asa, a Captured African. The appearance of Prince's text was an important moment in British print, since it was the first appearance of the autobiographical narrative of an enslaved Black woman. In her extraordinary and powerful testimony Mary Prince, who was temporarily living in London, recounted her experiences of a lifetime of enslavement in the West Indies (chiefly Bermuda and Antigua).

It opens with her birth in Bermuda and moves quickly to her experience of being sold away from her mother and siblings, passing through several households and working in various capacities, including in the salt ponds in Grand Turk Island before she was purchased by John Adams Wood and taken to live in Antigua. She describes the experience of being expected to carry out multiple duties and witnessing and being subjected to repeated acts of violence, especially being whipped.

When she was first sold away from her mother, she entered a household in Spanish Point:

> The next morning my mistress set about instructing me in my tasks. She taught me to do all sorts of household work; to wash and bake, pick cotton and wool, and wash floors, and cook. And she taught me (how can I ever forget it!) more than these; she caused me to know the exact difference between the smart of the rope, the cart-whip, and the cow-skin, when applied to my naked body by her own cruel hand. And there was scarcely any punishment more dreadful than the blows I received on my face and head from her hard heavy fist. She was a fearful woman, and a savage mistress to her slaves.

Prince was being instructed in a terrifying kind of knowledge, and she sought to explain the mutually constitutive relationship between her learned experience of torture and her training in "household work." The two are simply inseparable in her account, and they share the language of instruction within which she frames her depiction.

In this section of her text she reveals repeated examples of the terror and violence of enslavement, noting the random attacks made on an enslaved woman named Hetty, "the most active woman I ever saw," who was whipped so badly just before, and after, she went into labor that her child was stillborn—and Hetty also died shortly after this. Prince drew specific attention to the situation of two enslaved children, Jack and Cyrus, who were repeatedly beaten. She uses onomatopoeia to describe their experience: "Lick—lick—they were never secure one moment from a blow, and their lives were passed in continual fear."[86] But the most extended description of the violence to which she was subjected was when a cracked water jar she had been told to fill broke in half and she was whipped first by the wife of her enslaver and then, the next day, by her enslaver. She was tied to a ladder and his son stood by watching and counting the blows. Scenes of torture like this would become familiar in the many accounts of slavery circulating in print, such that, as Saidiya Hartman has argued, a few years later Frederick Douglass would establish "the centrality of violence to the making of the slave" as an "original generative act equivalent to the statement 'I was born.'"[87] Prince's testimony showed the casual and routine violence of enslavement.

Depictions of flogging were vividly described in another autobiographical text in the period. Moses Roper's *Narrative of the Adventures and Escape of Moses Roper from American Slavery* was first published in England in 1837 before appearing in the United States the following year. At this point the focus of British abolitionists was shifting away from slavery in the West Indies and towards slavery in the United States. Roper toured Britain and Ireland, describing his experiences during antislavery and religious meetings. He spoke in Leeds in October 1837 before embarking on a series of solo lectures, including one in Bradford in 1840, where he recited poetry by James Montgomery.[88] He was a tall and powerfully built man and his physical presence, combined with his text's refusal of victimhood, challenged ideas of abjected slave suffering, instead showing his refusal of such a category. His narrative included illustrations—two in the first edition, four in the 1838 and 1839 editions, and five in the 1840 edition. The final addition was a portrait of Roper himself, included as the frontispiece. These images, Martha Cutter has argued, use religious iconography to elevate his suffering and emphasize his agency, taking the reader/viewer "beyond the sensorium of slave torture."[89] This reconfiguration of the experience of the enslaved would be one of the contexts for the illustrations of John Antes.

Prince gave first-person testimony of her experience, intelligence, and resistance and revealed some of the ways in which the enslaved used traditional skills and knowledge, passed down by word of mouth, to alleviate their suffering. When she became so ill with rheumatism that she was unable to move, a doctor told her she needed to soak in hot water. An elderly enslaved woman who obviously had skills as a healer bathed her in hot water each evening as instructed, added an element drawn from her folk knowledge, boiling the bark of "some bush that was good for pains."[90] Prince herself moved skillfully within the local economy, trading in coffee and other goods with ships' captains and taking in laundry to make money to purchase her freedom. She operated in the manner of a self-employed factotum, understanding her personal worth and seeking methods to sustain herself in an environment that was overwhelmingly hostile. She was resourceful and able, not the supplicant and servile figure of the Wedgwood emblem. She also recounted the consequences of her encounter with Moravian missionaries in Antigua, part of a larger spiritual journey circumscribed by the politics of the various Protestant groups doing missionary work in the West Indies.

Prince describes initially attending a Methodist meeting in Antigua— unsurprisingly, since at that time nearly all of Antigua's 3,516 Methodists were Black women.[91] However, she eventually turned to the Moravian church where three female missionaries she calls Mrs. Richter, Mrs. Olufsen, and Mrs. Sauter taught literacy to a group of "all sorts of people, old and young, grey headed folks and children; but most of them . . . free people." She does not explain why she made this move, but it might have been due to the focus on reading and writing as well as the Moravians' focus on the spiritual equality of all church members, symbolically marked by calling each other Brother or Sister. It also is possible that her enslavers were less hostile to Moravians than they were to other Protestant missionaries. She moved between Protestant denominations and was baptized as an Anglican in August 1817, but she required her enslaver's written permission to attend Sunday school. Doubting she could get this, she instead moved to Moravian meetings.

She subsequently met and married a free Black man named Daniel James, in a Moravian ceremony, with Prince recounting, "We could not be married in the English Church. English marriage is not allowed to slaves; and no free man can marry a slave woman."[92] She obviously had solid knowledge of the local operations of Protestant denominations.

The first traceable moment of how her familiarity with the Moravian church in Antigua gave her access to wider Moravian networks came when she traveled from Antigua to London with the family of John Adams Wood, her abusive enslaver. She became friendly with the ship's steward and found that he had been in the same reading class as her husband. It is well established that Black sailors had access to news about abolition and rebellion that they circulated to wider communities. Though the steward had attended reading classes operated by missionaries, vital emancipatory knowledge was communicated to Prince by word of mouth. It is possible that he told her where she could find other Moravians in London, since within about three months of her arrival in 1828, after being ejected from the Wood household, she sought them out. She writes,

> When I came away, I went to the man (one Mash) who used to black the shoes of the family, and asked his wife to get somebody to go with me to Hatton Garden to the Moravian Missionaries: these were the only persons I knew in England. The woman sent a young girl with me to the mission house, and I saw there a gentleman called Mr. Moore. I told him my whole story, and how my owners had treated me, and asked him to take in my trunk with what few clothes I had. The missionaries were very kind to me—they were sorry for my destitute situation, and gave me leave to bring my things to be placed under their care. They were very good people, and they told me to come to the church.[93]

Prince's agency enabled her to start to take steps to claim freedom, connecting her to a series of largely unnamed non-elite figures far removed from the more official, and elite, abolitionist groupings and individuals. These radical participants who helped her actualize her freedom included the ship's steward who had also been taught by Moravians in Antigua; Mash the bootblack, who had seen firsthand how she was being mistreated and doubtless sympathized with her—as did the cook and a number of washerwomen who helped her with her washing; Mash's wife; and finally, the unnamed girl who took her to meet with Edward Moore, the Moravian mission agent in London. Leaving her trunk in the care of Moore, Prince took refuge with Mash and his wife, a laundress, who cared for her during a period of sickness and helped her find work. This group epitomizes the solidarity that animated abolition.

Details of the working-class networks within which she moved around this time are sketchy. A woman she identifies simply as "Hill" told her about the Anti-Slavery Society and then took her there to ask for help obtaining her manumission so that she could return to her husband in Antigua as a free woman. Through contact with the Anti-Slavery Society, her plight began to be known within wider antislavery circles, still circulating by word of mouth. In the winter of 1828, she was a visited by Quaker women who brought her "good warm clothing and money."[94]

Her prospects began to improve. After a series of jobs, she entered employment in the family of Thomas Pringle, the secretary of the Anti-Slavery Society. He and Susanna Strickland, now better known as Susanna Moodie, worked with Prince to prepare and publish her account.[95] But at the same time, Wood made scurrilous claims about her morality, both in England and Antigua, seeking to undermine Prince's position and her claims to freedom. Once more we see a series of networks being used to assist Prince in obtaining her freedom. Pringle approached Edward Moore to contact Joseph Newby, a Moravian missionary in Antigua, to negotiate with Wood directly. He also asked William Allen, a Quaker, to approach the governor of Antigua, Sir Patrick Ross, for his assistance to stop Wood's actions. Meanwhile, on the other side of the Atlantic, Prince was increasingly experiencing the consequences of Wood's anger, just as she had done when she was living in his household. Her situation became increasingly difficult.

In July 1832, a meeting of Moravian Elders led by Christian Ignatius Latrobe considered, and refused, her desire for readmission. They were willing to help her gain her manumission but not to have her as part of the congregation. Slurs about her relationship with a white man called Captain Abbot had hit their mark.[96] Prince was even publicly cross-examined about Abbot during the libel action *Wood v. Pringle* in March 1833, in a clear attempt to humiliate and silence her. The aim was to make her condemn herself in her own words in a court of law. She told the court that though she was a Moravian, she had "discharged herself [from the church community] in consequence of her connection with Captain Abbot."[97] The experience of being publicly questioned in this way must have tested her considerably, but she rose to the challenge.

Prince's narrative had a powerful impact due to her direct language, the detail she gave of being enslaved both in the West Indies and in London, and her obvious skills and intelligence. The furious response of figures support-ing West Indian planters opened her up to painful and damaging personal attacks, putting her at the center of a war of words and ideas in the period leading to the milestone of 1833. Since her *History* was short and reproducible, it was easy to distribute. When Moodie wrote to James Montgomery in May 1831, she enclosed a copy of Prince's text, writing, "I take this opportunity of enclosing a small tract, which will not fail to interest you as an advocate for the abolition of abhorred system of slavery. The narrative I took down from the lips of a very sensible black woman in the service of my dear friend Mr. Pringle."[98] Montgomery's long-standing abolitionism, Moravian background, and personal connection to the West Indies via his missionary parents no doubt made him highly receptive to the gift.

The final part of Prince's life currently remains a mystery. She vanishes from the historical record, leaving scholars still trying to discover what hap-pened in the last years of a remarkable woman. Such a notable archival ab-sence is emblematic of the absence of the many other individuals whose histories also remain difficult to recover and whose lives and aspirations may never be known. At the same time, this frustrating lack of knowledge is an invitation to undertake further work, and that offers the prospect of discov-ering more within the echoes of the vast connected library I have described in this book.

When Moodie frames Prince as "a very sensible black woman," she sets up both a hierarchy of intimacy and a sense of connectedness between herself, Prince, Montgomery, and "my dear friend Mr. Pringle." She suggests the ways in which their relationships are mediated by their shared commitment to ab-olition, something we have seen in other contexts. More striking is the way Moodie invokes the vivid embodiment of Prince. Moodie positions herself as a scrivener, transcribing words coming from Prince's own "lips." Not only is Prince positioned as the real source of the tract, via testimony that existed first as embodied speech, but also Moodie invokes the sense of process in which Prince's story moved from Prince's speech to Moodie's pen, from a handwritten text to the hands of a print-setter, and then from a printed tract back to a handwritten letter to Montgomery written with the knowledge that he will amplify it further by speech, pen, and print. In this way she articulates a claim that has also been at the heart of this book, putting embodied Black experience and Black-authored testimony at the heart of a transatlantic antislavery movement involving many voices and hands all working together across varied geographies and situations. Moodie is convinced that what she has been told by Prince needs to be repeated and amplified through varied overlapping networks and locations. She understands that Montgomery's advocacy is of value and is confident that she, and Prince, can expect it. But the vital and witnessing source is Prince herself; it is her story, it comes from her own lips, and her words are authoritative.

NOTES

‣‣‣‣‣‣‣‣‣‣‣‣‣‣‣‣‣‣

PROLOGUE

1. "Anti-slavery Soiree in the Leeds Town Hall," *Leeds Intelligencer* 106, no. 2809 (1 January 1859): 6, British Library Newspapers. All descriptions of the event in this chapter are from this source.

2. There is a substantial amount of scholarship in this area, but I have found the following works of particular help: Bernier, *Characters of Blood*; Huzzey, *Freedom Burning*; Kaplan and Oldfield, *Imagining Transatlantic Slavery*; Murray, *Advocates of Freedom*; Oldfield, *Transatlantic Abolition*; Rice and Crawford, *Liberating Sojourn*; Rice, *Scots Abolitionists*; Sweeney, *Frederick Douglass*.

3. Crowley, "Dissident," 2.

4. Holcomb, *Moral Commerce*, 7.

5. Sinha, *The Slave's Cause*, 1–3.

6. A pioneering work on this subject is Blackett, *Building an Antislavery Wall*. For an interactive map of Black abolitionists, see Hannah Murray, *Frederick Douglass in Britain and Ireland*, frederickdouglassinbritain.com.

7. Ware, *Beyond the Pale*, 71.

8. Jeannine Marie DeLombard, "The Claims of the Humanitarian, Legally Considered," 1778.

9. Midgley, *Women against Slavery*, 166–167.

10. See "The Corsican Brothers, The Slave Hunt (or, The Fate of St. Clair and the Happy Days of Uncle Tom)," 19 April 1853, https://www.leodis.net/viewimage/132750. The Leodis website is a fine resource for such playbills and for images of nineteenth-century Leeds. For a detailed account of responses to the novel, see Meer, *Uncle Tom Mania*.

11. "The Harpers Ferry Insurrection," *Leeds Mercury*, 29 November 1859, British Library Newspapers.

12. Armistead, *Piloted*, 1–2.

13. Roy, *Young Abolitionists*.

14. For work on the British Moravian church, see especially Mason, *Moravian Church*; Podmore, *Moravian Church in England*.

15. Jenny Uglow's group biography, *The Lunar Men*, gives a vivid sense of the contribution made to these fields by dissenters and others.

16. McHenry, *Forgotten Readers*, 3.

17. Moore, *Slavery*, 1; Augst and Carpenter, *Institutions of Reading*; Garvey, *Writing with Scissors*. On Black reading rooms, see Garvey, "Nineteenth-Century Abolitionists." A number of powerful works draw attention to the fragility and resistance of libraries or to the relation of libraries and archives. See Augst and Wiegand, "Library"; Mays, *Libraries*; Ovenden, *Burning the Books*; Partington and Smyth, *Book Destruction*; Raven, *Lost Libraries*.

18. For a fuller discussion, see Bennett, "Transatlantic Abolition."

19. Manguel, *Library at Night*, 107.

20. McHenry, *Forgotten Readers*, 10.

21. Ovenden, *Burning the Books*, 8.

22. Bly, "Indubitable Signs"; Fuentes, *Dispossessed Lives*; Gardner, "Accessing Early Black Print"; Hartman, *Scenes of Subjection*, "Venus in Two Acts," *Wayward Lives*; Newman, *Freedom Seekers*; Stoler, *Along the Archival Grain*; Trouillot, *Silencing the Past*.

23. Armistead, *Anthony Benezet*, 26.

24. Richard Blackett has shown how invaluable these networks and meeting sites were in the 1850s. Blackett, *Making Freedom*, 13.

25. Sinha, *The Slave's Cause*, 2.

26. "Anti-slavery Soiree."

27. Garvey, *Writing with Scissors*; Hickman, "Redundancy." Gustafson is quoted in Gikandi, "Rethinking the Archive," 81–82.

28. Notable recent examples include Almeida, *Reimagining the Transatlantic*; Erben, *Harmony of the Spirits*; Gruesz, *Cotton Mather's Spanish Lessons*. The transnational turn has been lauded as marking a decisive shift away from earlier, exceptionalist, paradigms to develop a more "worlded" American Studies too. See Gilroy, *Black Atlantic*; Giles, *Transatlantic Insurrections*; Manning and Taylor, *Transatlantic Literary Studies*; Levander and Levine, *Hemispheric American Studies*; Pisarz-Ramirez and Heide, *Hemispheric Encounters*; Fluck, Pease, and Rowe, *Re-framing the Transnational*.

29. "Anti-slavery Soiree."

30. Babbage, *Ninth Bridgewater Treatise*, 11.

I. SEWING THE SEEDS OF ANTISLAVERY

1. See Thompson, *History of Ackworth School*; Barber, *Narrative*.

2. In her fine book *Quaker School Girl Samplers from Ackworth* (p. 34), Carol Humphrey mistakenly describes Eliza and Thomas as siblings.

3. Thompson, *History of Ackworth School*, 131–133. For further details about what the school was like in this period, see Ford, *Memoir of Thomas Pumphrey*, 2–5.

4. Celia Wolfe, email to author, November 25, 2020. The committee minutes of 28 October 1816 note that "considering . . . the reports of different Committees who have visited the Schools, we are of the judgment that a change in that department is desirable. It is therefore concluded to give Thomas Beavington notice to leave the Institution."

5. Samplers serve as what has been called in another context "the meeting place of both written and material expression." Senchyne, *Intimacy of Paper*, 5. I borrow this memorable turn of phrase from a description of rag paper.

6. See, for instance, Parker, *Subversive Stitch*; Frye, *Pens and Needles*. For more on antislavery and abolitionist embroidery, see Gardner, *Embroidering Emancipation*. Works on British samplers and schools that I have found especially useful include the work of Carol Humphrey as well as Rana, "Stories behind the Stitches." With regard to American samplers, I have found a number of texts helpful, including Van Horn, "Samplers, Gentility, and the Middling Sort," and Howell, "Spirits of Emulation." See also the admiration expressed for accurate copying in embroidery in "Account of Miss Linwood," *Monthly Magazine, and American Review* 2, no. 6 (1 June 1800): 476–478, American Historical Periodicals from the American Antiquarian Society.

7. A similar point is made by Margaret Renkl, discussing her early abandonment of the techniques taught to her as a girl and her turn back to understanding the importance of items of domestic and material culture and what they can tell us about history. See Renkl, *Graceland, at Last,* 197–200.

8. Senchyne, *Intimacy of Paper,* 26.

9. Goggin, "An Essamplaire Essai."

10. See Ulrich, *Age of Homespun.*

11. Letter from Anna H. Richardson, Newcastle upon Tyne, England, to Mary Carpenter [1852], September 5, Anti-Slavery Collection, Boston Public Library.

12. Kelley, "Difference of Colour," 168.

13. Steel, *Historical Sketch,* 125. After attending the school as a girl, Rachel Richardson returned in 1834, after her marriage to Thomas Pumphrey, remaining there until her premature death in 1842. She worked alongside Pumphrey, who was the school's superintendent for nearly three decades.

14. Grubb, *Some Account,* 263.

15. Barbauld, *Hymns,* 60–62.

16. Barbauld, *Epistle,* 8.

17. Roy, *Young Abolitionists,* 113–114.

18. For more details about D'Silver and her sampler, see Barnes, "Schoolgirl Embroideries and Black Girlhood," 202; "Mary D'Silver, Negro School, Philadelphia, Pennsylvania, 1793," *Samplings,* http://samplings.com. American samplers sewed by Black schoolgirls are hugely outnumbered by those sewed by white schoolgirls, but they are still being found and researched. One such item is the sampler sewed by Olevia Rebecca Parker at the Lombard Street School in Philadelphia in 1852. See Gustafson, "Endnotes: African American Schoolgirl Embroidery."

19. See "There Is a Woman in Every Color: Black Women in Art," Bowdoin College, https://courses.bowdoin.edu/there-is-a-woman-in-every-color-2021/category/mary-dsilver.

20. See ibid., 77. Lewis discussed this in the *Non-Slaveholder* five decades later. See also Lewis, *Memoir,* 52.

21. Lewis, *Memoir,* 36. Describing the reading habits of Friends in the last decades of the eighteen century and first of the nineteenth, Anne Ogden Boyce wrote, "The door of a Friend's house was kept carefully closed against the entrance of prose fiction; but, by a happy inadvertence, a window was left open which overlooked the fair garden of Poesy. . . . [T]he poet after their own heart was Cowper. His love of the country, and of quiet domestic life,—his hatred of oppression and of cruelty, whether to man, beast, or creeping thing,—were in unison with the whole spirit of Quakerism. His poems were a reading-book in every Friends' school, and a valued possession in every Friend's home." Boyce, *Records of a Quaker Family,* 40. For more on Friends' reading habits,

see 35–45. For a discussion of the way Lucretia Mott was introduced to Cowper's work by Susanna Marriott, a Quaker teacher from England, see Roy, *Young Abolitionists*, 110–112.

22. Lewis, *Memoir*, 57.

23. Gould, "Early Black Atlantic Writing," 112.

24. See Holcomb, *Moral Commerce*, 73.

25. "An Account of 2 Anti-slavery Meetings, held in the Girls' Wing, Ackworth School," Third Month 1826, Ackworth School Records, C678/11/8/5/2, West Yorkshire Archives.

26. "Mary Frances Heaton," *Arts Café*, https://www.artscafeevents.org/mfh2. Stitched-up-theatre has written a new opera about her, titled *The Unravelling Fantasia of Miss H.*

27. Huzzey and Miller, "Petitions, Parliament and Political Culture." In an article on Elizabeth Parker's protest sampler (c. 1830), Maureen Daly Goggin discusses the model of the mythical Philomena, who turns to sewing to expose her rape by her brother-in-law, Tereus, after he cuts off her tongue to silence her. See Goggin, "Stitching a Life," 37–38. See also Remer, "Lesson Object as Object Lesson."

28. See Philip Gould's discussion of the way the petitions of the enslaved often emphasized the impact of enslavement on families. Gould, "Early Black Atlantic Writing," 111.

29. Zaeske, *Signatures of Citizenship*, 19.

30. Cuffee, *Memoir of Captain Paul Cuffee*.

31. She was highly regarded for her embroidered copies of well-known paintings. See Holcomb, *Moral Commerce*, 38.

32. For a detailed example of some of these petitions and of how antislavery petitioning was taking shape in Plymouth, see Huzzey, "Microhistory"; Huzzey and Miller, "Petitions, Parliament and Political Culture."

33. Holcomb, *Moral Commerce*, 89. See also her discussion of Walter Mifflin's antislavery petitions of 1786 and 1792, 71.

34. *Bradford Observer*, 7 August 1834, quoted in Gleadle and Hanley, "Children against Slavery," 103, 105.

35. On the importance of emulation and sampler-making, see Howell, *Against Self-Reliance*, 133–146.

36. Barnes, "Schoolgirl Embroideries," 299; Weaver, "Fashioning Freedom." See also Johnson, "African American Women and Their Quilts"; Thavolia Glymph's discussions of the way enslaved domestic workers developed power over tasking their labor, in Glymph, *Out of the House of Bondage*, 8; and Koritha Mitchell's discussion of what she terms "homemade citizenship" throughout her book *From Slave Cabins to the White House*.

37. Barnes, "Schoolgirl Embroideries," 302.

38. "Fugitives from Slavery.—Remarkable Return in the Census," *Illustrated London News* 18, no. 479 (19 April 1851): 316, Gale Primary Sources, *Illustrated London News* Historical Archive, 1842–2003.

39. Finley, *Intimate Economy*, 67. See Shirley Yee's discussion of Black women's domestic duties in Yee, *Black Women Abolitionists*, 40–59, especially 52–53.

40. Finley, *An Intimate Economy*, 47.

41. Miles, *All That She Carried*, xv, 5–6.

42. *Black Dolls*, 25 February 2022–5 June 2022, New-York Historical Society Museum and Library, https://www.nyhistory.org/exhibitions/black-dolls-0.

43. See Carol Humphrey's extensive and detailed discussion in Humphrey, *Quaker School Girl Samplers*, 44–106.

44. Humphrey writes that Jones was "revered by the pupils, not least for the strength of her Quaker ministry." Ibid., 50.

45. See, for instance, details of the charitable sewing classes offered in Blackburn, Lancashire, in 1862. "The Strangers' Friend Society Sewing Classes," *Blackburn Standard*, 26 November 1862, British Library Newspapers.

46. Schaffer, *Novel Craft*, 5–6.

47. Goggin, "Stitching a Life," 33.

48. See Schaffer, *Novel Craft*, 16–19.

49. Kelley, "Difference of Colour," 157.

50. Holcomb, *Moral Commerce*, 100. The group had earlier been known as the Female Society for Birmingham. Ibid., 97. See also Everill, *Not Made by Slaves*, 188.

51. Hingston Fox, *Dr. John Fothergill and his Friends*. See chapter 22 in particular.

52. Crabtree, *Holy Nation*, 95–130; Howell, *Against Self-Reliance*, 116–156.

53. Thompson, *History of Ackworth School*, 27; Humphrey, *Quaker School Girl Samplers*, 9.

54. For more on Biddle and his relationship to Ackworth and to the development of Quaker schools in the United States, see Crabtree, *Holy Nation*, chapter 7, "Walled Gardens: Friends' Schools." Sarah Grubb wrote a detailed account of the school and sent this to an American correspondent. See Grubb, *Some Account*, 251–275.

55. Lewis, *Friends' Review*, 5.

56. Biddle, *Plan for a School*, 22. See also Crabtree, *Holy Nation*, 54–62.

57. Stoker, "Ellenor Fenn," 820, 833.

58. Ford, *Memoir of Thomas Pumphrey*, 344. A selection of Pumphrey's verse was published in an appendix at the end of the memoir.

59. Boyce, *Records of a Quaker Family*, 178–179.

60. For further details, see Thompson, *History of Ackworth School*, 102–104. Another key text was *Lessons for Youth*, which was printed both in London and New York and was circulating in the last decade of the eighteenth century.

61. Holton, *Quaker Women*, 21.

62. Lewis, *Memoir*, 38.

63. Ackworth School Visitors Book 1796–1804, Ackworth School Records, C678/1/5/1/1, West Yorkshire Archives.

64. For more on the foundation of Fulneck, see Stead, *Moravian Settlement at Fulneck, 1742–1790*.

65. Martineau, *Retrospect of Western Travel*, 1:105.

66. Van Broekhoven, "Better than a clay club," 38. Henry Richardson quoted an extract from Weld's work in his free produce tract *A Revolution of the Spindles, for the Overthrow of Slavery* (1848), initially published in Newcastle but subsequently reissued in the *North Star* and the *Non-Slaveholder*. See *A Revolution of the Spindles, for the Overthrow of American Slavery* [Macliver and Bradley], [1848], Slavery and Anti-slavery.

67. Baker, *Building America*, 124–125.

68. The novelist Fanny Burney noted that Benjamin and his brother Christian Ignatius visited

her parents, and Benjamin recounted his initial difficulties in adjusting to family life after his child-hood experiences. See Burney, *Diary and Letters of Madame D'Arblay,* 580–581.

69. Frye, *Pens and Needles,* 26. Frye's work has been very helpful for thinking about needlecraft more broadly. Other works that have assisted me include Lackey, "I use the woman's figure naturally."

70. Stinebeck, "Understanding the Forgotten Poetry of American Samplers," 1193.

71. Dorr, *Lanmere,* 40.

72. Heaps, "Remember Me." In her history of the Richardson family, Anne Ogden Boyce used the 1715 genealogical sampler, sewn by the eleven-year-old Isobel Vasie, to piece together family history. Boyce, *Records of a Quaker Family,* 11.

73. Doody, *Frances Burney,* 23.

74. See Parker, *Subversive Stitch,* 189–215.

75. Humphrey, *Friends. A Common Thread,* 59–60. Gleadle and Hanley cite other examples of British antislavery samplers sewn by girls in this period. See Gleadle and Hanley, "Children against Slavery," 102.

76. See Humphrey, *Quaker School Girl Samplers,* 22, 33–36. For more on the sources of the most common extracts used at Ackworth, see 211–212. With regard to the bellflower motif, Humphrey notes that "often this little floral motif is thought of as a distinctive element of American Quaker samplers with Ruth James of Westtown School, Pennsylvania, including it in the border of her work of 1800 just a year after the foundation of that school" (34).

77. For more on how to read the codes of sewn work, see Frye, *Pens and Needles,* 14–15.

78. For a lengthy discussion of medallion samplers, see Humphrey, *Quaker School Girl Samplers,* 44–106.

79. Ford, *Memoir of Thomas Pumphrey,* 17.

80. Armistead, *Select Miscellanies,* iii–iv.

81. See Humphrey, *Quaker School Girl Samplers,* 189–194.

82. A photograph of the page is reproduced in ibid., 3.

83. Jane's siblings were Sarah (b. 1816), Esther (1818), Rachel (1819), Richard (1824), and Mary (1827). Esther left the Priestmans' employ when her religious beliefs became increasingly evangelical. Holton, *Quaker Women,* 58.

84. For more details, see Murray, *Advocates of Freedom,* 129–130.

85. Mood, "Women in the Quaker Community," 209–210.

86. Letter from John Sharp to Joseph Sharp, 17 July 1815, Sharp Family Tree, C617/6, and John Sharp Letters, C617/3, Sharp Family papers, West Yorkshire Archives.

87. The ship's manifest reveals that the family carried with them with ten trunks, beds and bedding, and scythes, a saw, and other tools, and that the vessel's chief cargo comprised 482 crates and 42 hogsheads of earthenware.

88. Letter from John Sharp to Joseph Sharp, 30 September 1815, Sharp Family papers, C617/3. Smedley was an American-born Friend whose mercantile business was ultimately unsuccessful. See Cope, *Genealogy of the Smedley Family,* 141.

89. Holcomb, *Moral Commerce,* 54, also 42–44.

90. Gould, "Early Black Atlantic Writing," 112.

91. The Sharp family records are contained in the West Yorkshire Archives and at the Historical Society of Pennsylvania; the loose sheet copy of the poem is in Wakefield, while the commonplace

book is in Philadelphia. See Sharp Family Records Including Correspondence and Description of Emigration Journey to America of Joseph Sharp, C617, West Yorkshire Archives; John Sharp Commonplace Book 1810, 2147, vol. 3, folder 1, Blackburne and Sharp Families Papers, Historical Society of Pennsylvania.

92. Letter from John Sharp to his father and sisters in Leeds, 9 July 1815, from Philadelphia, Sharp Family papers, C617, Sharp Family records.

93. Van Broekhoven, "'Better than a Clay Club,'" 34.

94. Sharp family records, (C617)/4, West Yorkshire Archives.

95. Ibid.

2. A TIRELESS LABORER

1. Everill, *Not Made by Slaves*, 173.

2. "A Revolution of the Spindles, for the Overthrow of American Slavery," Macliver and Bradley, [1848], Slavery and Anti-slavery.

3. O'Donnell, "There's Death in the Pot!"; Holcomb, *Moral Commerce*, 188–189.

4. Scott and Megoran, "Newcastle Upon Tyne Peace Society." See also Holton, *Quaker Women*, 50. More on these families of Newcastle Friends can be found in Boyce, *Records of a Quaker Family*; Richardson, *Memoir*; Mood, "Women in the Quaker Community." See also Steel, *Historical Sketch*.

5. Ann Rhoads, *Record of a Trip to England 1847*, Rhoads Family Papers, HC.MC-1033, box 3, pp. 40–41, Haverford College. Ann Rhoads described staying with "our dear friends" Jonathan and Rachel Priestman (connected to the Richardsons through marriage) in Newcastle. For details of the tricky relationships between the Richardson and Priestman families, see Holton, *Quaker Women*, 106–107.

6. Still, *Underground Rail Road*, 720.

7. Minto, *Autobiographical Notes*, 355.

8. Douglas, "A Cherished Friendship," 266.

9. Still, *Underground Rail Road*, 592.

10. *Annual Monitor for 1893*, 104.

11. I am especially thinking of Midgley, *Women against Slavery*; Holcomb, *Moral Commerce*; Mood, "Women in the Quaker Community"; and Holton, *Quaker Women*. In addition, feminist scholars have discussed the intersectionality of campaigning. See, for instance, Ware, *Beyond the Pale*.

12. *Annual Monitor for 1893*, 104.

13. Minto, *Autobiographical Notes*, 352.

14. Quoted in *Annual Monitor for 1893*, 104–105 (emphasis in the original).

15. Boyce, *Records of a Quaker Family*, 181.

16. Quoted in *Annual Monitor* for 1893, 105 (emphasis in the original).

17. Anna admired Anna Deborah, describing her in a letter to Ann Rhoads, after Deborah's premature death, as "a highly cultivated and very fine young woman." Letter from Anna Richardson to Ann Rhoads, 25 October 1872, Anna H. Richardson, 1872–1873, HC.MC-1033, box 2, Rhoads Family Papers.

18. Richardson, *Memoir*, 97–100, 20. The diary entry was written on 24 August 1852. The month before her description of the carriage journey she wrote to a friend, recommending *Uncle Tom's*

Cabin. Letter to H. M. Peile, 7 April 1852, 16. For details of Stowe's visit, see Richardson, *Memoir,* 95–101.

19. See, for instance, Sweeney, *Frederick Douglass;* Sweeney and Rice, "Liberating Sojourns?"; Murray, *Advocates of Freedom;* Blackett, *Building an Antislavery Wall.*

20. See, for instance, Gerzina, *Black England;* Kaufman, *Black Tudors;* Newman, *Freedom Seekers.*

21. Holcomb, *Moral Commerce,* 38–40.

22. Pocock, "From Enslavement to Freedom."

23. Pumphrey and Pumphrey, *Henry and Anna Richardson,* 11.

24. Bennett, "England/New England."

25. Still, *Underground Rail Road,* 592.

26. Duane, *Educated for Freedom,* 148–155.

27. Greenspan, *William Wells Brown,* 309–310. Greenspan's account is the most detailed to date.

28. Anna H. Richardson, "Anti-slavery Memoranda," [J. G. Forster, 1860?], Slavery and Anti-slavery.

29. James, E. Crawford, "A Card," *Liberator,* 23 April 1858, 67, Slavery and Anti-slavery. William Bell Scott wrote, "It was within her power to collect any amount of money within a few weeks—I mean such as five hundred pounds or more, to be sent away at any crisis in American slavery affairs or temperance." Minto, *Autobiographical Notes,* 353.

30. See indexed references in Gould, *Diary of a Contraband.*

31. "To Our British Subscribers," *North Star,* 2 October 1851, Slavery and Anti-slavery; Richardson, "Anti-slavery Memoranda." Midgley writes that "she provided up-to-date information to nearly a hundred newspaper editors." Midgley, *Women against Slavery,* 138. "Monthly Summary," *Anti-Slavery Monthly Reporter,* 9, no. 5 (1 May 1861): 97, Nineteenth Century U.K. Periodicals.

32. Holcomb, *Moral Commerce,* 42–44, 63.

33. See Gleadle and Hanley, "Children against Slavery," 98; Sheller, "Bleeding Humanity and Gendered Embodiments"; Holcomb, *Moral Commerce,* 89–106.

34. Midgley, "Dissenting Voice," 95, 100. The Rhoadses stayed with the Tukes in York when they visited England in 1847. They visited (and greatly admired) the York Retreat.

35. For details of how one boy scholar experienced his time at the school, see Howitt, *Boy's Country-Book,* chapters 15–17.

36. For a description of his feelings about the appointment and its circumstances, see Ford, *Memoir of Thomas Pumphrey,* 51–56.

37. "Ellen Richardson," *Annual Monitor for 1897,* 127–128. The word "Spartan" is also used by Anne Ogden Boyce in a description of the cold outdoor baths the scholars took three mornings a week, a mile from the school, without towels or any mode of drying themselves other than running outside. Boyce, *Records of a Quaker Family,* 184.

38. Stanley Holton argues that in this way an individual could "strengthen their own family by extending the resources available to it." Holton, *Quaker Women,* 19.

39. Letter from Anna Richardson to Ann Rhoads, 25 October 1872. Henry's brother Isaac was a long-term invalid who died prematurely in 1840 on the Isle of Wight, where he had moved to recover his health. Jane was the mother of Anna Deborah, who had died by this time.

40. *Annual Monitor for 1893,* 106.

41. Holton, *Quaker Women,* 6.

42. Richardson, *Memoir,* 2–4.

43. Letter to Kate O'Brien, 17 January 1860, in Richardson, *Memoir,* 172.

44. Richardson, *Memoir,* 213. For details of their correspondence, see 213–226.

45. Alfred Homes, "The Friends' Book Society," in Steel, *Historical Sketch,* 95–99.

46. Richardson, *Memoir,* 5–6.

47. Letter from Wilson Armistead, 1854, Letters to Henry Wadsworth Longfellow, box 3 (194), Houghton Library, Harvard.

48. Steel, *Historical Sketch,* 129. For more on Bragg, see indexed references in Holton, *Quaker Women.*

49. William Harris Robinson, "Recollections of Newcastle Meeting Sixty Years Ago," in Steel, *Historical Sketch,* 59–73, at 63, 66. Several secretaries to the Newcastle Literary and Scientific Society were Quakers. For more details of the Book Society, see Homes "Friends' Book Society," 95–99.

50. Confirmation of this can be found in the Sharp Family Papers in the West Yorkshire Archives.

51. Richardson, "To a Boy," 43.

52. Mood, "Women in the Quaker Community," 212–213.

53. For more on Newcastle's ragged school, see Prahms, *Newcastle Ragged and Industrial School.* Throughout the 1840s a number of such schools were opened, including a celebrated ragged school in Bristol founded by Mary Carpenter.

54. "Letter from Henry H. H. Garnet," *Non-Slaveholder,* 1 October 1850, 226, Slavery and Anti-slavery.

55. Roy, *Young Abolitionists,* 16.

56. "Anti-slavery Bazaar, Philadelphia," *Anti-Slavery Monthly Reporter,* 1 September 1846, 143, Nineteenth Century U.K. Periodicals.

57. Blackett, *Building an Antislavery Wall,* 9.

58. Richardson, *Memoir,* 64; Pumphrey, *Henry and Anna Richardson,* 23–33

59. Julie Holcomb has challenged earlier understandings of free produce, arguing that it had a range of participants and advocates, encompassing "women and black abolitionists as well as Quakers." Holcomb, *Moral Commerce,* 3–4.

60. *Address to the Members of the Religious Society of Friends,* 10.

61. For Sturge's involvement with free produce, see Billington, "British Humanitarians," 316–320.

62. See "Ackworth General Meeting and Other Anniversaries Held There, on the 2nd and 3d Ultimo," *British Friend,* August 1851, 195.

63. Letter from Elihu Burritt, 29 September 1849, George W., Correspondence, 1846–1890, 1233 Taylor, Taylor Family Papers, Haverford College.

64. Burritt, "Wall of Fire."

65. Elihu Burritt, *The Advocate of Peace and Universal Brotherhood* 1, no. 1 (1 January 1846), American Historical Periodicals from the American Antiquarian Society.

66. "Circular of the Newcastle Ladies' Free Produce Association," *Non-Slaveholder,* 1 June 1848, 123; and Anna H. Richardson, "On the Disuse of Slave Labour Produce," *Anti-Slavery Monthly Reporter,* 1 May 1848, 74, both in Slavery and Anti-slavery.

67. The Richardsons had initially wanted Henry Bibb to come to England and lecture about free produce, but they were unsuccessful. Billington, "British Humanitarians," 321.

68. "Letter from Henry H. H. Garnet." 1 October 1850, 226.

69. "Circular from Anna H. Richardson," *Non-Slaveholder*, 1 June 1850, 128, Slavery and Anti-slavery.

70. *Annual Monitor for 1893*, 64, 114. Ellen's obituary notes that "One of her last public efforts was the reprinting and wide circulation of a 'National Peace Anthem' for the use of schools.'" "Ellen Richardson," *Annual Monitor for 1897*, 137–138.

71. Mentia Taylor, "Friendly Addresses to Spanish Ladies," *Anti-Slavery Monthly Reporter*, 15 January 1866, 20, Nineteenth Century U.K. Periodicals.

72. Letter from Anna H. Richardson, Newcastle upon Tyne, England, to Mary Carpenter [1852], September 5, Anti-slavery Collection, Boston Public Library.

73. See De Rosa, *Domestic Abolitionism*; Roy, *Young Abolitionists*.

74. A footnote uses a male pronoun on a single occasion, but beyond that it is difficult to ascribe the tract's authorship with certainty. The note reads, "About three years ago, the writer, having been informed that chains and fetters were made in Birmingham expressly for the slave-trade, gave a commission to a friend to procure him samples of the varieties on sale. These were shortly afterwards received, and the construction of some of them sufficiently bespeaks their purpose—as iron collars for the neck, to one of which a long chain is attached; fetters for the ankles, to admit of walking but not of running; &c., &c." Richardson, *Who Are the Slaveholders?*, 7.

75. "Where is the Christian family that could stand the brunt of such an onset? Mrs. Stowe had swayed their minds as though she played upon a musical instrument. They had laughed and wept, despaired and exulted, melted into tenderness, and burned with indignation, as the narrative proceeded. They had trembled with Eliza in her elopement with her doomed child; laughed at Sam's devices for retarding the pursuit of the fugitives; sympathised with Aunt Chloe when her 'old man' was torn from her, and cried 'shame!' at the brutal Haley as he put the fetters upon Uncle Tom. They had been delighted with Tom's good fortune at New Orleans, and enraptured with Little Eva his guardian angel. They had admired the dashing amiability of St. Clare, while they scouted the heartless selfishness of his wife. They had marvelled at the military tactics of 'friend Phineas,' and rejoiced at the downfall of Tom Loker. They had smiled at the hobgoblinry of Topsy, and shuddered at poor Prue's horrid death. They had wept by the death-bed of the infant evangelist; melted under the heartfelt prayers of Uncle Tom; mourned the cruel fate of St. Clare, and deprecated the avaricious policy of his widow. They had traced poor Tom from the palace to the auction-block; accompanied him to Legree's plantation; execrated the proceedings of that fiend incarnate; thrilled with horror over Cassie's story; agonised with Uncle Tom in his sufferings, and boiled with indignation at his cruel martyrdom. The whole party, from the eldest to the youngest, had hung upon the narrative with intense interest; and it had left upon their hearts a deep and vivid impression of the heinous character of American slavery, suggesting the inquiry so natural to all well-regulated minds, 'Can *we* do anything for its mitigation?'" Ibid., 2–3.

When Stowe and her entourage subsequently toured Britain in 1856, they stayed with members of the extended Richardson family in Edinburgh and then Newcastle. For details, see Richardson, *Memoir*, 97–101. Anna D. Richardson recommends the novel in a letter to a friend dated 28 July 1852.

76. Richardson, *Who Are the Slaveholders?*, 3.

77. See De Rosa, *Domestic Abolitionism*, 79–106.

78. Richardson, *Who Are the Slaveholders?*, 3.

79. Ibid., 7 (emphasis in original). See also Blackett, *Building an Antislavery Wall*, 16, for de-

tails on the way Moses Roper, Henry Garnet, and James Pennington all displayed instruments of torture for sensational effect.

80. The *Guardian* newspaper's six-part Cotton Capital series (28 March–8 May 2023), available in print and as a podcast, explores this further. https://www.theguardian.com/news/series /cotton-capital-podcast.

81. Richardson, *Who Are the Slaveholders?*, 8.

82. For more on the importance of the inter-American realm, see Belton, "A Deep Interest in Your Cause."

83. Ibid., 10.

84. Ibid., 11.

85. See Holcomb, *Moral Commerce,* 116–117.

86. The article is reproduced in Hartman, "Tid-Bits of Northern Kentucky History." All subsequent quotations from "A Short Sketch" (with original emphasis) are also from this source. The article originally appeared in a Kentucky paper, *The Daily and Weekly News,* in 1858. Many of the details about Bailey come from this source. For additional details about him, see Bailey, "To the Friends of Emancipation!"

87. Quoted in Trill, Chedgzoy, and Osborne, *Lay By Your Needles,* 1.

88. See indexed references in Harrold, *Abolitionists and the South.*

89. Quoted in De Rosa, *Domestic Abolitionism,* 112–113.

90. "William S. Bailey," *Anti-Slavery Monthly Reporter,* 1 October 1859, 238, Slavery and Antislavery.

91. William Shreve Bailey to Anna H. Richardson, 19 November 1859, in Richardson, *Anti-slavery Memoranda.*

92. "Monthly Summary," *Anti-Slavery Monthly Reporter,* 1 March 1861, 49, Nineteenth Century U.K. Periodicals.

93. "William Shreve Bailey," *Anti-Slavery Monthly Reporter,* 1 May 1861, 112, Nineteenth Century U.K. Periodicals.

94. Bailey and Chamerovzow, "Letter from W. S. Bailey of Kentucky," 227.

95. Richardson, *Little Laura,* 4–5.

96. Ibid., 1. Clare Midgley notes that Henry Richardson's poor health meant that Anna had to reduce her work on free produce, and Elihu Burritt became editor of *The Slave* in place of Henry. Midgley, *Women against Slavery,* 139.

97. Ibid., 2–3.

98. Ibid., 2, 9–10, 12.

99. De Rosa, *Domestic Abolitionism,* 114, 134. She notes that the girl protagonists of these texts developed the model offered by the fictional Little Eva, calling them "heroic, nonconformists who use their voices for political activism that liberates the slaves and themselves."

100. Burritt, *Olive Leaflets.*

101. Quoted in De Rosa, *Domestic Abolitionism,* 109–110.

102. Richardson, *Anti-slavery Memoranda,* 2.

103. Richardson, *Little Laura,* 4.

104. Burritt capitalized on this move, publishing in 1846 a collection of short reflections, tales, and other prose pieces titled *Sparks from the Anvil.*

105. Advertisement, *Anti-Slavery Monthly Reporter*, 1 April 1857, 96, Nineteenth Century U.K. Periodicals. Wilson Armistead invited "Orders for the above, or Donations towards their gratuitous circulation."

3. THE QUIET ABOLITIONIST

1. Stoler, *Along the Archival Grain*, 1.

2. Gikandi, "Rethinking the Archive of Enslavement," 93.

3. Gardner, "Accessing Early Black Print," 29.

4. Rediker, *The Fearless Benjamin Lay*, 2. See also Rice, *Creating Memorials, Building Identities*.

5. Lois Brown urges us to use multiple sources when writing Black historiography, "published materials" and "public materials," including "newspapers, city directories, maps, shops and stock inventories, census reports, wills, and legal documents." Brown, "Death-Defying Testimony," 132.

6. Huzzey, *Freedom Burning*, 219. See also indexed entries on Armistead in Rice, *Scots Abolitionists* (1981).

7. Shepperson, "Abolitionism and African Political Thought," 24.

8. Armistead, *Memoirs of James Logan*, v.

9. Burritt, *Sparks from the Anvil*, x–xi.

10. Armistead, *Anthony Benezet*, 138–139.

11. *Catalogue of the Books, Belonging to the Friends of Leeds Particular Meeting* (emphasis in the original).

12. See Taylor and Loeb, "Librarian Is My Occupation."

13. Hodges, *David Ruggles*, 135.

14. Hochman, "Investing in Literature."

15. Karcher, *First Woman of the Republic*, 221.

16. Pfaelzer, "Hanging Out."

17. Newman, *Freedom Seekers*, 217.

18. For more on scrapbooks, see Ellen Gruber Garvey's fine book, *Writing with Scissors*.

19. "Joseph Barker, of Ohio, (Late of Wortley, near Leeds,) Having in Several Public Lectures Stated That 'The Last Edition of The,'" *Friend* 13, no. 147 (March 1855): 56, Gale Primary Sources, Nineteenth Century Collections Online.

20. "Local and Other News," *Leeds Intelligencer*, 20 January 1866, 5; "The Harpers Ferry Insurrection," *Leeds Mercury*, 29 November 1859, both in British Library Newspapers. Armistead wrote many other letters too. See, for instance, "Letter from Wilson Armistead," *National Anti-slavery Standard*, 1 June 1861, Slavery and Anti-slavery.

21. "Lectures on American Slavery," 10 December 1853, 2.; "Leeds Anti-slavery Association," 22 May 1858, 9; and "Anti-slavery Soiree in the Leeds Town Hall," 1 January 1859, 6, all from *Leeds Intelligencer*, in British Library Newspapers.

22. "Mrs. Stowe in Leeds," *Anti-slavery Bugle*, 15 October 1853, Slavery and Anti-slavery.

23. Midgley, *Churches and the Working Classes*, 120–121. This was a decade after the passing of the Toleration Act of 1689, which allowed Nonconformists freedom of worship. For the figures from the 1851 census, see "Census of 1851," *British Friend*, July 1851, 165–166.

24. This would be a central element of the rest of his short life; his abolitionist activities would be commented on in *The Liberator* throughout the 1850s. See, for instance, "Twentieth National Anti-slavery Bazaar," *Liberator,* 20 January 1854, 2; "Prof. Allen in Leeds, England," *Liberator,* 5 May 1854, 1; "The Twenty-First National Anti-slavery Bazaar," *Liberator,* 26 January 1855, 1. A detailed bibliography of Armistead's writing is reproduced in Joseph Smith's *A Descriptive Catalogue of Friends' Books* (1867). Smith credits Armistead for helping him with his work, and in the section describing Armistead's own publications there are several explanatory notes by Armistead himself.

25. Hall, *A Flora of Liverpool,* 153, 185.

26. Armistead, "Meteorological Observations," *British Friend,* 31 January 1845, 8, Gale Primary Sources, Nineteenth Century Collections Online.

27. Armistead, *Tribute,* xxxiii.

28. Ibid., 74.

29. Ibid., xiv. The letter to Thompson requesting Grégoire's work relegates this to a postscript. The body of his short letter focuses on Phillis Wheatley Peters. He writes, "Hast thou a memoir of poems of Phillis Wheatley an African female which I believe also contains a portrait. If so I should like to borrow it & would inform thee how to send it.—If not can thou tell me where I should be likely to meet with a copy." Wilson Armistead to Thomas Thompson, 1 April 1847, Gibson v.211, Library of the Society of Friends, London.

30. "Negroes Are Men!," *Liberator,* 20 April 1849, 62, Slavery and Anti-slavery.

31. "Multiple News Items," *Pennsylvania Freeman,* 11 May 1848, 155, Slavery and Anti-slavery.

32. Cushing, *Initials and Pseudonyms,* 288.

33. Allot, "Wilson Armistead, 1819–1869," 162.

34. Smith, *Descriptive Catalogue,* 128.

35. Tuvar, *Tales and Legends,* 8–9. He returns to the poem in a tale titled "Emma and Sir Eglamore. A Legend of Ullswater," and also discusses Wordsworth and Coleridge in "The Beauty of Buttermore; or, Tragedy in Real Life."

36. Ibid., 197.

37. Gurney, "Conversation on Geology," 181–189.

38. Massey, *For Space,* 137 (emphasis in original).

39. Tuvar, *Tales and Legends,* 259–260.

40. Steel, *Historical Sketch,* 171.

41. "A Friend of the Negro," *Garland of Freedom,* 55. The poem positioned immediately after Bragg's is simply attributed to "Mary," which might signify it was written by his wife, Mary (Bragg) Armistead. Armistead also included several stanzas of a poem Jane Bragg wrote in 1834, celebrating the Slavery Abolition Act in *A "Cloud of Witnesses,"* 115.

42. Armistead, *Five Hundred Thousand Strokes for Freedom,* 4.

43. Ibid., 5. In 1859, he described Anthony Benezet as a "humble, active and practical a Christian." Armistead, *Anthony Benezet,* vi.

44. See Bennett, "Transatlantic Abolition and the Unquiet Library."

45. Asher, *Incidents in the Life of the Rev. J. Asher,* 2.

46. Armistead, "Statue of William Penn," *British Friend,* 1 July 1865, 179, Gale Primary Sources, Nineteenth Century Collections Online.

47. Armistead, *Piloted*, 5.

48. Armistead, *Memoirs of James Logan*, 188. He used Water Hall as a distribution center for anti-slavery texts. He also assiduously drew attention to other sources. A notice at the end of *A "Cloud of Witnesses"* states, "The London Publishers of the Leeds Anti-slavery Tracts are W. and F. G. Cash, 5, Bishopsgate Street; and WILLIAM TWEEDIE, 337, Strand—from whom they may be obtained through application to any country Booksellers, also from JANE JOWETT, Friends' Meeting Yard, Leeds."

49. "Anti-slavery Prize Essay," *Liberator*, 21 July 1854, 114, Slavery and Anti-slavery. The announcement of the prize was made elsewhere—for instance in the *North Star* on 16 June 1854. Its progress was reported subsequently. See, for instance, Wilson and Lupton, "American Slavery."

50. "Selections," *Liberator*, 7 October 1859, Slavery and Anti-slavery. Details of the Leeds Anti-Slavery Society had been circulated in an article two years earlier, in which Armistead was described as its president. "British Abolitionist Movements," *Anti-Slavery Monthly Reporter*, 1 June 1857, 132, Nineteenth Century U.K. Periodicals.

51. Editorial, *Leeds Intelligencer*, 10 February 1866, 5, British Library Newspapers.

52. "'Guilty or Not Guilty?' A Few Facts and Feelings Regarding the Religious Bodies of America in the Matter of Slavery," 1855, John Rylands University Library, University of Manchester; and National Freedmen's-Aid Union of Great Britain and Ireland, *The Freedmen's-Aid Reporter* (London: F. Bowyer Kitto, [1867?]), both in Slavery and Anti-slavery.

53. Nicholls, "Richard Cobden and the International Peace Movement," 354. The 1851 (London) Congress was extensively covered in the August 1851 edition of the *British Friend*.

54. Women (and sometimes male supporters) protested at a piece of recordkeeping that acknowledged their obligations as wives and the mothers of children without according them the privileges of citizenship. Other examples of this kind of guerrilla inscription include Dorothea Rock's assertion that "I, Dorothea Rock, in the absence of the male occupier, refuse to fill up this Census paper as, in the eyes of the Law, women do not count, neither shall they be counted." Liddington and Crawford, "Women do not count, neither shall they be counted," 106, 108, 111–112.

55. Blackett, "Fugitive Slaves in Britain," 42.

56. England and Wales Census, 1851. Brown was staying in the household of Elizabeth and Philipp Clark. Also on the property that night were other family members, a number of servants, and eight other lodgers. Two lodgers were from Ireland, one from Scotland, and the others, with the exception of Brown and a Danish lodger, were from England.

57. Key texts include Woo, *Master Slave Husband Wife*; Blackett, "Fugitive Slaves in Britain"; McCaskill, "The Profits and Perils of Partnership"; McCaskill, *Love, Liberation, and Escaping Slavery*; Salenius, "Transatlantic Interracial Sisterhoods."

58. Craft, *Running a Thousand Miles for Freedom*, 2.

59. "Singular Escape of Two Slaves from Georgia," *Newcastle Guardian and Tyne Mercury* 161 (10 March 1849), British Library Newspapers. The letter was written in Philadelphia and dated 30 December 1848. Similar pieces were published in the *Newcastle Courant* on 30 March 1849 and the *Hull Packet and East Riding Times*, 6 April 1849.

60. Armistead, "Reminiscences," November 1850, 261. The *Hibernia*'s sister ship, the *Cambria*, had carried Frederick Douglass west to east across the Atlantic five years earlier and would carry Ellen and William Craft in December 1850.

61. He discussed Dickens's meeting with Laura Bridgman of the Perkins Institute when he made his own visit there. Ibid., March 1852, 57.

62. William Cooper Nell to Amy Post, 15 July 1850, Rare Books, Special Collections, and Preservation, River Campus Libraries, University of Rochester.

63. Armistead, "Reminiscences," March 1852, 57–58.

64. Ibid., April 1851, 94. He had letters of introduction for the three.

65. Armistead, "Concluding Chapter of Additional Evidence," 133–162.

66. Davis and Bilder, "Library of Robert Morris," 22.

67. Armistead, *Tribute*, 140–141. Armistead went on to quote a poem by Vashon in *Autographs for Freedom*.

68. Armistead, *Tribute*, 95–96. For evidence, see the difference between the 1846 and 1849 editions of Adams's *New Directory of the City of Boston*. The later edition is integrated.

69. Ibid., 96.

70. The evidence these schedules gave about the lives of enslaved African Americans would be used by abolitionists. See Clarke, *Present Condition of the Coloured People of the United States*. It is not clear whether Armistead knew that slave schedules existed.

71. Carby, *Imperial Intimacies*, 260–261.

72. U.S. National Archives and Records Administration, "1850 Census Records," series M432, roll 336, Massachusetts: City of Boston.

73. For more on the consequences of the law and the experience of this volatile period, see Blackett, *Captive's Quest for Freedom*, 42–87.

74. "William and Ellen Crafts [*sic*] the Fugitive Slaves from Boston," *Liverpool Mercury*, January 1851, British Library Newspapers.

75. Collison, *Shadrach Minkins*, 84–85, 130–133, 193–196. Armistead writes of his visit to the Perkins Institute and Asylum for the Blind and his meeting with its director, Grindley Howe, in "Reminiscences," February 1852, 30–32.

76. See indexed references in von Frank, *Trials of Anthony Burns*.

77. "Advertisements & Notices," *Aberdeen Journal*, 12 February 1851. Further details of their appearance locally are given in elsewhere. See, for instance, "Local Intelligence," *Aberdeen Journal*, 12 February 1851; "American Slavery," *Dundee Courier*, 29 January 1851. All in British Library Newspapers.

78. For more on this, see Foreman, "Who's Your Mama?"; Millette, "Exchanging Fugitive Identity."

79. For more on this, see Morgan, "Celebrity Boundaries," 163.

80. See "Afro-alienation Acts," in Brooks, *Bodies in Dissent*, 3–6.

81. "Anti-slavery Meeting in Newcastle," *Newcastle Guardian and Tyne Mercury*, 15 March 1851, British Library Newspapers.

82. "Public Meeting in York, on the Question of American Slavery," *Yorkshire Gazette*, 29 March 1851, British Library Newspapers.

83. *British Friend*, May 1851, 106 (emphasis in original).

84. "Remarkable Return in the Census—Disgrace to America," *Hereford Journal*, 30 April 1851; "Remarkable Return in the Census—Disgrace to America," *Cheltenham Chronicle*, 1 May 1851;

"American Slavery," *Bristol Mercury and West Counties Advertiser,* 30 August 1851. See also "Fugitive Slaves," *Bristol Mercury,* 12 April 1851. All in British Library Newspapers. On the Crafts' work in the West Country, see Blackett, "Fugitive Slaves," 48–49.

85. "He must be a person of intelligence and activity; he must read and write well, and have some knowledge of arithmetic; he must not be infirm or of such weak health as may render him unable to undergo the requisite exertion; he should not be younger than 18 years of age or older than 65; he must be temperate, orderly and respectable, and be such a person as is likely to conduct himself with strict propriety, and to deserve the goodwill of the inhabitants of his district." Higgs, *Making Sense of the Census Revisited,* 16–17. Much of the following information is taken from Higgs's book.

86. Cheshire, *The Results of the Census of Great Britain in 1851,* 12.

87. Higgs, *Making Sense of the Census Revisited,* 18.

88. Liddington and Crawford, "Women do not count, neither shall they be counted," 117.

89. *Poll Book of the Leeds Borough Election of 1847,* 3, 5; *Poll Book of the Leeds Borough Election, July, 1841.*

90. See Fraser, "Areas of Urban Politics," 763–788, and "Politics and Society in the Nineteenth Century," 270–300.

91. "Births, Deaths, Marriages and Obituaries," *Leeds Mercury,* 2 February 1856, British Library Newspapers.

92. "Election of Clerk to the Guardians, Last Night," *Leeds Mercury,* 14 February 1856, British Library Newspapers.

93. "Death of Mr. Wilson Armistead, of Leeds," *Leeds Mercury,* 20 February 1868, British Library Newspapers.

4. MOBILE MORAVIANS AND BRITISH ANTISLAVERY

1. See McCorkle, "John Antes"; Stolba, "Evidence for Quartets by John Antes."

2. Vogt, "Everywhere at Home."

3. These include Atwood, *Community of the Cross;* Faull, *Moravian Women's Memoirs* and "Self-Encounters"; Sensbach, *A Separate Canaan* and *Rebecca's Revival.*

4. Hartman, "Venus in Two Acts," 3. Brockden's Lebenslauf is reproduced in Faull, *Moravian Women's Memoirs,* 77–78. See also Catron, "Early Black-Atlantic Christianity"; Moglen, "Enslaved City on a Hill."

5. Jones, *Jubilee Memorial,* 17.

6. For more on the Religious Tract Society, see Fyfe, "A Short History of the Religious Tract Society," 13–35.

7. In 1747, five Greenlanders visited Europe and were painted by Johann Valentin Haidt. After two of the group died in Herrnhut, in what today is Germany, the three surviving visitors went to Fetter Lane in London before returning to Greenland. In 1771, Jens Haven, the founder of the Labrador Mission, visited Fetter Lane with his Inuit wife and children, where they attended a love feast, a simple ritual meal, wearing traditional dress. Podmore, *Fetter Lane Moravian,* 12–13. See also Harbsmeier, "Bodies and Voices."

8. For more on Osman Bey, see indexed reference in Engel, "Ottoman Egypt."

9. Antes, *Confidence in God,* 11–12.

10. Baepler, *White Slaves*, 24–31.

11. Of particular relevance here is the work of Wood, *Blind Memory*.

12. "Issue of Half a Million Anti-slavery Tracts," *British Friend*, 1 November 1853, 3, Nineteenth Century Collections Online.

13. Williams, *Liberty's Captives*, 276. The narrative is reproduced on 270–284.

14. Antes, *Extract*, 3.

15. Hamlin, *Benjamin Henry Latrobe*, 7. See the fine account of this congregation in Jon F. Sensbach, *A Separate Canaan*.

16. Antes, *Extract*, 4.

17. He wrote, "In answer to my prayer, the Lord appeared with healing and comfort to my soul. His love was shed abroad in my heart, and I found, that, by His strength made perfect in my weakness, I could resist and overcome, in the hour of temptation; insomuch that, sinful as I felt myself to be, sin had no longer any dominion over me." Antes, *Extract*, 5.

18. For what Moravian archives can add to this well-known moment of violence in early America, see Gordon, "The Paxton Boys and the Moravians."

19. For details, see Choules and Smith, *Origin and History of Missions*.

20. Antes, *Observations*, 68. In a footnote describing an observation made by the French historian Constantin-François de Chasseboeuf, comte de Volney, he challenges Volney's estimation of when the events he described took place, writing that he "kept a regular diary of all such occurrences, during the twelve years of my stay in that country" (92). Benjamin Henry Latrobe similarly lost a large part of his substantial library, making it difficult to piece together details of his early architectural development in its crucial formative period in England before he emigrated permanently to the United States.

21. Stolba, "Evidence," 572.

22. Ibid., 566, 572.

23. Thorp, "Chattel with a Soul."

24. Evidence suggests that he could speak Italian, though not Arabic, before he went to Egypt. See Antes, *Extract*, 8, 10. Antes's nephew Benjamin Henry Latrobe was educated in England and Germany, where he studied modern languages—German, French, and Italian—as well as mathematics, botany, music, Hebrew, and ancient Greek. As part of the church's encouragement of practical skills, Latrobe pursued studies in draftsmanship and drawing, and when he turned his back on the church in his late teens, he was able to develop this skill further, becoming one of the most significant architects in the early United States after his emigration in 1796.

25. Stolba, "Evidence," 572.

26. See Erben, *Harmony of the Spirits*, 14, n.12. See also Wiggin, *Babel of the Atlantic*, 14–18.

27. Even in such a perilous situation, he tried to draw on established hospitality protocols that might have offered him some protection. He recounted, "When I came near him I addressed him with the usual phrase, 'I am under your protection'; to which, if they are not maliciously inclined, they answer, 'You are welcome.' But, instead of answering at all, he stared furiously at me, and said, 'Who are you?' I replied; 'I am an Englishman.'" *Confidence in God*, 9–10.

28. Antes, *Observations*, 3.

29. Ibid., 4.

30. Ibid., 9–10.

31. Several sources suggest that Latrobe had undertaken what was evidently a difficult and time-consuming job, in which he had to take dictation from Bruce for long hours with very little rest. He worked for him from May 1788 to June 1789. For instance, Latrobe called his work "a very tedious and disagreeable task . . . I had once or twice the misfortune to offend him in endeavouring to expunge a few grammatical errors." Moorehead, *Blue Nile*, 46–48. See also Hulton, Hepper, and Friis, *Luigi Balugani's Drawings*, 38; Friis, "Traveling among Fellow Christians," 170. It is clear from Antes's work that he had read Bruce as well as other Western writers on Egypt and that he often disagreed with their comments.

32. Antes, *Observations*, 17.

33. They "must, therefore, address themselves to an European to be their interpreter, or hire a Greek or an Armenian for that purpose. These latter are, upon the whole, not sensible of the importance of giving always a correct and satisfactory answer: they are, perhaps, at the same time, as well as many of the Europeans, ignorant where to apply for proper information." Ibid., 11.

34. Ibid., 23.

35. On the significance of the act, see Podmore, *Moravian Church in England*, 228–265.

36. For more detail, see Podmore, *Moravian Church in England*, 230–237.

37. Holland and Everett, *Memoirs*, 19.

38. Moravian Church, Fulneck Congregation, *Brotherly Agreement and Declaration*, 19.

39. Equiano, *Interesting Narrative*, xviii–xix.

40. On the establishment of an English identity, see in particular Young, *Idea of English Ethnicity*, 1–10.

41. Regier, *Exorbitant Enlightenment*, 163.

42. Donald McCorkle, quoted in ibid., 154. See Patrick Erben's discussion of the Delaware hymnal in Erben, *Harmony of the Spirits*, 312–314.

43. Podmore, *Moravian Church in England*, 124.

44. On the Fetter Lane Society, see Beachy, "Manuscript Missions," 38. See also Wakefield, "Olaudah Equiano's Ecclesiastical World."

45. Holland and Everett, *Memoirs*, 56.

46. This has given rise to considerable critical debate. See, for instance, Beachy, "Manuscript Missions," 44; Fogleman, *Jesus Is Female*; Podmore, *Moravian Church in England*, 132–136; Regier, *Exorbitant Enlightenment*, 154–156. Fogleman's claims have been challenged by some other scholars, notably by Atwood, "Little Side Holes," 61–75. Also see the discussion in Atwood, *Community of the Cross*, 11–19.

47. Writing of his activities in Bristol in August 1756, Brother Andrew Parminter notes, "To the Society I read some Diaspora Accounts." Dresser, "Moravians in Bristol," 115.

48. See Jensz, "Overcoming Objections to Print," 13–14; Beachy, "Manuscript Missions," 33–49.

49. This has now been well established. See, for instance, Mason, *Moravian Church*, especially chapters 1 and 2; Sensbach, *Rebecca's Revival*, 235–237; Ahlbäck, "Overly Candid Missionary Historian," 192. On the systematic and ruthless way the Unity Archives were revised and controlled in the post-Zinzendorf period, see Peucker, "Selection and Destruction"; Atwood, "Apologizing for the Moravians."

50. Gerbner, *Christian Slavery*, 147. For her full discussion of the start of the mission and its aftermath, see 146–163. Defining Christian slavery, she writes, "At the most basic level, it was an

attempt to Christianize and reform slavery. Protestant theologians and missionaries drew on biblical descriptions of slavery as well as the ideal of the godly household to encourage slave owners to assume responsibility for the spiritual lives of their enslaved laborers. They also noted that Christian slavery had a long and well-established history in Europe and the Catholic American colonies. As missionaries faced opposition from slave owners, however, the meaning of 'Christian slavery' shifted. Missionaries increasingly emphasized the beneficial aspects of slave conversion, arguing that Christian slaves would be more docile and harder working than their 'heathen' counterparts. They also sought to pass legislation that confirmed the legality of owning enslaved Christians. Over time, they integrated race into their arguments for Christian slavery. Since the ideology of Protestant Supremacy used religion to differentiate between slavery and freedom, missionaries suggested that race, rather than religion, was the defining feature of bondage" (3). See also Sensbach, *Rebecca's Revival*, 49. Holmes and others also discuss the meeting between Ulrich and the Moravians.

51. Sensbach, *Rebecca's Revival*, 234–247, and 244.

52. Sensbach, "Slavery, Race, and the Global Fellowship," 234.

53. Armistead, *Tribute*, 437.

54. This remains titled, by an earlier archivist, "Catalogue of Real Estate 1758–1797 (inclusively slaves)."

55. Moglen, "Enslaved City on a Hill," 162.

56. Ahlbäck, "Overly Candid Missionary Historian," 191–192.

57. Sensbach, *Rebecca's Revival*, 237. Ahlbäck argues that this is true of Brossart's work but not of Oldendorp's original.

58. Gerbner, *Christian Slavery*, 179–180.

59. Ahlbäck, "Overly Candid Missionary Historian," 195.

60. Armistead, *A "Cloud of Witnesses,"* 33.

61. Copley, *History of Slavery*, 191. She omits the date though.

62. Ibid., 247; Armistead, *A "Cloud of Witnesses,"* 53.

63. Jones, *Jubilee Memorial*, 98. See page 95 for details of his work on the tracts on Antes.

64. Holland and Everett, *Memoirs*, 33. For a full description, see 31–33.

65. Mortimer, *Marrying by Lot*, ix.

66. Holland and Everett, *Memoirs*, 26.

67. Ibid., 123.

68. Ibid., 128 (emphasis in original).

69. Montgomery, *Poetical Works*, 3.

70. Boyce, *Records of a Quaker Family*, 31; Holland and Everett, *Memoirs*, 165–173, 198–201, 215–216, 267–281.

71. John Parrish, Joseph Moore, Jacob Lindley, William Savery, William Hartshorne, and John Elliot to David Zeisberger and Moravian Indians settled on the River La French, 26 June 1793, Autograph Book no. 6.30, Moravian Archives, Bethlehem, Pennsylvania.

72. Armistead, *Anthony Benezet*, 85. It seems unlikely that Armistead knew and suppressed that information, since he had long expressed religious tolerance, writing in his preface to the *Tribute*, "It may be observed, that in making the Biographical selection for this work, the author has been governed by no sectarian prejudice. With due regard to the primary object in view, he has embraced, in support of the proposition maintained, all classes, irrespective of their particular religious tenets."

Armistead, *Tribute*, xv. On Benezet's relationship with the Moravians, see Jackson, "How the Quakers Worked," and *Let This Voice Be Heard*, 8–9.

73. Armistead, *Tribute*, xv.

74. Ackroyd, *Blake*, 85–86. On the connections between a number of these dissenters, see Hay, *Dinner with Joseph Johnson*; Uglow, *Lunar Men*.

75. Hay, *Dinner with Joseph Johnson*, 284–285.

76. Ibid., 283.

77. Cutter, *Illustrated Slave*, 141–152, at 141.

78. Gould, "Early Black Atlantic Writing," 107–122.

79. See Davies and Schuchard, "Recovering the Lost Moravian History of William Blake's Family." In a discussion of the complexity of Moravian attitudes to dissent, Davies opines, "Not only is E. P. Thompson's Muggletonian hypothesis now seem [*sic*] to be entirely mistaken, but the Moravian discoveries go much deeper, challenging the accepted understanding of Blake's relation to dissent." Davies, "Lost Moravian History," 1314.

80. Davies, "Lost Moravian History," 1315. For more on Blake's relationship to the Moravians, see Schuchard, "Young William Blake"; Regier, *Exorbitant Enlightenment*.

81. Mason, *Moravian Church and the Missionary Awakening*, 120–121.

82. Quoted in Davies, "Jonathan Spilsbury," 106. His invitation is addressed to a Brother Montgomery, and though this person's identity remains uncertain, he might have been the brother of James Montgomery.

83. Cronshagen, "Loyal Heart to God and Governor," 4, 11, 17–18, 23; and "We Do Not Need Any Slaves."

84. Hoermann, "A Very Hell of Horrors?," 187–188. See also Cutter, *Illustrated Slave*, 32–47; Wood, *Blind Memory*, 230–239.

85. Ibid., 234.

86. Prince, *History of Mary Prince*, 65–66.

87. Hartman, *Scenes of Subjection*, 3.

88. Sweeney and Baker, "I am not a beggar."

89. Cutter, *Illustrated Slave*, 115–134.

90. Prince, *History of Mary Prince*, 79.

91. Sensbach, *Rebecca's Revival*, 242.

92. Prince, *History of Mary Prince*, 83–84.

93. Ibid., 89

94. Ibid., 91.

95. Strickland became Susanna Moodie after she married and emigrated to Canada and focused her writing on Canadian topics.

96. For full details about this, see Thomas, "New Information on Mary Prince in London."

97. Prince, *History of Mary Prince*, 1.

98. Susanna Moodie to James Montgomery, 1 May 1831, in Bird, "Susanna Moodie's Last Letter about Mary Prince," 287.

BIBLIOGRAPHY

⬤⬤➤➤➤➤➤➤➤➤➤➤➤➤➤

MANUSCRIPTS AND ARCHIVAL COLLECTIONS

Boston Public Library, Anti-Slavery Collection.
Harvard College Library, Houghton Library, Letters to Henry Wadsworth Longfellow, 1761–1904, Longfellow, Henry Wadsworth, 1807–1882, recipient.
Haverford College, Rhoads Family Papers, 1822–1955.
Haverford College, Taylor Family Papers, 1755–1930.
Historical Society of Pennsylvania, Blackburne and Sharp Families Papers.
Library of the Society of Friends, London.
Moravian Archives, Bethlehem, Pennsylvania.
West Yorkshire Archives, Sharp Family, records including Correspondence and Description of Emigration Journey to America of Joseph Sharp.
West Yorkshire Archives, Ackworth School Records.

ONLINE SOURCES

American Historical Periodicals from the American Antiquarian Society, Gale Primary Sources, https://www.gale.com/intl/primary-sources/american-historical-periodicals.
British Library Newspapers, Gale Primary Sources, https://www.gale.com/intl/primary-sources/british-library-newspapers.
Leodis by Leeds Libraries, photographic archive, https://www.leodis.net.
Nineteenth Century Collections Online, Gale Primary Sources, https://www.gale.com/intl/primary-sources/nineteenth-century-collections-online.
Nineteenth Century U.K. Periodicals, Gale Primary Sources, https://www.gale.com/intl/primary-sources/19th-century-uk-periodicals.

Slavery and Anti-slavery: A Transnational Archive, Gale Primary Sources, https://www .gale.com/intl/primary-sources/slavery-and-anti-slavery.

BOOKS AND ARTICLES

A Catalogue of the Books, Belonging to the Friends of Leeds Particular Meeting. Leeds: J. Binns, 1794.

Ackroyd, Peter. *Blake.* London: Minerva, 1995.

An Address to the Members of the Religious Society of Friends, on the Propriety of Abstaining from the Use of the Produce of Slave Labour. Philadelphia: Merrihew and Gunn, 1838.

Ahlbäck, Anders. "The Overly Candid Missionary Historian: C. G. A. Oldendorp's Theological Ambivalence over Slavery in the Danish West Indies." In *Ports of Globalisation, Places of Creolisation: Nordic Possessions in the Atlantic World during the Era of the Slave Trade,* edited by Holger Weiss, 191–217. Leiden: Brill, 2016.

Allot, Wilfred. "Wilson Armistead, 1819–1869." *Journal of the Friends' Historical Society* 50 (Summer 1963): 158–163.

Almeida, Jocelyn M. *Reimagining the Transatlantic, 1780–1890.* Farnham: Ashgate, 2011.

Anecdotes in the Life of John Antes, Giving an Account of His Residence in Egypt, and His Sufferings from the Inhumanity of Osman Bey. London: Religious Tract Society, n.d.

The Annual Monitor for 1893. London: Edward Hicks, 1892.

The Annual Monitor for 1897. London: Hedley Bros., 1896.

Antes, John. *Extract of the Narrative of the Life of our Late, Dear and Venerable Brother, John Antes, Written by Himself.* London: W. M'Dowall, 1811.

———. *Observations of the Manners and Customs of the Egyptians.* London: John Stockdale, 1800.

Armistead, Wilson. *Anthony Benezet.* London: A. W. Bennett, 1859.

———. *A "Cloud of Witnesses" against Slavery and Oppression.* London: William Tweedie, 1853.

———. "Concluding Chapter of Additional Evidence." In *God's Image in Ebony: Being a Series of Biographical Sketches, Facts, Anecdotes, etc., Demonstrative of the Mental Powers and Intellectual Capacities of the Negro Race,* edited by H. G. Adams, 33–162. London: Partridge and Oakey, 1854.

———, ed. *Five Hundred Thousand Strokes for Freedom: A Series of Anti-slavery Tracts, of which Half a Million Are Now First Issued by the Friends of the Negro.* London: W and F. Cash, 1853.

———. *Memoirs of James Logan; a Distinguished Scholar and Christian Litigator.* London: Charles Gilpin, 1851.

———. "Meteorological Observations." *British Friend,* 31 January 1845, 8.

————. "Reminiscences of a Visit to the United States, in the Summer of 1850." *British Friend*, November 1850 and passim.

————. *Select Miscellanies, Chiefly Illustrative of the History, Christian Principles, and Sufferings, of the Society of Friends*. London: Charles Gilpin, 1851.

————. "Statue of William Penn." *British Friend*, 1 July 1865, 179.

————. *A Tribute for the Negro: Being a Vindication of the Moral, Intellectual, and Religious Capabilities of the Coloured Portion of Mankind; with Particular Reference to the African Race*. Manchester: William Irwin, 1848.

Armistead, J. J. *Piloted; Being a Series of Notes and Experiences from the Author's Life*. London: Headley Bros., 1906.

Asher, J. *Incidents in the Life of the Rev. J. Asher, Pastor of Shiloh (Coloured) Baptist Church, Philadelphia, U.S.* London: Charles Gilpin, 1850.

Atwood, Craig D. "Apologizing for the Moravians: Spangenberg's *Idea Fidei Fratrum*." *Journal of Moravian History* 8 (Spring 2010): 53–88.

————. *Community of the Cross: Moravian Piety in Colonial Bethlehem*. University Park: Pennsylvania State University Press, 2004.

————. "Little Side Holes: Moravian Devotional Cards of the Mid-eighteenth Century." *Journal of Moravian History* 6 (Spring 2009): 61–75.

Augst, Thomas, and Kenneth Carpenter, eds. *Institutions of Reading: The Social Life of Libraries in the United States*. Amherst: University of Massachusetts Press, 2007.

Augst, Thomas, and Wayne A. Wiegand, eds. "The Library as an Agency of Culture." *American Studies* 42, no. 3 (2001).

Babbage, Charles. *The Ninth Bridgewater Treatise*. London: John Murray, 1838.

Baepler, Paul, ed. *White Slaves, African Masters: An Anthology of American Barbary Captivity Narratives*. Chicago: University of Chicago Press, 1999.

Bailey, William Shreve. "To the Friends of Emancipation!: The Re-establishment of 'The Free South' Newspaper in Kentucky." Newport, KY, 1858.

Bailey, Wm. Shreve, and L. A. Chamerovzow. "Letter from W. S. Bailey of Kentucky." *Anti-Slavery Monthly Reporter; Under the Sanction of the British and Foreign Anti-Slavery Society*, 2 December 1861.

Baker, Jean H. *Building America: The Life of Benjamin Henry Latrobe*. New York: Oxford University Press, 2020.

Barbauld, Anna Letitia. *Epistle to William Wilberforce, Esq. on the Rejection of the Bill for Abolishing the Slave Trade*. London: J. Johnson, 1791.

————. *Hymns in Prose for Children*. London: J. Johnson, 1781.

Barber, James Henry, ed. *A Narrative of the Proceedings at the Celebration of the Centenary of Ackworth School, 26th and 27th of Sixth Month, 1879*. London: Samuel Harris, 1879.

Barnes, Kelli Racine. "Schoolgirl Embroideries and Black Girlhood in Antebellum Philadelphia." *Journal of Textile Design Research and Practice* 9, no. 3 (2021): 298–320.

Beachy, Robert. "Manuscript Missions in the Age of Print: Moravians Community in the Atlantic World." In *Pious Pursuits: German Moravians in the Atlantic World,* edited by Michele Gillespie and Robert Beachy, 33–49. New York: Berghahn Books 2007.

Belton, Lloyd. "A Deep Interest in Your Cause": The Inter-American Sphere of Black Abolitionism and Civil Rights." *Slavery & Abolition* 42, no. 3 (2021): 589–609.

Bennett, Bridget. "England/New England: A Quaker and a Fugitive from Slavery Encounter Each Other on a Train, 1850." In *Crossings in Nineteenth-Century American Culture: Junctures of Times, Space, Self and Politics,* edited by Edward Sugden, 158–173. Edinburgh: Edinburgh University Press, 2022.

———. "Transatlantic Abolition and the Unquiet Library: Print Culture and the Making of a "Celebrated Philanthropist." In *American Philanthropy at Home and Abroad: New Directions in the History of Giving,* edited by Ben Offiler and Rachel Williams, 67–85. London: Bloomsbury Academic, 2023.

Bernier, Celeste-Marie. *Characters of Blood: Black Heroism in the Transatlantic Imagination.* Charlottesville: University of Virginia Press, 2012.

Biddle, Owen. *A Plan for a School or an Establishment Similar to that at Ackworth in Yorkshire Great Britain.* Philadelphia: Joseph Crukshank, 1790.

Billington, Louis. "British Humanitarians and American Cotton, 1840–1860." *Journal of American Studies* 11, no. 3 (1977): 313–334.

Bird, Eleanor Lucy. "Susanna Moodie's Last Letter about Mary Prince." *Notes and Queries* 66, no. 2 (2019): 285–289.

Blackett, R. J. M. *Building an Antislavery Wall: Black Americans in the Atlantic Abolitionist Movement, 1830–1860.* Baton Rouge: Louisiana State University Press, 1983.

———. *The Captive's Quest for Freedom: Fugitive Slaves, the 1850 Fugitive Slave Law, and the Politics of Slavery.* New York: Cambridge University Press, 2018.

———. "Fugitive Slaves in Britain: The Odyssey of William and Ellen Craft." *Journal of American Studies* 12, no. 1 (1978): 41–62.

———. *Making Freedom: The Underground Railroad and the Politics of Freedom.* Chapel Hill: University of North Carolina Press, 2013.

Bly, Antonio T. "Indubitable Signs": Reading Silence as *Text* in New England Runaway Slave Advertisements." *Slavery & Abolition* 42, no. 2 (2021): 240–268.

The Boston Directory: Adams's Boston Directory. Boston: George Adams, 1848–1849.

Boyce, Anne Ogden. *Records of a Quaker Family: The Richardsons of Cleveland.* London: Samuel Harris, 1889.

Brooks, Daphne A. *Bodies in Dissent: Spectacular Performances of Race and Freedom, 1850–1910.* Durham, NC: Duke University Press, 2006.

Brown, Lois. "Death-Defying Testimony: Women's Private Lives and the Politics of Public Documents." *Legacy: A Journal of American Women Writers,* 27, no. 1 (2010): 130–139.

Burney, Frances. *Diary and Letters of Madame D'Arblay.* Edited by Charlotte Barrett. London: Bickers and Son, 1842.

Burritt, Elihu. *The Advocate of Peace and Universal Brotherhood* 1, no. 1 (1 January 1846).

———, ed. *Olive Leaflets.* New York: S. S. & W. Wood, 1852–1855[?].

———. *Sparks from the Anvil.* Worcester: Henry J. Howland, 1846.

Carby, Hazel V. *Imperial Intimacies: A Tale of Two Islands.* London: Verso, 2019.

Catron, John. "Early Black-Atlantic Christianity in the Middle Colonies: Social Mobility and Race in Moravian Bethlehem." *Pennsylvania History: A Journal of Mid-Atlantic Studies* 76, no. 3 (2009): 301–345.

Cheshire, Edward. *The Results of the Census of Great Britain in 1851.* London: John William Parker and Son, 1854.

Choules, John Overton, and Thomas Smith. *The Origin and History of Missions.* Boston: S. Walker, 1832.

Clarke, James Freeman. *Present Condition of the Colored People of the United States.* New York: Anti-Slavery Society, 1859.

Collison, Gary. *Shadrach Minkins: From Fugitive Slave to Citizen.* Cambridge, MA: Harvard University Press, 1997.

Confidence in God, Illustrated in the Life of John Antes. A Missionary in Egypt. London: Religious Tract Society, n.d.

Cope, Gilbert. *Genealogy of the Smedley Family.* Lancaster, PA: Wickersham, 1901.

Copley, Esther. *A History of Slavery and its Abolition.* London: Houlston and Stoneman, 1839.

Crabtree, Sarah. *Holy Nation: The Transatlantic Quaker Ministry in an Age of Revolution.* Chicago: University of Chicago Press, 2015.

Craft, William. *Running a Thousand Miles for Freedom; or, the Escape of William and Ellen Craft from Slavery.* London: William Tweedie, 1860.

Cronshagen, Jessica. "'A Loyal Heart to God and Governor': Missions and Colonial Policy in the Surinamese Saramaccan Mission (c. 1750–1813)," *Journal of Moravian History* 19, no. 1 (2019): 1–24.

———. "'We Do Not Need Any Slaves; We Use Oxen and Horses': Children's Letters from Moravian Communities in Central Europe to Slaves' Children in Suriname (1829)." In *Beyond Exceptionalism: Traces of Slavery and the Slave Trade in Early Modern Germany, 1650–1850,* edited by Rebekka Mallinckrodt, Josef Köstlbauer, and Sarah Lentz, 264–286. Berlin: De Gruyter Oldenbourg, 2021.

Crowley, T. "'Dissident': A Brief Note." *Critical Quarterly* 53, no. 2 (2011): 1–11

Cuffee, Paul. *Memoir of Captain Paul Cuffee, a Man of Color.* Liverpool: Egerton Smith, 1811.

Cushing, William. *Initials and Pseudonyms: A Dictionary of Literary Disguises.* New York: Thomas Y. Crowell, 1885.

Cutter, Martha J. *The Illustrated Slave: Empathy, Graphic Narrative, and the Visual Culture of the Transatlantic Abolition Movement, 1800–1852.* Athens: University of Georgia Press, 2017.

De Rosa, Deborah. *Domestic Abolitionism and Juvenile Literature, 1830–1865.* New York: State University of New York Press, 2003.

Davies, Keri. "Jonathan Spilsbury and the Lost Moravian History of William Blake's Family." *Blake/ An Illustrated Quarterly* 40, no. 3 (2006–2007): 100–109

———. "The Lost Moravian History of William Blake's Family: Snapshots from the Archive." *Literature Compass* 3, no. 6 (2006): 1297–1319.

Davies, Keri, and Martha Keith Schuchard. "Recovering the Lost Moravian History of William Blake's Family." *Blake: An Illustrated Quarterly* 38, no. 1 (2004): 36–43.

Davis, Laurel, and Mary Sarah Bilder. "The Library of Robert Morris, Antebellum Civil Rights Lawyer and Activist." *Law Library Journal* 111, no. 4 (2019): 461–508. Boston College Law School Faculty Papers.

DeLombard, Jeannine Marie. "The Claims of the Humanitarian, Legally Considered." *American Literary History* 35, no. 4 (2021):1776–1785.

Doody, Margaret Anne. *Frances Burney: The Life in the Works.* Cambridge: Cambridge University Press, 1988.

Dorr, Julia C. R. *Lanmere.* New York: Mason Brothers, 1856.

Douglas, Janet. "A Cherished Friendship: Julia Griffiths Crofts and Frederick Douglass." *Slavery & Abolition* 33, no. 2 (2012): 265–274.

Dresser, Madge. "Moravians in Bristol." In *Reformation and Revival in Eighteenth-Century Bristol,* edited by Jonathan Barry and Kenneth Morgan, 105–148. Bristol: Bristol Record Society, 1994.

Duane, Anna Mae. *Educated for Freedom: The Incredible Story of Two Fugitive Schoolboys Who Grew Up to Change a Nation.* New York: New York University Press, 2020.

Engel, Mücahide Nihal. "Ottoman Egypt in the mid Eighteenth Century—Local Interest Groups and Their Connection with and Rebellions against the Sublime Porte and Resistance to State Authority." PhD diss., University of Birmingham, 2017.

Equiano, Olaudah. *The Interesting Narrative and Other Writings.* Edited by Vincent Carretta. New York: Penguin, 2003.

Erben, Patrick M. *A Harmony of the Spirits: Translation and the Language of Community in Early Pennsylvania.* Chapel Hill: University of North Carolina Press and Omohundru Institute of Early American History and Culture, 2012.

Everill, Bronwen. *Not Made by Slaves: Ethical Capitalism in the Age of Abolition.* Cambridge, MA: Harvard University Press, 2020.

Faull, Katherine M., trans. *Moravian Women's Memoirs: Their Related Lives, 1750–1820.* Syracuse, NY: Syracuse University Press, 1997.

———. "Self-Encounters: Two Eighteenth-Century Memoirs from Moravian Bethlehem." In *Beyond Douglass: New Perspectives on Early African American Literature*, edited by Michael J. Drexler and Ed White, 21–53. Lewisburg: Bucknell University Press, 2008.

Finley, Alexandra J. *An Intimate Economy: Enslaved Women, Work, and America's Domestic Slave Trade*. Chapel Hill: University of North Carolina Press, 2020.

Fluck, Winfried Donald E. Pease and John Carlos Rowe, eds. *Re-framing the Transnational Turn in American Studies*. Hanover: Dartmouth College Press, 2011.

Fogleman, Aaron Spencer. *Jesus Is Female: Moravians and the Challenge of Radical Religion in Early America*. Philadelphia: University of Pennsylvania Press, 2007.

Ford, John, ed. *Memoir of Thomas Pumphrey, for Twenty-Seven Years Superintendent of Ackworth School*. London: A. W. Bennett, 1864.

Foreman, P. Gabrielle. "Who's Your Mama? 'White' Genealogies, Early Photography, and Anti-passing Narratives of Slavery and Freedom." *American Literary History* 19, no. 3 (2002): 505–539.

Foster, Frances Smith. "A Narrative of the Interesting Origins and (Sometimes) Surprising Developments of African-American Print Culture." *American Literary History* 4, no. 4 (2005): 714–740.

Fox, R. Hingston. *Dr. John Fothergill and his Friends: Chapters in Eighteenth Century Life*. London: Macmillan, 1919.

Fraser, Derek. "Areas of Urban Politics." In *The Victorian City*, edited by H. J. Dyos and Michael Wolff, 763–788. London: Routledge and Kegan Paul, 1973.

———. "Politics and Society in the Nineteenth Century." In *A History of Modern Leeds*, edited by Derek Fraser, 270–300. Manchester: Manchester University Press, 1980.

Friis, Ib. "Traveling among Fellow Christians (1768–1833): James Bruce, Henry Salt and Eduard Rüppell in Abyssinia." *Humanisca* 4, no. 2 (2013): 161–194.

Frye, Susan. *Pens and Needles: Women's Textualities in Early Modern England*. Philadelphia: University of Pennsylvania Press, 2010.

Fuentes, Marisa J. *Dispossessed Lives: Enslaved Women, Violence, and the Archive*. Pennsylvania: University of Pennsylvania Press, 2016.

Fyfe, Aileen. "A Short History of the Religious Tract Society." In *From the Dairyman's Daughter to Worrals of the WAAF: The Religious Tract Society*, edited by Dennis Butts and Pat Garret, 13–35. Cambridge: Lutterworth Press, 2006.

Gardner, Eric. "Accessing Early Black Print." *Legacy: A Journal of American Women Writers* 33, no. 1 (2016): 25–30.

Gardner, Naomi. *Embroidering Emancipation: Female Abolitionists and Material Culture in Britain and the USA, c.1780–1865*. PhD diss., Royal Holloway, University of London, 2016.

The Garland of Freedom: A Collection of Poems, Chiefly Anti-Slavery, Selected from Various Authors. London: W. and F. G. Cash; William Tweedie, 1853.

Garvey, Ellen Gruber. "Nineteenth-Century Abolitionists and the Databases They Created," *Legacy: A Journal of American Women Writers* 27, no. 2 (2010): 357–366.

——. *Writing with Scissors: American Scrapbooks from the Civil War to the Harlem Renaissance.* New York: Oxford University Press, 2013.

Gerbner, Katharine. *Christian Slavery: Conversion and Race in the Protestant Atlantic World.* Philadelphia: University of Pennsylvania Press, 2018.

Gikandi, Simon. "Rethinking the Archive of Enslavement." *Early American Literature* 50, no. 1 (2015): 81–102.

Giles, Paul. *Transatlantic Insurrections: British Culture and the Formation of American Culture, 1730–1860.* Philadelphia: University of Pennsylvania Press, 2001.

Gilroy, Paul. *The Black Atlantic: Modernity and Double Consciousness.* London: Verso, 1993.

Gleadle, Kathryn, and Ryan Hanley. "Children against Slavery: Juvenile Agency and the Sugar Boycotts in Britain." *Transactions of the RHS* 30 (2020): 97–117.

Glymph, Thavolia. *Out of the House of Bondage: The Transformation of the Plantation Household.* Cambridge: Cambridge University Press, 2008.

Goggin, Maureen Daly. "An Essamplaire Essai on the Rhetoricity of Needlework Sampler-Making: A Contribution to Theorizing and Historicizing Rhetorical Praxis." *Rhetoric Review* 21, no. 4 (2002): 309–338.

—— "Stitching a Life in 'Pen of Steele and Silken Inke': Elizabeth Parker's circa 1830 Sampler." In *Women and the Material Culture of Needlework and Textile, 1750–1950,* edited by Maureen Daly Goggin and Beth Fowkes Tobin, 31–49. Farnham: Ashgate, 2009.

Gordon, Scott Paul. "The Paxton Boys and the Moravians: Terror and Faith in the Pennsylvania Backcountry." *Journal of Moravian History* 14, no. 2 (2014): 119–152.

Gould, Philip. "Early Black Atlantic Writing and the Cultures of Enlightenment." In *Beyond Douglass: New Perspectives on Early African American Literature,* edited by Michael J. Drexler and Ed White, 107–121. Lewisburg: Bucknell University Press, 2008.

Gould, William B. *Diary of a Contraband: The Civil War Passage of a Black Sailor,* edited by William B. Gould IV. Stanford: Stanford University Press, 2002.

Greenspan, Ezra. *William Wells Brown: An African American Life.* New York: W. W. Norton 2014.

Gerzina, Gretchen. *Black England: Life Before Emancipation.* London: John Murray, 1995.

Grubb, Sarah. *Some Account of the Life and Religious Labours of Sarah Grubb.* London: James Phillips, 1794.

Gruesz, Kristin Silva. *Cotton Mather's Spanish Lessons: A Story of Language, Race, and Belonging in the Early Americas.* Cambridge, MA: Harvard University Press, 2022.

Gustafson, Eleanor H. "Endnotes: African American Schoolgirl Embroidery." *Samplings,* http://samplings.com/curator-archives/LombardStreetSchoolSampler.

Gurney, John Joseph. "Conversation on Geology. Extracted from a Manuscript Entitled "Colloquia Edinesia." In *The Aurora Borealis, a Literary Annual,* edited by Members of the Society of Friends, 181–189. Newcastle: Charles Empson, 1833.

Hall, T. B. *A Flora of Liverpool.* London: Whitaker.

Hamlin, Talbot. *Benjamin Henry Latrobe.* New York: Oxford University Press, 1955.

Harbsmeier, Michael. "Bodies and Voices from Ultima Thule: Inuit Explorations of the Kablunat from Christian IV to Knud Rasmussen." In *A Cultural History of Nordic Scientific Practices,* edited by Michael Bravo and Sverker Sörlin, 33–71. Canton, MA: Science History Publications, 2002.

Harrold, Stanley. *The Abolitionists and the South, 1831–1861.* Lexington: University Press of Kentucky, 1995.

Hartman, Margaret Strebel. "Tid-Bits of Northern Kentucky History: Wm. S. Bailey of Newport, and His Anti-Slavery Newspapers," July 1987, https://www.nkyviews .com/campbell/pdf/Bailey_Anti-Slavery_Newspaper.pdf.

Hartman, Saidiya V. *Scenes of Subjection: Terror, Slavery, and Self-Making in Nineteenth-Century America.* New York: Oxford University Press, 1997.

———. "Venus in Two Acts." *Small Axe* 12, no. 2 (2008): 1–14.

———. *Wayward Lives, Beautiful Experiments: Intimate Histories of Riotous Black Girls, Troublesome Women, and Queer Radicals.* New York: W. W. Norton, 2019.

Hay, Daisy. *Dinner with Joseph Johnson: Books and Friendships in a Revolutionary Age.* London: Chatto and Windus, 2022.

Heaps, Jennifer Davis. "'Remember Me': Six Samplers in the National Archives." National Archives, *Prologue Magazine* 34, no. 3 (Fall 2002). https://www.archives.gov /publications/prologue/2002/fall/samplers-1.html.

Hickman, Jared. "On the Redundancy of 'Transnational American Studies.'" In *The Oxford Handbook of Nineteenth-Century American Literature,* edited by Russ Castronovo, 269–288. Oxford: Oxford University Press, 2012.

Higgs, Edward. *Making Sense of the Census Revisited: Census Records for England and Wales 1801–1901.* London: Institute of Historical Research, 2005.

Hochman, Barbara. "Investing in Literature: Ernestine Rose and the Harlem Branch Public Library of the 1920s." *Legacy: A Journal of American Women Writers* 31, no. 1 (2014): 93–106.

Hodges, Graham Russell Gao. *David Ruggles: A Radical Black Abolitionist and the Underground Railroad in New York City.* Chapel Hill: University of North Carolina Press, 2010.

Hoermann, Ralph. "'A Very Hell of Horrors?': The Haitian Revolution and the Early Transatlantic Haitian Gothic." *Slavery & Abolition* 37, no. 1 (2016): 183–205.

Holcomb, Julie L. *Moral Commerce: Quakers and the Transatlantic Boycott of the Slave Labor Economy.* Ithaca, NY: Cornell University Press, 2016.

Holland, John, and James Everett. *Memoirs of the Life and Writings of James Montgomery,* vol. 1. London: Longman, Brown, Green and Longmans, 1854.

Holmes, John. *Historical Sketches of the Missions of the United Brethren for Propagating the Gospel among the Heathen, from their Commencement to the Year 1817.* Dublin: R. Napper, 1818.

Holton, Sandra Stanley. *Quaker Women: Personal Life, Memory and Radicalism in the Lives of Women Friends, 1800–1920.* Abingdon: Routledge, 2007.

Howell, William Huntting. *Against Self-Reliance: The Arts of Dependence in the Early United States.* Philadelphia: University of Pennsylvania Press, 2015.

———— "Spirits of Emulation: Readers, Samplers, and the Republican Girl, 1787–1810." *American Literature* 81, no. 3 (2009): 497–526.

Howitt, William, ed. *The Boy's Country-Book: Being the Real Life of a Country Boy, Written by Himself.* London: Longman, Orme, Brown, Green, and Longmans, 1839.

Humphrey, Carol. *Friends. A Common Thread: Samplers with Quaker Influence.* Witney: Witney Antiques, 2008.

————. *Quaker School Girl Samplers from Ackworth.* Needlepoint and Ackworth School Estates, 2006.

Hulton, Paul, F. Nigel Hepper, and Ib Friis, eds. *Luigi Balugani's Drawings of African Plants: From a Collection Made by James Bruce of Kinnaird on His Travels to Discover the Source of the Nile 1767–1773.* New Haven, CT: Yale Center for British Art, 1991.

Huzzey, Richard. *Freedom Burning: Anti-slavery and Empire in Victorian Britain.* Ithaca, NY: Cornell University Press, 2012.

————. "A Microhistory of British Antislavery Printing." *Social Science History* 43, no. 3 (2019): 599–623.

Huzzey, Richard, and Henry Miller. "Petitions, Parliament and Political Culture: Petitioning in the House of Commons, 1780–1918." *Past and Present: A Journal of Historical Studies* 248, no. 1 (2020): 123–164.

Jackson, Maurice. "How the Quakers Worked with Moravians, Germans, the French, the British, and Enslaved and Free Africans All in the Antislavery Cause." In *Babel of the Atlantic,* edited by Bethany Wiggin, 228–246. University Park: Pennsylvania State University Press, 2019.

————. *Let This Voice Be Heard: Anthony Benezet, Father of Atlantic Abolitionism.* Philadelphia: University of Pennsylvania Press, 2009.

Jensz, Felicity. "Overcoming Objections to Print: The Moravian Periodical Accounts and the Pressure of Publishing in Eighteenth-Century Britain," *Journal of Moravian History* 15, no. 1 (2015): 1–28.

Johnson, Pearlie M. "African American Women and Their Quilts: Exploring Three Centuries of Hand-Made Quilts in Kentucky." *The Griot* 35, no. 1 (2016): 1–16.

Jones, William. *The Jubilee Memorial of the Religious Tract Society.* London: Religious Tract Society, 1850.

Karcher, Carolyn L. *The First Woman of the Republic: A Cultural Biography of Lydia Maria Child.* Durham, NC: Duke University Press, 1994.

Kaufman, Miranda. *Black Tudors: The Untold Story.* London: Oneworld, 2017.

Kelley, Mary. "'The Difference of Colour': Reading and Writing Abolitionism." *Social Dynamics* 45, no. 1 (2019): 156–173.

Lackey, Joanna. "I use the woman's figure naturally": Figuring Women's Work in Elizabeth Barrett Browning's *Aurora Leigh.*" *Nineteenth-Century Gender Studies* 8, no. 3 (2012). http://www.ncgsjournal.com/issue83/lackey.html

Lessons for Youth, Selected for the Use of Ackworth, and other Schools. New York: Isaac Collins, 1798.

Levander, Caroline F., and Robert S. Levine, eds. *Hemispheric American Studies.* New Brunswick: Rutgers University Press, 2008.

Lewis, Enoch, ed. *Friends' Review: A Religious, Literary and Miscellaneous Journal* 1, no. 1 (September 1847).

Lewis, Joseph J. *A Memoir of Enoch Lewis.* West Chester, PA: F. S. Hickman, 1882.

Liddington, Jill, and Elizabeth Crawford. "'Women do not count, neither shall they be counted': Suffrage, Citizenship and the Battle for the 1911 Census." *History Workshop Journal* 71, no. 1 (Spring 2011): 98–127.

Manguel, Alberto. *The Library at Night.* New Haven, CT: Yale University Press, 2006.

Manning, Susan, and Andrew Taylor, eds. *Transatlantic Literary Studies: A Reader.* Baltimore: Johns Hopkins University Press, 2007.

Martineau, Harriet. *Retrospect of Western Travel.* 3 vols. London: Saunders and Otley, 1838.

Mason, J. C. S. *The Moravian Church and the Missionary Awakening in England, 1760–1800.* Woodbridge: Boydell Press, 2001.

Massey, Doreen. *For Space.* London: Sage, 2005.

Mays, Sas, ed. *Libraries, Literatures, and Archives.* New York: Routledge, 2014.

McCaskill, Barbara. *Love, Liberation, and Escaping Slavery: William and Ellen Craft in Cultural Memory.* Athens: University of Georgia Press, 2015.

———. "The Profits and Perils of Partnership in the 'Thrilling' Saga of William and Ellen Craft." *MELUS: Multi-Ethnic Literature of the US* 38, no. 1 (2013): 76–97.

McCorkle, Donald M. "John Antes: 'American Dilettante.'" *Musical Quarterly* 42, no. 4 (1956): 486–499.

McHenry, Elizabeth. *Forgotten Readers: Recovering the Lost History of African American Literary Societies.* Durham, NC: Duke University Press, 2002.

Meer, Sarah. *Uncle Tom Mania: Slavery, Minstrelsy and Transatlantic Culture in the 1850s.* Athens: University of Georgia Press, 2005.

Midgley, Clare. "The Dissenting Voice of Elizabeth Heyrick: An Exploration of the Links between Gender, Religious Dissent, and Anti-slavery Radicalism." In *Women, Dissent, and Anti-slavery in Britain and America, 1790–1865*, edited by Elizabeth J. Clapp and Julie Roy Jeffrey, 88–110. Oxford: Oxford University Press, 2011.

———. *Women against Slavery: The British Campaign, 1780–1870*. London: Routledge, 1992.

Midgley, Patricia. *The Churches and the Working Classes: Leeds 1870–1920*. Newcastle: Cambridge Scholars, 2012.

Miles, Tiya. *All That She Carried: The Journey of Ashley's Sack, a Black Family Keepsake*. New York: Random House, 2022.

Millette, HollyGale. "Exchanging Fugitive Identity: William and Ellen Craft's Transatlantic Reinvention (1850–69)." In *Imagining Transatlantic Slavery*, edited by Cora Kaplan and John Oldfield, 61–76. Basingstoke: Palgrave Macmillan, 2010.

Minto, W., ed. *Autobiographical Notes of the Life of William Bell Scott*. New York: Harper and Bros., 1892.

Mitchell, Koritha. *From Slave Cabins to the White House: Homemade Citizenship in African American Culture*. Urbana: University of Illinois Press, 2020.

Moglen, Seth. "Enslaved City on a Hill: The Archive of Moravian Slavery and the Practical Past." *History of the Present: A Journal of Critical History* 6, no. 2 (2016): 155–183.

Montgomery, James. *The Poetical Works of James Montgomery*. London: Orme Brown, Green and Longmans, 1841.

Mood, Jonathan. "Women in the Quaker Community: The Richardson Family of Newcastle, c. 1815–1860." *Quaker Studies* 9, no. 2 (2005): 204–219.

Moore, Sean D. *Slavery and the Making of Early American Libraries: British Literature, Political Thought, and the Transatlantic Book Trade, 1731–1814*. Oxford: Oxford University Press, 2019.

Moorehead, Alan. *The Blue Nile*. London: Four Square, 1965.

Moravian Church, Fulneck Congregation, *Brotherly Agreement and Declaration, Concerning the Rules and Orders of the Brethren's Congregation at Fulneck*, 1777.

Morgan, Simon. "Celebrity Boundaries: Harriet Beecher Stowe as Literary Celebrity and Anti-slavery Campaigner." *Celebrity Studies* 8, no. 1 (2017): 162–166.

Mortimer, C. B. *Marrying by Lot: A Tale of the Primitive Moravians*. New York: G. P. Putnam and Son, 1868.

Murray, Hannah-Rose. *Advocates of Freedom: African American Transatlantic Abolitionism in the British Isles*. Cambridge: Cambridge University Press, 2020.

Newman, Simon. *Freedom Seekers: Escaping from Slavery in Restoration London*. London: University of London Press, 2022.

Nicholls, David. "Richard Cobden and the International Peace Movement, 1848–1853." *Journal of British Studies* 30, no. 4 (1991): 351–376.

O'Donnell, Elizabeth A. "'There's Death in the Pot!' The British Free Produce Movement and Religious Society of Friends, with Particular Reference to the North-East of England." *Quaker Studies* 13, no. 2 (2009): 184–204.

Oldfield, J. R. *Transatlantic Abolition in the Age of Revolution: An International History of Anti-slavery, c. 1787–1820.* Cambridge: Cambridge University Press, 2013.

Ovenden, Richard. *Burning the Books: A History of Knowledge Under Attack.* London: John Murray, 2020.

Parker, Rozsika. *The Subversive Stitch: Embroidery and the Making of the Feminine.* London: Women's Press, 1984.

Partington, Gill, and Adam Smyth, eds. *Book Destruction from the Medieval to the Contemporary.* Basingstoke: Palgrave Macmillan, 2014.

Peucker, Paul. "Selection and Destruction in Moravian Archives Between 1760 and 1810." *Journal of Moravian History* 12, no. 2 (2012): 170–215.

Pfaelzer Jean. "Hanging Out: A Research Methodology." *Legacy: A Journal of American Woman Writers* 27, no. 1 (2010): 140–159.

Pisarz-Ramirez, Gabriele, and Markus Heide, eds. *Hemispheric Encounters: The Early United States in a Transnational Perspective.* Frankfurt: Peter Lang, 2016.

Pocock, Nigel. "From Enslavement to Freedom: Five Young Girls from Antigua." Equiano Centre, October 2013. https://www.ucl.ac.uk/equiano-centre/black-presence-blog /previous-posts/october-2013

Podmore, Colin, ed. *The Fetter Lane Moravian Congregation London, 1742–1992.* London: Fetter Lane Moravian Congregation, 1992.

———. *The Moravian Church in England, 1728–1760.* Oxford: Clarendon Press, 1998.

The Poll Book of the Leeds Borough Election of 1847. Leeds: T. W Green, 1847.

The Poll Book of the Leeds Borough Election, July 1841. Leeds: J. Swallow, Corn-Exchange, 1841.

Prahms, Wendy. *Newcastle Ragged and Industrial School.* Stroud: Tempus, 2006.

Prince, Mary. *The History of Mary Prince a West Indian Slave, Related by Herself.* Edited by Moira Ferguson. Ann Arbor: University of Michigan Press, 1997.

Pumphrey, Thomas, and Emma R. Pumphrey. *Henry and Anna Richardson: In Memoriam.* Newcastle, 1892.

Rana, Leena A. "Stories behind the Stitches: Schoolgirl Samplers of the Eighteenth and Nineteenth Centuries." *Textile: The Journal of Cloth and Culture* 12, no. 2 (2014): 158–179.

Raven, James, ed. *Lost Libraries: The Destruction of Great Book Collections since Antiquity.* Basingstoke: Palgrave Macmillan, 2004.

Rediker, Marcus. *The Fearless Benjamin Lay: The Quaker Dwarf Who Became the First Revolutionary Abolitionist.* London: Verso, 2017.

Regier, Alexander. *Exorbitant Enlightenment: Blake, Hamman, and Anglo-German Constellations.* Oxford: Oxford University Press, 2018.

Remer, Ashley E. "Lesson Object as Object Lesson: The Embroidery Sampler." *Journal of the History of Childhood and Youth* 12, no. 3 (2019): 345–352.

Renkl, Margaret. *Graceland, at Last: Notes on Hope and Heartache from the American South.* Minneapolis: Milkweed Editions, 2021.

Rice, Alan J. *Creating Memorials, Building Identities: The Politics of Memory in the Black Atlantic.* Liverpool: Liverpool University Press, 2010.

Rice, Alan J., and Martin Crawford, eds. *Liberating Sojourn: Frederick Douglass and Transatlantic Reform.* Athens: University of Georgia Press, 1999.

Rice, C. Duncan. *The Scots Abolitionists, 1833–1861.* Baton Rouge: Louisiana State University Press, 1981.

Richardson, Anna H. "Anti-slavery Memoranda." [J. G. Forster, 1860?].

———. *Little Laura, the Kentucky Abolitionist.* Newcastle: T. Pigg, 1859.

———. *Who Are the Slaveholders?.* Newcastle: Selkirk and Rhago, 1852[?].

Richardson, Henry. "To a Boy, on Hearing Him Whistling in the Streets 'The Bonnets of Blue,' during the Prevalence of the Cholera." In *The Aurora Borealis, a Literary Annual,* edited by Members of the Society of Friends. Newcastle: Charles Empson, 1833.

Richardson, John W., ed. *Memoir of Anna Deborah Richardson with Extracts from Her Letters.* Newcastle: J. M. Carr, 1877.

Roy, Michaël. *Young Abolitionists: Children of the Antislavery Movement.* New York: New York University Press, 2024.

Salenius, Sirpa. "Transatlantic Interracial Sisterhoods: Sarah Remond, Ellen Craft, and Harriet Jacobs in England." *Frontiers* 38, no. 1 (2017): 166–196.

Schaffer, Talia. *Novel Craft: Victorian Domestic Handicraft and Nineteenth-Century Fiction.* New York: Oxford University Press, 2011.

Schuchard, Martha Keith. "Young William Blake and the Moravian Tradition of Visionary Art." *Blake/An Illustrated Quarterly* 40, no. 3 (2006/2007): 84–100.

Scott, Matthew, and Nick Megoran. "The Newcastle Upon Tyne Peace Society (1817–50)." *Northern History* 54, no. 2 (2017): 1–17.

Sensbach, Jon F. *A Separate Canaan: The Making of an Afro-Moravian World in North Carolina, 1763–1840.* Chapel Hill: University of North Carolina Press, 1998.

———. *Rebecca's Revival: Creating Black Christianity in the Atlantic World.* Cambridge, MA: Harvard University Press, 2005.

———. "Slavery, Race, and the Global Fellowship: Religious Radicals Confront the Modern Age." In *Pious Pursuits: German Moravians in the Atlantic World,* edited by Michele Gillespie and Robert Beachy, 223–236. New York: Berghahn Books, 2007.

Senchyne, Jonathan. *The Intimacy of Paper in Early Nineteenth-Century American Literature.* Amherst: University of Massachusetts Press, 2020.

Sheller, Mimi. "Bleeding Humanity and Gendered Embodiments: From Anti-slavery

Sugar Boycotts to Ethical Consumers." *Humanity: An International Journal of Human Rights Humanitarianism and Development* 2, no. 2 (2011): 171–192.

Shepperson, George. "Abolitionism and African Political Thought." *Transition* 12 (1964): 22–26.

Sinha, Manisha. *The Slave's Cause: A History of Abolition.* New Haven: Yale University Press, 2016.

Smith, Joseph. *A Descriptive Catalogue of Friends' Books.* London: Joseph Smith, 1867.

Stauffer, John, Celeste-Marie Bernier, and Zoe Trodd. *Picturing Frederick Douglass: An Illustrated History of the Nineteenth Century's Most Photographed American.* New York: W. W. Norton, 2015.

Stead, Geoffrey. *The Moravian Settlement at Fulneck, 1742–1790.* Leeds: Thoresby Society, 1999.

Stedman, J. G. *Narrative of a Five Years' Expedition, against the Revolted Negroes of Surinam.* London: J. Johnson, 1796.

Steel, John William, ed. *A Historical Sketch of the Society of Friends "In Scorn Called Quakers" in Newcastle and Gateshead, 1653–1898.* London: Headley Brothers, 1899.

Still, William. *The Underground Rail Road.* Philadelphia: People's Publishing Company 1871.

Stinebeck, David. "Understanding the Forgotten Poetry of American Samplers." *Journal of Popular Culture* 52, no. 5 (2019): 1183–1199.

Stolba, K. Marie. "Evidence for Quartets by John Antes, American-Born Moravian Composer." *Journal of the American Musicological Society* 33, no. 3 (1980): 565–574.

Stoler, Ann Laura. *Along the Archival Grain: Epistemic Anxieties and Colonial Common Sense.* Princeton, NJ: Princeton University Press, 2008.

Stoker, David. "Ellenor Fenn as 'Mrs. Teachwell' and 'Mrs. Lovechild': A Pioneer Late Eighteenth-Century Children's Writer, Educator, and Philanthropist." *Princeton University Library Chronicle* 68, no. 3 (2007): 817–850.

Sweeney, Fionnghuala. *Frederick Douglass and the Atlantic World.* Liverpool: Liverpool University Press, 2007.

Sweeney, Fionnghuala, and Bruce E. Baker. "'I am not a beggar': Moses Roper, Black Witness and the Lost Opportunity of British Abolitionism." *Slavery & Abolition* 42, no. 3 (2022): 632–667.

Sweeney, Fionnghuala, and Alan J. Rice. "Liberating Sojourns?: African Americans and Transatlantic Abolition, 1845–1865." *Slavery & Abolition* 33, no. 2 (2021): 181–189.

Taylor, Jaime, and Zachary Loeb. "Librarian Is My Occupation: A History of the People's Library of Occupy Wall Street." In *Informed Agitation: Library and Information Skills in Social Justice Movements and Beyond,* edited by Melissa Morrone, 271–288. Sacramento, CA: Library Juice Press, 2013.

Taylor, Mentia. "Friendly Addresses to Spanish Ladies." *Anti-Slavery Monthly Reporter; Under the Sanction of the British and Foreign Anti-Slavery Society*, 15 January 1866.

Thomas, Sue. "1831 Reviews of *The History of Mary Prince.*" *Notes and Queries* 66, no. 2 (2019): 282–285.

——— "New Information on Mary Prince in London." *Notes and Queries* 58, no. 1 (2011): 82–85.

Thompson, Henry. *A History of Ackworth School during its First Hundred Years: Preceded by a Brief Account of the Fortunes of the House whilst Occupied as a Foundling Hospital.* London: Samuel Harris, 1879.

Thorp, Daniel B. "Chattel with a Soul: The Autobiography of a Moravian Slave." *Pennsylvania Magazine of History and Biography* 3, no. 112 (1988): 433–451.

Trill, Susanne; Kate Chedgzoy, and Melanie Osborne, eds. *Lay By Your Needles Ladies, Take the Pen: Writing Women in England, 1500–1700.* London: Arnold, 1997.

Trouillot, Michel-Rolph. *Silencing the Past: Power and the Production of History.* Boston: Beacon Press, 1995.

Tuvar, Lorenzo [pseud.]. *Tales and Legends of the English Lakes and Mountains: Collected from the Best and Most Authentic Sources.* London: Longmans, 1852.

Uglow, Jenny. *The Lunar Men: The Friends Who Made the Future 1730–1810.* London: Faber and Faber, 2002.

Ulrich, Laurel Thatcher. *The Age of Homespun: Objects and Stories in the Creation of an American Myth.* New York: Alfred A. Knopf, 2002.

Van Broekhoven, Deborah. "'Better than a clay club': The Organisation of Anti-slavery Fairs, 1835–60." *Slavery & Abolition* 19, no. 1 (1998): 24–45.

Van Horn, Jennifer. "Samplers, Gentility, and the Middling Sort." *Winterthur Portfolio* 40, no. 4 (2005): 219–248.

Vogt, Peter. "'Everywhere at Home': The Eighteenth-Century Moravian Movement as a Transatlantic Religious Community." *Journal of Moravian History* 1 (2006): 7–29.

von Frank, Albert J. *The Trials of Anthony Burns: Freedom and Slavery in Emerson's Boston.* Cambridge, MA: Harvard University Press, 1998.

Wakefield, Hannah. "Olaudah Equiano's Ecclesiastical World." *Early American Literature* 55, no. 3 (2020): 651–684.

Ware, Vron. *Beyond the Pale: White Women, Racism, and History.* London: Verso, 1992.

Weaver, Karol K. "Fashioning Freedom: Slave Seamstresses in the Atlantic World." *Journal of Women's History* 24, no. 1 (2012): 44–59.

Wiggin, Bethany, ed. *Babel of the Atlantic.* University Park: Pennsylvania State University Press, 2019.

Williams, Daniel E., ed. *Liberty's Captives: Narratives of Confinement in the Print Culture of the Early Republic.* Athens: University of Georgia Press, 2006.

Wilson, John, and Joseph Lupton. "American Slavery." *Anti-Slavery Monthly Reporter; Under the Sanction of the British and Foreign Anti-Slavery Society*, 1 July 1854.

Woo, Ilyon. *Master Slave Husband Wife: An Epic Journey from Slavery to Freedom.* New York: Simon & Schuster, 2023.

Wood, Marcus. *Blind Memory: Visual Representations of Slavery in England and America, 1780–1865.* Manchester: Manchester University Press.

Yee, Shirley. *Black Women Abolitionists: A Study in Activism, 1828–1860.* Knoxville: University of Tennessee Press, 1993.

Young, Robert J. C. *The Idea of English Ethnicity.* Malden: Blackwell, 2008.

Zaeske, Susan. *Signatures of Citizenship: Petitioning, Antislavery, and Women's Political Identity.* Chapel Hill: University of North Carolina Press, 2003.

INDEX

> ▶▶▶▶▶▶▶▶▶▶▶▶▶▶▶▶

www.ingramcontent.com/pod-product-compliance
Lightning Source LLC
Chambersburg PA
CBHW030300100426
42812CB00002B/511